D0875771

ENGLISH HISTORY TOLD BY ENGLISH POETS

ENGLISH HISTORY TOLD BY ENGLISH POETS

A READER FOR SCHOOL USE

COMPILED BY

KATHARINE LEE BATES

AND

KATHARINE COMAN

Granger Index Reprint Series

BOOKS FOR LIBRARIES PRESS
FREEPORT, NEW YORK

First Published 1902
Reprinted 1969

STANDARD BOOK NUMBER:
8369-6097-1

LIBRARY OF CONGRESS CATALOG CARD NUMBER:
71-103082

MANUFACTURED
BY
HALLMARK LITHOGRAPHERS, INC.
IN THE U.S.A.

"England, thy name is story."

PREFACE

Iт is hoped that this volume will find a place as a reading-book in connection with the study of English history.

Poets are spirited historians; they enlist imagination and sympathy in the cause of the fading past. They turn the task of memory to pastime. They are not always accurate, but neither are more sedate chroniclers. The dulness of a record was never yet proof of its veracity.

The London populace of Elizabethan times learned English history from the stage. The reigns of the Plantagenets, the Wars of the Roses, and the reigns of the Tudors were set forth in a long series of chronicle plays and historical dramas. In these, as in the lyrics and ballads that more commonly express the Stuart reigns, the tendency is to concentrate attention on royal and noble personages rather than on the life of the nation as a whole. It is a stately and a tragic story as the poets tell it, — too stately and too tragic to give an altogether just impression of the growth of a great people ; but it furnishes the dramatic outline to which a fuller knowledge may easily relate itself.

The present book illustrates, by carefully chosen selections from English poetry, the history of England from Queen Boadicea to Queen Victoria. Notes introductory to the selections carry on a connected account of principal events and make manifest the historic bearing of each poem. Further notes, at the end of the book, explain allusions and difficulties in the text, and also set the poets right in flagrant cases of misreporting. As one of the editors has derived her ideas of English history chiefly from English literature, and the other has suffered the modern, scientific training on "sources," this volume represents a battle-field, where values of fact and values of poetry have both been stoutly championed. The honors of war are divided. While, on the one hand, the historian fears that the book will lead young readers to believe that the Jacobites were the most important characters in English history, the literary editor, on the other, has submitted to the insertion of a few selections whose only art is to tell the truth.

The space limit has necessitated the omission of a number of famous poems, as Gray's "The Bard," and the whole splendid group of imperial ballads and lyrics, as " The Charge of the Light Brigade," " The Defence of Lucknow," " Ave Imperatrix."

The editors have had scrupulous regard to accuracy of wording, sparing no pains to find and follow authoritative texts, although at the cost of uniformity in capitalization, punctuation, and even in spelling.

Grateful acknowledgments are rendered to Mr. Andrew Lang for permission to use " Three. Portraits of Prince Charles," to Mr. Henry Newbolt for permission to use " Drake's Drum " (taken from " The Island Race," published by John Lane), to Messrs. Longmans, Green and Company for permission to use selected stanzas from William Morris's " The Day is Coming," to Mr. James Lincoln for permission to use " Simon de Montfort " and " England," and also, in case of the latter, — published in the *Atlantic Monthly* of April, 1900, — to Messrs. Houghton, Mifflin and Company, and finally to The Macmillan Company for large privileges of quotation from the poetic works of Lord Tennyson.

CONTENTS

xi

CONTENTS

ENGLISH HISTORY AS TOLD BY ENGLISH POETS

CYMBELINE

WILLIAM SHAKESPEARE

CUNOBELINUS, king of the Trinovantes, was the most powerful of the British chiefs known to Roman historians. He was grandson to the Cassivelaunus who had fought successfully against Julius Cæsar. One of his sons, Caractacus, for nine years defied the Roman army that, under Aulus Plautius, finally conquered the Britons. There is no further historical basis for Shakespeare's play. The scene represents the reception (43 A.D.) of Caius Lucius, the emissary of the emperor, at the court of Cymbeline. Lucius demands a renewal of the tribute paid to Julius Cæsar, and regards Cymbeline's refusal as amounting to a declaration of war.

ACT III

SCENE I. BRITAIN. *A Room of State in Cymbeline's Palace.*

(*Enter, at one side, Cymbeline, Queen, Cloten, and Lords; at the other, Caius Lucius and Attendants.*)

Cym. Now say, what would Augustus Cæsar with us?
Luc. When Julius Cæsar — whose remembrance yet
Lives in men's eyes, and will to ears and tongues
Be theme and hearing ever — was in this Britain,
And conquer'd it, Cassibelan, thine uncle, —
Famous in Cæsar's praises no whit less

1

Than in his feats deserving it, — for him
And his succession granted Rome a tribute
Yearly three thousand pounds; which by thee lately
Is left untender'd.

   Queen.   And, to kill the marvel,
Shall be so ever.

   Clo.   There be many Cæsars
Ere such another Julius.   Britain is
A world by itself; and we will nothing pay
For wearing our own noses.

   Queen.   That opportunity
Which then they had to take from 's, to resume
We have again. — Remember, sir, my liege,
The kings your ancestors; together with
The natural bravery of your isle, which stands
As Neptune's park, ribbèd and palèd in
With rocks unscalable and roaring waters,
With sands that will not bear your enemies' boats,
But suck them up to the top-mast.   A kind of con-
     quest
Cæsar made here; but made not here his brag
Of '*came* and *saw* and *overcame*': with shame, —
The first that ever touch'd him, — he was carried
From off our coast, twice beaten; and his shipping —
Poor ignorant baubles! — on our terrible seas,
Like egg-shells mov'd upon their surges, crack'd
As easily 'gainst our rocks: for joy whereof
The fam'd Cassibelan, who was once at point, —
O, giglot [1] fortune! — to master Cæsar's sword,

<hr />

[1] fickle.

Made Lud's town with rejoicing fires bright
And Britons strut with courage.

Clo. Come, there's no more tribute to be paid:
our kingdom is stronger than it was at that time;
and, as I said, there is no more such Cæsars: other
of them may have crooked noses; but to owe [1] such
straight arms, none.

Cym. Son, let your mother end.

Clo. We have yet many among us can gripe as
hard as Cassibelan: I do not say I am one; but I
have a hand. Why tribute? Why should we pay
tribute? If Cæsar can hide the sun from us with a
blanket, or put the moon in his pocket, we will pay
him tribute for light; else, sir, no more tribute, pray
you now.

Cym. You must know
Till the injurious Romans did extort
This tribute from us, we were free: Cæsar's ambi-
    tion, —
Which swell'd so much that it did almost stretch
The sides o' the world, — against all color here
Did put the yoke upon 's; which to shake off
Becomes a warlike people, whom we reckon
Ourselves to be.

Clo.   We do.

Cym.   Say then to Cæsar,
Our ancestor was that Mulmutius which
Ordain'd our laws, — whose use the sword of Cæsar
Hath too much mangled; whose repair and franchise

[1] own.

Shall, by the power we hold, be our good deed,
Though Rome be therefore angry: Mulmutius made
    our laws,
Who was the first of Britain which did put
His brows within a golden crown, and call'd
Himself a king.
    Luc.   I am sorry, Cymbeline,
That I am to pronounce Augustus Cæsar, —
Cæsar, that hath more kings his servants than
Thyself domestic officers, — thine enemy:
Receive it from me then: War and confusion
In Cæsar's name pronounce I 'gainst thee: look
For fury not to be resisted.

BOADICEA

WILLIAM COWPER

THE Romans proved cruel masters. Under Suetonius (63 A.D.) they took possession of Mona, the sacred island of the Druids, destroyed their temples and massacred the priests. The sacrilege was resented by all the British tribes. The Iceni, led by their warrior queen Boudicca, who, with her daughters, had suffered gross cruelty at the hands of the Roman soldiers, rose in revolt. They were joined by the Trinovantes and other neighboring tribes. Camulodunum, the strong Roman colony in the east, was sacked and the inhabitants put to the sword. Before Suetonius could rally his troops, London and Verulamium were reduced to ashes. Finally an army of ten thousand Roman soldiers was brought against the Britons, and the natives were overwhelmed. The heroic queen took her own life.

When the British warrior queen,
    Bleeding from the Roman rods,
Sought, with an indignant mien,
    Counsel of her country's gods,

Sage beneath a spreading oak
  Sat the Druid, hoary chief;
Every burning word he spoke
  Full of rage, and full of grief:

" Princess! if our aged eyes
  Weep upon thy matchless wrongs,
'Tis because resentment ties
  All the terrors of our tongues.

" Rome shall perish, — write that word
  In the blood that she has spilt;
Perish hopeless and abhorr'd,
  Deep in ruin as in guilt.

" Rome, for empire far renown'd,
  Tramples on a thousand states;
Soon her pride shall kiss the ground, —
  Hark! the Gaul is at her gates.

" Other Romans shall arise,
  Heedless of a soldier's name;
Sounds, not arms, shall win the prize;
  Harmony the path to fame.

" Then the progeny that springs
  From the forests of our land,
Arm'd with thunder, clad with wings,
  Shall a wider world command.

" Regions Cæsar never knew
  Thy posterity shall sway;
Where his eagles never flew,
  None invincible as they."

Such the bard's prophetic words,
    Pregnant with celestial fire,
Bending as he swept the chords
    Of his sweet but awful lyre.

She, with all a monarch's pride,
    Felt them in her bosom glow,
Rush'd to battle, fought and died;
    Dying, hurl'd them at the foe.

" Ruffians, pitiless as proud,
    Heaven awards the vengeance due ;
Empire is on us bestowed,
    Shame and ruin wait for you ! "

THE PASSING OF ARTHUR

LORD TENNYSON

THE Roman troops were withdrawn from Britain in 410. Forty years later the unhappy land was invaded by barbarians from oversea, — Jutes, Angles, and Saxons. The Britons were demoralized by centuries of subjection, and could make but feeble resistance. Led by Ambrosius Aurelian, a Briton who had learned generalship from the Romans, they rallied to the defence of the south country. He, or, as some authorities hold, his nephew, Uther Pendragon, is the King Arthur about whose valor and brave deeds so many marvellous stories have been told. Twelve great battles were fought and won in the long struggle against the Saxons. The crowning victory of Mount Badon (520) checked the progress of the invasion. A peace was agreed upon that might have lasted for many years but for the treachery of Modred, King Arthur's nephew, who rebelled against his rule and called in the assistance of the pagan foe. The last great battle against the traitor and his allies was fought at Camlan in Cornwall. There Arthur was fatally wounded, and the British resistance was broken.

Then spake King Arthur to Sir Bedivere:
" Far other is this battle in the west
Whereto we move, than when we strove in youth,
And thrust the heathen from the Roman wall,
And shook him thro' the north.   Ill doom is mine
To war against my people and my knights.
The king who fights his people fights himself.
And they my knights, who loved me once, the stroke
That strikes them dead is as my death to me.
Yet let us hence, and find or feel a way
Thro' this blind haze, which ever since I saw
One lying in the dust at Almesbury,
Hath folded in the passes of the world."

Then rose the King and moved his host by night,
And ever push'd Sir Modred, league by league,
Back to the sunset bound of Lyonesse —
A land of old upheaven from the abyss
By fire, to sink into the abyss again;
Where fragments of forgotten peoples dwelt,
And the long mountains ended in a coast
Of ever-shifting sand, and far away
The phantom circle of a moaning sea.
There the pursuer could pursue no more,
And he that fled no further fly the King;
And there, that day when the great light of heaven
Burn'd at his lowest in the rolling year,
On the waste sand by the waste sea they closed.
Nor ever yet had Arthur fought a fight
Like this last, dim, weird battle of the west.

A deathwhite mist slept over sand and sea:
Whereof the chill to him who breathed it, drew
Down with his blood, till all his heart was cold
With formless fear; and ev'n on Arthur fell
Confusion, since he saw not whom he fought,
For friend and foe were shadows in the mist,
And friend slew friend not knowing whom he slew:
And some had visions out of golden youth,
And some beheld the faces of old ghosts
Look in upon the battle; and in the mist
Was many a noble deed, many a base,
And chance and craft and strength in single fights,
And ever and anon with host to host
Shocks, and the splintering spear, the hard mail hewn,
Shield-breakings, and the clash of brands, the crash
Of battle-axes on shatter'd helms, and shrieks
After the Christ, of those who falling down
Looked up for heaven, and only saw the mist;
And shouts of heathen and the traitor knights,
Oaths, insult, filth, and monstrous blasphemies,
Sweat, writhings, anguish, laboring of the lungs
In that close mist, and cryings for the light,
Moans of the dying, and voices of the dead.

Last, as by some one death-bed after wail
Of suffering, silence follows, or thro' death
Or deathlike swoon, thus over all that shore,
Save for some whisper of the seething seas,
A dead hush fell; but when the dolorous day
Grew drearier toward twilight falling, came

A bitter wind, clear from the North, and blew
The mist aside, and with that wind the tide
Rose, and the pale king glanced across the field
Of battle : but no man was moving there ;
Nor any cry of Christian heard thereon,
Nor yet of heathen ; only the wan wave
Brake in among dead faces, to and fro
Swaying the helpless hands, and up and down
Tumbling the hollow helmets of the fallen,
And shiver'd brands that once had fought with Rome,
And rolling far along the gloomy shores
The voice of days of old and days to be.

Then spake King Arthur to Sir Bedivere,
And whiter than the mist that all day long
Had held the field of battle was the King :

" Hearest thou this great voice that shakes the world,
And wastes the narrow realm whereon we move,
And beats upon the faces of the dead,
My dead, as tho' they had not died for me ? —
O Bedivere, for on my heart hath fall'n
Confusion, till I know not what I am,
Nor whence I am, nor whether I be king.
Behold, I seem but king among the dead."

Then spake the bold Sir Bedivere : " My King,
King everywhere ! and so the dead have kings,
There also will I worship thee as king.
Yet still thy life is whole, and still I live
Who love thee : but who hates thee, he that brought

The heathen back among us, yonder stands,
Modred, unharm'd, the traitor of thine house."

Then spake the King: "My house hath been my doom.
But call not thou this traitor of my house
Who hath but dwelt beneath one roof with me.
My house are rather they who sware my vows,
Yea, even while they brake them, own'd me king.
And well for thee, saying in my dark hour,
When all the purport of my throne hath fail'd,
That quick or dead thou holdest me for king.
King am I, whatsoever be their cry;
And one last act of knighthood shalt thou see
Yet, ere I pass."   And uttering this the King
Made at the man: then Modred smote his liege
Hard on that helm which many a heathen sword
Had beaten thin; while Arthur at one blow,
Striking the last stroke with Excalibur,
Slew him, and all but slain himself, he fell.

So all day long the noise of battle roll'd
Among the mountains by the winter sea;
Until King Arthur's Table, man by man,
Had fall'n in Lyonesse about their lord,
King Arthur.   Then, because his wound was deep,
The bold Sir Bedivere uplifted him,
And bore him to a chapel nigh the field,
A broken chancel with a broken cross,
That stood on a dark strait of barren land:
On one side lay the Ocean, and on one
Lay a great water, and the moon was full.

Then spake King Arthur to Sir Bedivere :
" The sequel of to-day unsolders all
The goodliest fellowship of famous knights
Whereof this world holds record.   Such a sleep
They sleep — the men I loved.   I think that we
Shall nevermore, at any future time,
Delight our souls with talk of knightly deeds,
Walking about the gardens and the halls
Of Camelot, as in the days that were.
I perish by this people which I made,
Tho' Merlin sware that I should come again
To rule once more ; but let what will be, be.
I am so deeply smitten thro' the helm
That without help I cannot last till morn.
Thou therefore take my brand Excalibur,
Which was my pride : for thou rememberest how
In those old days, one summer noon, an arm
Rose up from out the bosom of the lake,
Clothed in white samite, mystic, wonderful,
Holding the sword — and how I row'd across
And took it, and have worn it, like a king ;
And, wheresoever I am sung or told
In aftertime, this also shall be known :
But now delay not : take Excalibur,
And fling him far into the middle mere :
Watch what thou seëst, and lightly bring me word."

    *   *   *   *   *   *   *   *

Then quickly rose Sir Bedivere, and ran,
And, leaping down the ridges lightly, plunged
Among the bulrush-beds, and clutch'd the sword,

And strongly wheel'd and threw it. The great brand
Made lightnings in the splendor of the moon,
And flashing round and round, and whirl'd in an arch,
Shot like a streamer of the northern morn,
Seen where the moving isles of winter shock
By night, with noises of the northern sea.
So flash'd and fell the brand Excalibur;
But ere he dipt the surface, rose an arm
Clothed in white samite, mystic, wonderful,
And caught him by the hilt, and brandish'd him
Three times, and drew him under in the mere.
And lightly went the other to the King.

   Then spoke King Arthur, drawing thicker breath:
" Now see I by thine eyes that this is done.
Speak out: what is it thou hast heard, or seen?"

   And answer made the bold Sir Bedivere:
" Sir King, I closed mine eyelids, lest the gems
Should blind my purpose, for I never saw,
Nor shall see, here or elsewhere, till I die,
Not tho' I live three lives of mortal men,
So great a miracle as yonder hilt.
Then with both hands I flung him, wheeling him;
But when I look'd again, behold an arm,
Clothed in white samite, mystic, wonderful,
That caught him by the hilt, and brandish'd him
Three times, and drew him under in the mere."

   And answer made King Arthur, breathing hard:
" My end draws nigh; 'tis time that I were gone.

Make broad thy shoulders to receive my weight,
And bear me to the margin ; yet I fear
My wound hath taken cold, and I shall die."

So saying, from the pavement he half rose,
Slowly, with pain, reclining on his arm,
And looking wistfully with wide blue eyes
As in a picture.   Him Sir Bedivere
Remorsefully regarded thro' his tears,
And would have spoken, but he found not words ;
Then took with care, and kneeling on one knee,
O'er both his shoulders drew the languid hands,
And rising bore him thro' the place of tombs.

But, as he walk'd, King Arthur panted hard,
Like one that feels a nightmare on his bed
When all the house is mute.   So sigh'd the King,
Muttering and murmuring at his ear, " Quick, quick !
I fear it is too late, and I shall die."
But the other swiftly strode from ridge to ridge,
Clothed with his breath, and looking, as he walk'd,
Larger than human on the frozen hills.
He heard the deep behind him, and a cry
Before.   His own thought drove him like a goad.
Dry clash'd his harness in the icy caves
And barren chasms, and all to left and right
The bare black cliff clang'd round him, as he based
His feet on juts of slippery crag that rang
Sharp smitten with the dint of armèd heels —
And on a sudden, lo ! the level lake,
And the long glories of the winter moon.

Then saw they how there hove a dusky barge,
Dark as a funeral scarf from stem to stern,
Beneath them; and descending they were ware
That all the decks were dense with stately forms,
Black-stoled, black-hooded, like a dream — by these
Three Queens with crowns of gold: and from them
     rose
A cry that shiver'd to the tingling stars,
And, as it were one voice, an agony
Of lamentation, like a wind that shrills
All night in a waste land, where no one comes,
Or hath come, since the making of the world.

Then murmur'd Arthur, " Place me in the barge ; "
So to the barge they came.   There those three Queens
Put forth their hands, and took the King, and wept.
But she, that rose the tallest of them all
And fairest, laid his head upon her lap.
And loos'd the shatter'd casque, and chafed his hands,
And call'd him by his name, complaining loud,
And dropping bitter tears against his brow
Striped with dark blood ; for all his face was white
And colorless, and like the wither'd moon
Smote by the fresh beam of the springing east;
And all his greaves and cuisses dash'd with drops
Of onset; and the light and lustrous curls —
That made his forehead like a rising sun
High from the daïs-throne — were parch'd with dust;
Or, clotted into points and hanging loose,
Mix'd with the knightly growth that fringed his lips.

So like a shatter'd column lay the King :
Not like that Arthur who, with lance in rest,
From spur to plume a star of tournament,
Shot thro' the lists at Camelot, and charged
Before the eyes of ladies and of kings.

Then loudly cried the bold Sir Bedivere :
"Ah ! my Lord Arthur, whither shall I go ?
Where shall I hide my forehead and my eyes ?
For now I see the true old times are dead,
When every morning brought a noble chance,
And every chance brought out a noble knight.
Such times have been not since the light that led
The holy Elders with the gift of myrrh.
But now the whole Round Table is dissolved
Which was an image of the mighty world ;
And I, the last, go forth companionless,
And the days darken round me, and the years,
Among new men, strange faces, other minds."

And slowly answered Arthur from the barge :
"The old order changeth, yielding place to new,
And God fulfils himself in many ways,
Lest one good custom should corrupt the world.
Comfort thyself : what comfort is in me ?
I have lived my life, and that which I have done
May He within himself make pure ! but thou,
If thou shouldst never see my face again,
Pray for my soul.   More things are wrought by
    prayer

Than this world dreams of. Wherefore, let thy voice
Rise like a fountain for me night and day.
For what are men better than sheep or goats
That nourish a blind life within the brain,
If, knowing God, they lift not hands of prayer
Both for themselves and those who call them friends?
For so the whole round earth is every way
Bound by gold chains about the feet of God.
But now farewell.   I am going a long way
With these thou seëst — if indeed I go
(For all my mind is clouded with a doubt) —
To the island-valley of Avilion :
Where falls not hail, or rain, or any snow,
Nor ever wind blows loudly : but it lies
Deep-meadow'd, happy, fair with orchard-lawns
And bowery hollows crown'd with summer sea,
Where I will heal me of my grievous wound."

So said he, and the barge with oar and sail
Moved from the brink, like some full-breasted swan
That, fluting a wild carol ere her death,
Ruffles her pure cold plume, and takes the flood
With swarthy webs.   Long stood Sir Bedivere
Revolving many memories, till the hull
Look'd one black dot against the verge of dawn,
And on the mere the wailing died away.

GLAD TIDINGS

WILLIAM WORDSWORTH

To convert the heathen conquerors to Christianity, Pope Gregory I. sent Augustine to Britain (597). The missionaries landed at Thanet in Kent, where they were hospitably received by King Ethelbert. The procession of priests in white vestments, chanting the litany and bearing aloft a silver cross and a banner on which was painted the crucifixion, made a deep impression on the mind of the king. He gave Augustine permission to preach the word of God throughout Kent. Within the next hundred years all Britain was converted to Christianity.

For ever hallowed be this morning fair,
Blest be the unconscious shore on which ye tread,
And blest the silver Cross, which ye, instead
Of martial banner, in procession bear;
The Cross preceding Him who floats in air,
The pictured Saviour! — By Augustin led,
They come, — and onward travel without dread,
Chanting in barbarous ears a tuneful prayer, —
Sung for themselves and those whom they would
    free!
Rich conquest waits them : — the tempestuous sea
Of Ignorance, that ran so rough and high,
And heeded not the voice of clashing swords,
These good men humble by a few bare words,
And calm with fear of God's divinity.

ALFRED AND HIS DESCENDANTS

WILLIAM WORDSWORTH

No sooner had the English established themselves in Britain, adopted Christianity, and settled down to an orderly life, than their land was overrun by new barbarians. These were the Danes, daring sea-rovers, who had abandoned their own bleak country and come south to seek booty and conquest along the rich Channel coasts. Among the kings who strove to defend England against the Danes, Alfred, king of Wessex, was the most glorious. His hard-fought victories, the wisdom of his rule, his zealous care for learning and for religion, won for him, alone among English kings, the title of "the Great." Among the descendants of Alfred, his son, Edward the Elder, his daughter, Ethelflæda, Lady of Mercia, his great-grandson, Edgar the Peaceful, proved worthy of their high inheritance.

I

Behold a pupil of the Monkish gown,
The pious ALFRED, King to Justice dear!
Lord of the harp and liberating spear;
Mirror of Princes! Indigent Renown
Might range the starry ether for a crown
Equal to *his* deserts, who like a year
Pours forth his bounty, like a day doth cheer,
And awes like night with mercy-tempered frown.
Ease from this noble miser of his time
No moment steals; pain narrows not his cares.
Though small his kingdom as a spark or gem
Of Alfred boasts remote Jerusalem,
And Christian India, through her widespread
    clime,
In sacred converse gifts with Alfred shares.

II

When thy great soul was freed from mortal chains,
Darling of England! many a bitter shower
Fell on thy tomb; but emulative power
Flowed in thy line through undegenerate veins.
The Race of Alfred covet glorious pains
When dangers threaten, dangers ever new!
Black tempests bursting, blacker still in view!
But manly sovereignty its hold retains;
The root sincere, the branches bold to strive
With the fierce tempest, while, within the round
Of their protection, gentle virtues thrive;
As oft, 'mid some green plot of open ground,
Wide as the oak extends its dewy gloom,
The fostered hyacinths spread their purple bloom.

CANUTE THE DANE

MICHAEL FIELD

EDGAR'S son, Ethelred the Unready, was a feeble king, and the realm was wrested from him by Swegen, king of Denmark. Canute, Swegen's son, reigned over England twenty-one years (1014–1035). The Danes were hated by the English as barbarians and pagans, but Canute became a Christian and proved a wise and able ruler.

ACT III

SCENE II

Canute (*a voice singing*). Is that a child
At babble with his vespers? — Silver sweet!
It minds me of the holy brotherhood,
Chanting adown the banks. As yesterday

I see all clear, how as they moved, they chanted,
And made a mute procession in the stream.

(*Gazing abstractedly on the water.*)

Merrily sang the monks of Ely,
As Canute the king passed by.
Row to the shore, knights, said the king,
And let us hear these churchmen sing.

Still are they singing ?   It was Candlemas,
My queen sat splendid at the prow and listened
With heaving breast.   'Twas then the passion seized
me
To emulate, to let her know my ear
Had common pleasure with her, and I trilled
The story out.   The look she turned on me !
The choir shall sing this music.   I resolved
In the glory of the verse to civilize
My blood, to sweeten it, to give it law,
To curb my wild thoughts with the rein of metre.
Row to the shore !   So pleasantly it ran,
A ripple on the wave.   I grew ambitious
To be a scholar like King Alfred, gather
Wise men about me, in myself possess
A treasure, an enchantment.   For an instant
I looked round royally, and felt a king.
The abbey-chant, the stream, the meadow-land,
The willows glimmering in the sun ; — a poet
Wins things to come so close.

KING CANUTE

WILLIAM MAKEPEACE THACKERAY

CANUTE was king not of England only, but of Scotland, Denmark, and the islands of the North Sea even to Iceland. The story of the rebuke given to his fawning courtiers illustrates the humility of a really great man.

King Canute was weary-hearted ; he had reigned for
      years a score,
Battling, struggling, pushing, fighting, killing much
      and robbing more ;
And he thought upon his actions, walking by the
      wild seashore.

'Twixt the Chancellor and Bishop, walked the King
      with steps sedate,
Chamberlains and grooms came after, silversticks and
      goldsticks great,
Chaplains, aides-de-camp, and pages, — all the officers
      of state.

Sliding after like his shadow, pausing when he chose
      to pause,
If a frown his face contracted, straight the courtiers
      dropped their jaws ;
If to laugh the King was minded, out they burst in
      loud hee-haws.

But that day a something vexed him ; that was clear
      to old and young ;
Thrice his Grace had yawned at table when his
      favorite gleemen sung,

And the Queen would have consoled him, but he
bade her hold her tongue.

"Something ails my gracious master!" cried the
Keeper of the Seal,
"Sure, my lord, it is the lampreys served to dinner,
or the veal?"
"Psha!" exclaimed the angry monarch, "Keeper,
'tis not that I feel.

" 'Tis the *heart*, and not the dinner, fool, that doth
my rest impair.
Can a king be great as I am, prithee, and yet know
no care?
Oh, I'm sick, and tired, and weary." —Some one cried,
" The King's armchair!"

Then toward the lackeys turning, quick my Lord
the Keeper nodded,
Straight the King's great chair was brought him by
two footmen able-bodied.
Languidly he sank into it; it was comfortably
wadded.

" Leading on my fierce companions," cried he, " over
storm and brine,
I have fought and I have conquered! where was
glory like to mine?"
Loudly all the courtiers echoed, "Where is glory like
to thine?"

" What avail me all my kingdoms?   Weary am I now
and old;

Those fair sons I have begotten long to see me dead
    and cold ;
Would I were, and quiet buried underneath the silent
    mould !

" Oh, remorse, the writhing serpent ! at my bosom
    tears and bites ;
Horrid, horrid things I look on, though I put out all
    the lights ;
Ghosts of ghastly recollections troop about my bed at
    nights.

"Cities burning, convents blazing, red with sacrilegious
    fires ;
Mothers weeping, virgins screaming vainly for their
    slaughtered sires."
" Such a tender conscience," cries the Bishop, " every
    one admires.

" Look, the land is crowned with minsters, which your
    Grace's bounty raised ;
Abbeys filled with holy men, where you and Heaven
    are daily praised ;
You, my lord, to think of dying ? on my conscience
    I'm amazed ! "

" Nay, I feel," replied King Canute, " that my end is
    drawing near."
" Don't say so," exclaimed the courtiers (striving each
    to squeeze a tear).
" Sure your Grace is strong and lusty, and may live
    this fifty year."

"Live these fifty years?" the Bishop roared, with
    actions made to suit.
"Are you mad, my good Lord Keeper, thus to speak
    of King Canute?
Men have lived a thousand years, and sure His Majesty
    will do't.

"Adam, Enoch, Lamech, Cainan, Mahaleel, Methusela
Lived nine hundred years apiece, and mayn't the King
    as well as they?"
"Fervently," exclaimed the Keeper, "fervently I trust
    he may."

"*He* to die?" resumed the Bishop.   "He a mortal
    like to *us?*
Death was not for him intended, though *communis
    omnibus;*
Keeper, you are irreligious for to talk and cavil thus.

"With his wondrous skill in healing ne'er a doctor
    can compete,
Loathsome lepers, if he touch them, start up clean
    upon their feet;
Surely he could raise the dead up, did his Highness
    think it meet.

"Did not once the Jewish captain stay the sun upon
    the hill,
And the while he slew the foemen, bid the silver moon
    stand still?
So, no doubt, could gracious Canute, if it were his
    sacred will."

" Might I stay the sun above us, good Sir Bishop ? "
    Canute cried ;
" Could I bid the silver moon to pause upon her
    heavenly ride ?
If the moon obeys my orders, sure I can command
    the tide !

" Will the advancing waves obey me, Bishop, if I make
    the sign ? "
Said the Bishop, bowing lowly : " Land and sea, my
    lord, are thine."
Canute turned towards the ocean — " Back ! " he said,
    " thou foaming brine.

" From the sacred shore I stand on, I command thee
    to retreat ;
Venture not, thou stormy rebel, to approach thy
    master's seat ;
Ocean, be thou still ! I bid thee come not nearer to
    my feet ! "

But the sullen ocean answered with a louder, deeper
    roar,
And the rapid waves drew nearer, falling sounding on
    the shore ;
Back the Keeper and the Bishop, back the King and
    courtiers bore.

And he sternly bade them never more to kneel to
    human clay,
But alone to praise and worship that which earth and
    seas obey ;

And his golden crown of empire never wore he from
    that day.
King Canute is dead and gone : Parasites exist alway.

HAROLD

LORD TENNYSON

EDWARD THE CONFESSOR, son of Ethelred and Emma, who had spent
his boyhood in exile at the Norman court, was elected king after the
death of Harthacanute.   He was Norman at heart, and had little con-
cern for the well-being of England.   Having no children, he promised
to leave the kingdom to his kinsman, William, Duke of Normandy.
Harold, Earl of Wessex, was preferred by the English, but William won
the crown through craft and violence.   Harold was tricked into swear-
ing to support the Norman's claim to the throne, and when, on Edward's
death, the Witan elected the Earl of Wessex king, William crossed the
Channel with a great army to seize the government.   Landing at
Pevensey, he met Harold's army at Senlac Hill and destroyed it (1066).
Harold himself was killed by a falling arrow that pierced his eye.

ACT I

SCENE I.   LONDON.   *The King's Palace.*

(*A comet seen through the open window.*)

King, Queen, the Lady Aldwyth, Harold, and Tostig.

Edward.   In heaven signs !
Signs upon earth ! signs everywhere ! your Priests
Gross, worldly, simoniacal, unlearn'd !
They scarce can read their Psalter ; and your churches
Uncouth, unhandsome, while in Normanland
God speaks thro' abler voices, as He dwells
In statelier shrines.   I say not this, as being
Half Norman-blooded, nor as some have held,

Because I love the Norman better — no,
But dreading God's revenge upon this realm
For narrowness and coldness: and I say it
For the last time perchance, before I go
To find the sweet refreshment of the Saints.
I have lived a life of utter purity:
I have builded the great church of Holy Peter:
I have wrought miracles — to God the glory —
And miracles will in my name be wrought
Hereafter. — I have fought the fight and go —
I see the flashing of the gates of pearl —
And it is well with me, tho' some of you
Have scorn'd me — ay — but after I am gone
Woe, woe to England! I have had a vision;
The seven sleepers in the cave at Ephesus
Have turn'd from right to left.
   Harold.   My most dear Master,
What matters? Let them turn from left to right
And sleep again.
   Tostig.   Too hardy with thy king!
A life of prayer and fasting well may see
Deeper into the mysteries of heaven
Than thou, good brother.
   Aldwyth (*aside*).   Sees he into thine,
That thou wouldst have his promise for the crown?
   Edward. Tostig says true; my son, thou art too hard,
Not stagger'd by this ominous earth and heaven:
But heaven and earth are threads of the same loom,
Play into one another, and weave the web
That may confound thee yet.

 Harold.   Nay, I trust not,
For I have served thee long and honestly.

 Edward. I know it, son ; I am not thankless : thou
Hast broken all my foes, lighten'd for me
The weight of this poor crown, and left me time
And peace for prayer to gain a better one.
Twelve years of service ! England loves thee for it.
Thou art the man to rule her !

 Aldwyth (*aside*).   So, not Tostig !

 Harold. And after those twelve years a boon, my
  king,
Respite, a holiday : thyself wast wont
To love the chase : the leave to set my feet
On board, and hunt and hawk beyond the seas !

 Edward. What, with this flaming horror overhead ?

 Harold. Well, when it passes then.

 Edward.   Ay if it pass.
Go not to Normandy — go not to Normandy.

 Harold. And wherefore not, my king, to Nor-
  mandy ?
Is not my brother Wulfnoth hostage there
For my dead father's loyalty to thee?
I pray thee, let me hence and bring him home.

ACT II

Scene II. Bayeux Palace.

Count William and William Malet.

 William. We hold our Saxon woodcock in the
  springe,

But he begins to flutter.   As I think
He was thine host in England when I went
To visit Edward.
   Malet.   Yea, and there, my lord,
To make allowance for their rougher fashions,
I found him all a noble host should be.
   William. Thou art his friend : thou knowst my
      claim on England
Thro' Edward's promise : we have him in the toils.
And it were well, if thou shouldst let him feel
How dense a fold of danger nets him round,
So that he bristle himself against my will.
   Malet. What would I do, my lord, if I were you ?
   William. What wouldst thou do ?
   Malet.   My lord, he is thy guest.
   William. Nay, by the splendor of God, no guest
      of mine.
He came not to see me, had passed me by
To hunt and hawk elsewhere, save for the fate
Which hunted *him* when that un-Saxon blast,
And bolts of thunder moulded in high heaven
To serve the Norman purpose, drave and crack'd
His boat on Ponthieu beach ; where our friend
      Guy
Had wrung his ransom from him by the rack,
But that I stept between and purchased him,
Translating his captivity from Guy
To mine own hearth at Bayeux, where he sits
My ransom'd prisoner.

        *   *   *   *   *   *   *

(*Enter William Rufus.*)

William Rufus.   Father.

William.   Well, boy.

William Rufus. They have taken away the toy
thou gavest me,

The Norman knight.

William.   Why, boy?

William Rufus.   Because I broke
The horse's leg — it was mine own to break;
I like to have my toys, and break them too.

William. Well, thou shalt have another Norman
knight!

William Rufus. And may I break his legs?

William.   Yea, — get thee gone!

William Rufus. I'll tell them I have had my way
with thee.   [*Exit.*

Malet. I never knew thee check thy will for aught
Save for the prattling of thy little ones.

William. Who shall be kings of England. I am
heir

Of England by the promise of her king.

Malet. But there the great Assembly choose their
king,

The choice of England is the voice of England.

William. I will be king of England by the laws,
The choice, and voice of England.

Malet.   Can that be?

William. The voice of any people is the sword
That guards them, or the sword that beats them down.
Here comes the would-be what I will be — kinglike —

Tho' scarce at ease; for, save our meshes break,
More kinglike he than like to prove a king.

(*Enter Harold, musing, with his eyes on the ground.*)

* * * * * * *

[*Exeunt Count William and Malet.*

* * * * * * *

Harold. (*A man-at-arms follows him.*)
I need thee not. Why dost thou follow me?
  Man-at-arms. I have the Count's commands to fol-
    low thee.
  Harold. What then? Am I in danger in this court?
  Man-at-arms. I cannot tell. I have the Count's
    commands.
  Harold. Stand out of earshot then, and keep me
    still
In eyeshot.
  Man-at-arms. Yea, Lord Harold. (*Withdraws.*)
  Harold.   And arm'd men
Ever keep watch beside my chamber door,
And if I walk within the lonely wood,
There is an arm'd man ever glides behind!

* * * * * * *

(*Muttering.*) Go not to Normandy, — go not to Nor-
  mandy!

      (*Enter Wulfnoth.*)

Poor brother! still a hostage!
  Wulfnoth.   Yea, and I
Shall see the dewy kiss of dawn no more
Make blush the maiden-white of our tall cliffs,

Nor mark the sea-bird rouse himself and hover
Above the windy ripple, and fill the sky
With free sea-laughter — never — save indeed
Thou canst make yield this iron-mooded Duke
To let me go.

    Harold.   Why, brother, so he will :
But on conditions.   Canst thou guess at them ?

    Wulfnoth.   Draw nearer, — I was in the corridor,
I saw him coming with his brother Odo
The Bayeux bishop, and I hid myself.

    Harold. They did thee wrong who made thee
        hostage ; thou
Wast ever fearful.

    Wulfnoth.   And he spoke — I heard him —
" This Harold is not of the royal blood,
Can have no right to the crown," and Odo said,
" Thine is the right, for thine the might : he is here,
And yonder is thy keep."

    Harold.   No, Wulfnoth, no.

    Wulfnoth. And William laugh'd and swore that
        might was right,
Far as he knew in this poor world of ours —
" Marry, the Saints must go along with us,
And, brother, we will find a way," said he —
Yea, yea, he would be king of England.

    Harold.   Never !

    Wulfnoth. Yea, but thou must not this way answer
        him.

    Harold. Is it not better still to speak the truth ?

    Wulfnoth. Not here, or thou wilt never hence
       nor I ;

For in the racing toward this golden goal
He turns not right or left, but tramples flat
Whatever thwarts him; hast thou never heard
His savagery at Alençon, — the town
Hung out raw hides along their walls, and cried
"Work for the tanner."

    Harold.   That had angered *me*,
Had I been William.

    Wulfnoth.   Nay, but he had prisoners,
He tore their eyes out, sliced their hands away,
And flung them streaming o'er the battlements
Upon the heads of those who walk'd within —
O speak him fair, Harold, for thine own sake.

    Harold. Your Welshman says, " The Truth against
    the World,"

Much more the truth against myself.

    Wulfnoth.   Thyself?

But for my sake, oh, brother! oh! for my sake!

    Harold. Poor Wulfnoth! do they not entreat thee
    well?

    Wulfnoth. I see the blackness of my dungeon loom
Across their lamps of revel, and beyond
The merriest murmurs of their banquet clank
The shackles that will bind me to the wall.

    Harold. Too fearful still.

    Wulfnoth.   Oh no, no, — speak him fair !

Call it to temporize; and not to lie;
Harold, I do not counsel thee to lie.
The man that hath to foil a murderous aim
May, surely, play with words.

·　*Harold.*　　　　　　　　　Words are the man.
Not ev'n for thy sake, brother, would I lie.
　Wulfnoth.　Then for thine Edith?
　Harold.　　　　　　　There thou prickst me deep.
　Wulfnoth.　And for our Mother England?
　Harold.　　　　　　　　　Deeper still.
　Wulfnoth.　And deeper still the deep-down oubli-
　　ette,
Down thirty feet below the smiling day —
In blackness — dogs' food thrown upon thy head.
And over thee the suns arise and set,
And the lark sings, the sweet stars come and go,
And men are at their markets, in their fields,
And woo their loves and have forgotten thee;
And thou art upright in thy living grave,
Where there is barely room to shift thy side,
And all thine England hath forgotten thee;
And he our lazy-pious Norman King,
With all his Normans round him once again,
Counts his old beads, and hath forgotten thee.

　　　*　　*　　*　　*　　*　　*　　*
　　　(*Enter William and Malet.*)
　　　*　　*　　*　　*　　*　　*　　*

　Harold.　　　　　　Then let me hence
With Wulfnoth to King Edward.
　William.　　　　　　So we will.
We hear he hath not long to live.
　Harold.　　　　　　It may be.
　William.　Why then the heir of England, who is he?
　Harold.　The Atheling is nearest to the throne.

William. But sickly, slight, half-witted and a child,
Will England have him king?

Harold.   It may be, no.

William. And hath King Edward not pronounced
his heir?

Harold. Not that I know.

William.   When he was here in Normandy,
He loved us and we him, because we found him
A Norman of the Normans.

Harold.   So did we.

William. A gentle, gracious, pure and saintly
man!
And grateful to the hand that shielded him,
He promised that if ever he were king
In England, he would give his kingly voice
To me as his successor.   Knowest thou this?

Harold. I learn it now.

William.   Thou knowest I am his cousin,
And that my wife descends from Alfred?

Harold.   Ay.

William. Who hath a better claim then to the
crown
So that ye will not crown the Atheling?

Harold. None that I know — if that but hung upon
King Edward's will.

William.   Wilt *thou* uphold my claim?

Malet (*aside to Harold*). Be careful of thine
answer, my good friend.

Wulfnoth (*aside to Harold*). Oh! Harold, for my
sake and for thine own!

Harold. Ay — if the king have not revoked his
   promise.

William. But hath he done it then ?

Harold. Not that I know.

William. Good, good, and thou wilt help me to the
   crown.

Harold. Ay — if the Witan will consent to this.

William. Thou are the mightiest voice in England,
   man,

Thy voice will lead the Witan — shall I have it ?

Wulfnoth (aside to Harold). Oh ! Harold, if thou
   love thine Edith, ay.

Harold.   Ay, if —

Malet (aside to Harold). Thine ' ifs ' will sear
   thine eyes out — ay.

William. I ask thee, wilt thou help me to the crown ?
And I will make thee my great Earl of Earls,
Foremost in England and in Normandy ;
Thou shalt be verily king — all but the name —
For I shall most sojourn in Normandy ;
And thou be my vice-king in England.   Speak.

Wulfnoth (aside to Harold). Ay, brother — for the
   sake of England — ay.

Harold.   My lord —

Malet (aside to Harold). Take heed now.

Harold. Ay.

William.   I am content,

For thou art truthful, and thy word thy bond.
To-morrow will we ride with thee to Harfleur.

                                  [*Exit William.*

Malet. Harold, I am thy friend, one life with thee,
And even as I should bless thee, saving mine,
I thank thee now for having saved thyself.

[*Exit Malet.*

Harold. For having lost myself to save myself,
Said 'ay' when I meant 'no,' lied like a lad
That dreads the pendent scourge, said 'ay' for 'no'!
Ay! No! — he hath not bound me by an oath —
Is 'ay' an oath? is 'ay' strong as an oath?
Or is it the same sin to break my word
As break mine oath? He call'd my word my bond!
He is a liar who knows I am a liar,
And makes believe that he believes my word —
The crime be on his head — not bounden — no.

(*Suddenly doors are flung open, discovering in an inner hall Count William in his state robes, seated upon his throne, between two bishops, Odo of Bayeux being one: in the centre of the hall an ark covered with cloth of gold; and on either side of it the Norman barons.*)

*   *   *   *   *   *   *

William. (*Descends from his throne and stands by the ark.*)

Let all men here bear witness of our bond!

(*Beckons to Harold, who advances. Enter Malet behind him.*)

Lay thou thy hand upon this golden pall!
Behold the jewel of St. Pancratius
Woven into the gold. Swear thou on this!

Harold. What should I swear? Why should I swear on this?

William (*savagely*). Swear thou to help me to the
crown of England.

Malet (*whispering Harold*). My friend, thou hast
gone too far to palter now.

Wulfnoth (*whispering Harold*). Swear thou to-day,
to-morrow is thine own.

Harold. I swear to help thee to the crown of
England —

According as King Edward promises.

William. Thou must swear absolutely, noble Earl.

Malet (*whispering*). Delay is death to thee, ruin
to England.

Wulfnoth (*whispering*). Swear, dearest brother,
I beseech thee, swear !

Harold (*putting his hand on the jewel*). I swear to
help thee to the crown of England.

William. Thanks, truthful Earl ; I did not doubt
thy word,

But that my barons might believe thy word,

And that the Holy Saints of Normandy

When thou art home in England, with thine own,

Might strengthen thee in keeping of thy word,

I made thee swear. — Show him by whom he hath
sworn.

(*The two bishops advance, and raise the cloth of
gold. The bodies and bones of Saints are seen lying
in the ark.*)

The holy bones of all the Canonized

From all the holiest shrines in Normandy !

Harold. Horrible !

ACT V

SCENE I. *A Tent on a Mound from which can be seen the Field of Senlac. Monks chanting in the distance.*

Edith and Stigand, Archbishop of Canterbury.

Edith. Are those the blessed angels quiring, father?

Stigand. No, daughter, but the canons out of Waltham,
The king's foundation, that have follow'd him.

Edith. O God of battles, make their wall of shields
Firm as thy cliffs, strengthen their palisades!
What is that whirring sound?

Stigand. The Norman arrow!

Edith. Look out upon the battle — is he safe?

Stigand. The king of England stands between his banners.
He glitters on the crowning of the hill.
God save King Harold!

Edith. — chosen by his people,
And fighting for his people!

Stigand. There is one
Come as Goliath came of yore — he flings
His brand in air and catches it again;
He is chanting some old war song.

Edith. And no David
To meet him?

Stigand. Ay, there springs a Saxon on him,
Falls — and another falls.

Edith. Have mercy on us!

Stigand. Lo! our good Gurth hath smitten him to
   the death.
Edith. So perish all the enemies of Harold!

                    Canons singing.

         *   *   *   *   *   *   *

English Cries. Harold and Holy Cross! Out! out!
Stigand. Our javelins
Answer their arrows.   All the Norman foot
Are storming up the hill.   The range of knights
Sit, each a statue on his horse, and wait.
   English Cries. Harold and God Almighty!
   Norman Cries.   Ha Rou! Ha Rou!

                    Canons singing.

         *   *   *   *   *   *   *

Stigand. Look, daughter, look.
Edith.   Nay, father, look for *me!*
Stigand. Our axes lighten with a single flash
About the summit of the hill, and heads
And arms are sliver'd off and splinter'd by
Their lightning — and they fly — the Norman flies.
   Edith. Stigand, O father, have we won the day?
   Stigand. No, daughter, no — they fall behind the
      horse —
Their horse are thronging to the barricades;
I see the gonfanon of Holy Peter
Floating above their helmets — ha! he is down!
   Edith. He down!   Who down?
   Stigand.   The Norman Count is down.
   Edith. So perish all the enemies of England!
   Stigand. No, no, he hath risen again — he bares
      his face —

Shouts something — he points onward — all their
    horse
Swallow the hill locust-like, swarming up.

    Edith. O God of battles, make his battle-axe keen
As thine own sharp-dividing justice, heavy
As thine own bolts that fall on crimeful heads
Charged with the weight of heaven wherefrom they
    fall!

Canons singing.

*   *   *   *   *   *   *

    Edith. O God of battles, they are three to one,
Make thou one man as three to roll them down!

Canons singing.

*   *   *   *   *   *   *

    Stigand. Yea, yea, for how their lances snap and
    shiver
Against the shifting blaze of Harold's axe!
War-woodman of old Woden, how he fells
The mortal copse of faces! There! And there!
The horse and horseman cannot meet the shield.
The blow that brains the horseman cleaves the horse,
The horse and horseman roll along the hill,
They fly once more, they fly, the Norman flies!

*   *   *   *   *   *   *

    Edith. O God, the God of truth hath heard my cry.
Follow them, follow them, drive them to the sea!

    Stigand. Truth! no; a lie; a trick, a Norman trick!
They turn on the pursuer, horse against foot,
They murder all that follow.

    Edith.   Have mercy on us!

Stigand. Hot-headed fools — to burst the wall of
   shields!
They have broken the commandment of the king!
   Edith. *His* oath was broken. — O holy Norman
   Saints,
Ye that are now of Heaven, and see beyond
Your Norman shrines, pardon it, pardon it,
That he forsware himself for all he loved,
Me, me and all! Look out upon the battle!
   Stigand. They press again upon the barricades.
My sight is eagle, but the strife so thick —
This is the hottest of it: hold, ash! hold, willow!
   English Cries. Out, out!
   Norman Cries.   Ha Rou!
   Stigand.   Ha! Gurth hath leapt upon him
And slain him: he hath fallen.
   Edith.   And I am heard.
Glory to God in the Highest! fallen, fallen!
   Stigand. No, no, his horse — he mounts another —
   wields
His war-club, dashes it on Gurth, and Gurth,
Our noble Gurth, is down!
   Edith.   Have mercy on us!
   Stigand. And Leofwin is down!
   Edith.   Have mercy on us!
O Thou that knowest, let not my strong prayer
Be weaken'd in thy sight, because I love
The husband of another!
   Norman Cries.   Ha Rou! Ha Rou!
   Edith. I do not hear our English war-cry.
   Stigand.   No.

Edith. Look out upon the battle — is he safe?

Stigand. He stands between the banners with the dead

So piled about him he can hardly move.

Edith (*takes up the war-cry*). Out! out!

Norman Cries. Ha Rou!

Edith (*cries out*). Harold and Holy Cross!

Norman Cries. Ha Rou! Ha Rou!

Edith. What is that whirring sound?

Stigand. The Norman sends his arrows up to Heaven,

They fall on those within the palisade!

Edith. Look out upon the hill — is Harold there?

Stigand. Sanguelac — Sanguelac — the arrow — the arrow! — away!

SCENE II. *Field of the Dead. Night.*

Edith, beside Harold's body. Count William and Malet.

Edith. And thou,

Thy wife am I for ever and evermore.

(*Falls on Harold's body and dies.*)

William. Death! — and enough of death for this one day,

The day of St. Calixtus, and the day,

My day, when I was born.

Malet. And this dead king's,

Who, king or not, hath kinglike fought and fallen,

His birthday, too. It seems but yestereven

I held it with him in his English halls,

His day, with all his rooftree ringing " Harold,"
Before he fell into the snare of Guy ;
When all men counted Harold would be king,
And Harold was most happy.

   William.   Thou art half English.
Take them away !
Malet, I vow I build a church to God
Here on this hill of battle ; let our high altar
Stand where their standard fell — where these two lie.
Take them away, I do not love to see them.
Pluck the dead woman off the dead man, Malet !

   Malet. Faster than ivy.   Must I hack her arms off ?
How shall I part them ?

   William. Leave them.   Let them be !

      *   *   *   *   *   *   *

Wrap them together in a purple cloak
And lay them both upon the waste seashore
At Hastings, there to guard the land for which
He did forswear himself — a warrior — ay,
And but that Holy Peter fought for us,
And that the false Northumbrian held aloof,
And save for that chance arrow which the Saints
Sharpen'd and sent against him — who can tell ? —
Three horses had I slain beneath me : twice
I thought that all was lost.   Since I knew battle,
And that was from my boyhood, never yet —
No, by the splendor of God — have I fought men
Like Harold and his brethren, and his guard
Of English.   Every man about his king
Fell where he stood.   They loved him : and, pray God

My Normans may but move as true with me
To the door of death. Of one self-stock at first,
Make them again one people — Norman, English ;
And English, Norman ; — we should have a hand
To grasp the world with, and a foot to stamp it —
Flat. Praise the Saints. It is over. No more blood !
I am King of England, so they thwart me not,
And I will rule according to their laws.

THE RED KING

CHARLES KINGSLEY

WILLIAM RUFUS, THE RED (1066–1087), was a man of fierce and cruel temper. Far from working for the happiness of his people, he plundered the rich and oppressed the poor. His greed of gold and his reckless pursuit of evil pleasures made him many enemies. This much-hated king was shot by an arrow, whether by accident or intentionally was never known, while hunting in the New Forest. A brother of William Rufus and a nephew had already been killed in this same forest, and men believed that a curse rested on the place.

The King was drinking in Malwood Hall,
There came in a monk before them all :
He thrust by squire, he thrust by knight,
Stood over against the dais aright ;
And, " The Word of the Lord, thou cruel Red King,
The word of the Lord to thee I bring.
A grimly sweven [1] I dreamt yestreen ;
I saw thee lie under the hollins green,
And through thine heart an arrow keen ;
And out of thy body a smoke did rise,
Which smirched the sunshine out of the skies :

[1] ominous dream.

So if thou God's anointed be
I rede thee unto thy soul thou see.
For mitre and pall thou hast y-sold,
False knight to Christ, for gain and gold;
And for this thy forest were digged down all,
Steading [1] and hamlet and churches tall;
And Christès poor were ousten forth,
To beg their bread from south to north.
So tarry at home, and fast and pray,
Lest fiends hunt thee in the judgment-day."

The monk he vanished where he stood;
King William sterte up wroth and wood [2];
Quod [3] he, " Fools' wits will jump together;
The Hampshire ale and the thunder weather
Have turned the brains for us both, I think;
And monks are curst [4] when they fall to drink.
A lothly sweven I dreamt last night,
How there hoved [5] anigh me a griesly knight,
Did smite me down to the pit of hell;
I shrieked and woke, so fast I fell.
There's Tyrrel as sour as I, perdie,
So he of you all shall hunt with me;
A grimly brace [6] for a hart to see."

The Red King down from Malwood came;
His heart with wine was all aflame,
His eyne were shotten, red as blood,
He rated and swore, wherever he rode.

[1] homestead.   [2] frantic.   [3] quoth.
[4] malicious.   [5] drew.   [6] terrible pair.

They roused a hart, that grimly brace ;
A hart of ten, a hart of grease,
Fled over against the kingès place.
The sun it blinded the kingès ee,
A fathom behind his hocks shot he :
"Shoot thou," quod he, "in the fiendès name,
To lose such a quarry were seven years' shame."
And he hove up his hand to mark the game.
Tyrrel he shot full light, God wot ;
For whether the saints they swerved the shot,
Or whether by treason, men knowen not,
But under the arm, in a secret part,
The iron fled through the kingès heart.
The turf it squelched where the Red King fell,
And the fiends they carried his soul to hell,
Quod "His master's name it hath sped him well."

Tyrrel he smited full grim that day,
Quod "Shooting of kings is no bairns' play ; "
And he smote in the spurs, and fled fast away.
As he pricked along by Fritham plain,
The green tufts flew behind like rain ;
The waters were out, and over the sward :
He swam his horse like a stalwart lord ;
Men clepen [1] that water Tyrrel's ford.
By Rhinefield and by Osmondsleigh,
Through glade and furze-brake fast drove he,
Until he heard the roaring sea ;
Quod he, "Those gay waves they call me."
By Mary's grace a seely [2] boat

[1] call. [2] frail.

On Christchurch bar did lie afloat ;
He gave the shipmen mark and groat,
To ferry him over to Normandie,
And there he fell to sanctuarie ;
God send his soul all bliss to see.

And fend [1] our princes every one,
From foul mishap and trahison ; [2]
But kings that harrow Christian men,
Shall England never bide again.

THE WHITE SHIP

DANTE GABRIEL ROSSETTI

HENRY I. (1100–1135), the fourth son of the Conqueror, was left by his father with a good sum in money, but no land; yet he became a great king. He succeeded to the throne of England on the death of William Rufus, and he later wrested the duchy of Normandy from his eldest brother Robert. It was a turbulent time, and the king was constantly at war with one or another of his powerful barons. At last he had reason to hope for peace. He had married his only son William to the daughter of his strongest adversary, Fulc of Anjou, and the barons of England and of Normandy had done homage to his son, recognizing him as heir to the throne. The wreck of the White Ship in the harbor of Honfleur (November 25, 1120) blasted all Henry's hopes, for he could not expect that the unruly barons would accept his daughter Matilda as their sovereign. At his death began a civil war that lasted for twenty years.

By none but me can the tale be told,
The butcher of Rouen, poor Berold.
  (*Lands are swayed by a King on a throne.*)
'Twas a royal train put forth to sea,
Yet the tale can be told by none but me.
  (*The sea hath no King but God alone.*)

1 guard.   2 treason.

King Henry held it as life's whole gain
That after his death his son should reign.

'Twas so in my youth I heard men say,
And my old age calls it back to-day.

King Henry of England's realm was he,
And Henry duke of Normandy.

The times had changed when on either coast
"Clerkly Harry" was all his boast.

Of ruthless strokes full many an one
He had struck to crown himself and son;
And his elder brother's eyes were gone.

And when to the chase his court would crowd,
The poor flung ploughshares on his road,
And shrieked: "Our cry is from King to God!"

But all the chiefs of the English land
Had knelt and kissed the Prince's hand.

And next with his son he sailed to France
To claim the Norman allegiance.

And every baron in Normandy
Had taken the oath of fealty.

'Twas sworn and sealed, and the day had come
When the King and the Prince might journey home.

For Christmas cheer is to home hearts dear,
And Christmas now was drawing near.

Stout Fitz-Stephen came to the King, —
A pilot famous in seafaring;

And he held to the King, in all men's sight,
A mark of gold for his tribute's right.

" Liege Lord ! my father guided the ship
From whose boat your father's foot did slip
When he caught the English soil in his grip,

" And cried : ' By this clasp I claim command
O'er every rood of English land ! '

" He was borne to the realm you rule o'er now
In that ship with the archer carved at her prow :

" And thither I'll bear, an' it be my due,
Your father's son and his grandson too.

"The famed White Ship is mine in the bay,
From Harfleur's harbor she sails to-day,

" With masts fair-pennoned as Norman spears
And with fifty well-tried mariners."

Quoth the King : " My ships are chosen each one,
But I'll not say nay to Stephen's son.

" My son and daughter and fellowship
Shall cross the water in the White Ship."

The King set sail with the eve's south wind,
And soon he left that coast behind.

The Prince and all his, a princely show,
Remained in the good White Ship to go.

With noble knights and with ladies fair,
With courtiers and sailors gathered there,
Three hundred living souls we were :

And I Berold was the meanest hind
In all that train to the Prince assign'd.

The Prince was a lawless shameless youth;
From his father's loins he sprang without ruth:

Eighteen years till then he had seen,
And the devil's dues in him were eighteen.

And now he cried: "Bring wine from below;
Let the sailors revel ere yet they row:

"Our speed shall o'ertake my father's flight
Though we sail from the harbor at midnight."

The rowers made good cheer without check;
The lords and ladies obeyed his beck;
The night was light, and they danced on the deck.

But at midnight's stroke they cleared the bay,
And the White Ship furrowed the water-way.

The sails were set, and the oars kept tune
To the double flight of the ship and the moon:

Swifter and swifter the White Ship sped
Till she flew as the spirit flies from the dead:

As white as a lily glimmered she
Like a ship's fair ghost upon the sea.

And the Prince cried, "Friends, 'tis the hour to sing!
Is a songbird's course so swift on the wing?"

And under the winter stars' still throng,
From brown throats, white throats, merry and strong,
The knights and the ladies raised a song.

A song, — nay, a shriek that rent the sky,
That leaped o'er the deep! — the grievous cry
Of three hundred living that now must die.

An instant shriek that sprang to the shock
As the ship's keel felt the sunken rock.

'Tis said that afar — a shrill strange sigh —
The King's ships heard it, and knew not why.

Pale Fitz-Stephen stood by the helm
'Mid all those folk that the waves must whelm.

A great King's heir for the waves to whelm,
And the helpless pilot pale at the helm!

The ship was eager and sucked athirst,
By the stealthy stab of the sharp reef pierc'd:

And like the moil round a sinking cup
The waters against her crowded up.

A moment the pilot's senses spin, —
The next he snatched the Prince 'mid the din,
Cut the boat loose, and the youth leaped in.

A few friends leaped with him, standing near.
" Row! the sea's smooth and the night is clear! "

"What! none to be saved but these and I?"
" Row, row as you'd live!   All here must die!"

Out of the churn of the choking ship,
Which the gulf grapples and the waves strip,
They struck with the strained oars' flash and dip.

'Twas then o'er the splitting bulwarks' brim
The Prince's sister screamed to him.

He gazed aloft, still rowing apace,
And through the whirled surf he knew her face.

To the toppling decks clave one and all
As a fly cleaves to a chamber-wall.

I Berold was clinging anear;
I prayed for myself and quaked with fear,
But I saw his eyes as he looked at her.

He knew her face and he heard her cry,
And he said, " Put back! she must not die! "

And back with the current's force they reel
Like a leaf that's drawn to a water-wheel.

'Neath the ship's travail they scarce might float,
But he rose and stood in the rocking boat.

Low the poor ship leaned on the tide:
O'er the naked keel as she best might slide,
The sister toiled to the brother's side.

He reached an oar to her from below,
And stiffened his arms to clutch her so.

But now from the ship some spied the boat,
And " Saved! " was the cry from many a throat.

And down to the boat they leaped and fell:
It turned as a bucket turns in a well,
And nothing was there but the surge and swell.

The Prince that was and the King to come,
There in an instant gone to his doom,

Despite of all England's bended knee
And maugre the Norman fealty!

He was a Prince of lust and pride;
He showed no grace till the hour he died.

When he should be King, he oft would vow,
He'd yoke the peasant to his own plough.
O'er him the ships score their furrows now.

God only knows where his soul did wake,
But I saw him die for his sister's sake.

By none but me can the tale be told,
The butcher of Rouen, poor Berold.
 (*Lands are swayed by a King on a throne.*)
'Twas a royal train put forth to sea,
Yet the tale can be told by none but me.
 (*The sea hath no King but God alone.*)

And now the end came o'er the waters' womb
Like the last great Day that's yet to come.

With prayers in vain and curses in vain,
The White Ship sundered on the mid-main:

And what were men and what was a ship
Were toys and splinters in the sea's grip.

I Berold was down in the sea ;
And passing strange though the thing may be,
Of dreams then known I remember me.

Blithe is the shout on Harfleur's strand
When morning lights the sails to land :

And blithe is Honfleur's echoing gloam
When mothers call the children home :

And high do the bells of Rouen beat
When the Body of Christ goes down the street.

These things and the like were heard and shown
In a moment's trance 'neath the sea alone ;

And when I rose, 'twas the sea did seem,
And not these things, to be all a dream.

The ship was gone and the crowd was gone,
And the deep shuddered and the moon shone,

And in a strait grasp my arms did span
The mainyard rent from the mast where it ran ;
And on it with me was another man.

Where lands were none 'neath the dim sea-sky,
We told our names, that man and I.

" O I am Godefroy de l'Aigle hight,
And son I am to a belted knight."

" And I am Berold the butcher's son
Who slays the beasts in Rouen town."

Then cried we upon God's name, as we
Did drift on the bitter winter sea.

But lo! a third man rose o'er the wave,
And we said, "Thank God! us three may He save!"

He clutched to the yard with panting stare,
And we looked and knew Fitz-Stephen there.

He clung, and "What of the Prince?" quoth he.
"Lost, lost!" we cried.　He cried, "Woe on me!"
And loosed his hold and sank through the sea.

And soul with soul again in that space
We two were together face to face:

And each knew each, as the moments sped,
Less for one living than for one dead:

And every still star overhead
Seemed an eye that knew we were but dead.

And the hours passed; till the noble's son
Sighed, "God be thy help! my strength's foredone!"

"O farewell, friend, for I can no more!"
"Christ take thee!" I moaned; and his life was o'er.

Three hundred souls were all lost but one,
And I drifted over the sea alone.

At last the morning rose on the sea
Like an angel's wing that beat tow'rds me.

Sore numbed I was in my sheepskin coat;
Half dead I hung, and might nothing note,
Till I woke sun-warmed in a fisher-boat.

The sun was high o'er the eastern brim
As I praised God and gave thanks to Him.

That day I told my tale to a priest,
Who charged me, till the shrift were releas'd,
That I should keep it in mine own breast.

And with the priest I thence did fare
To King Henry's court at Winchester.

We spoke with the King's high chamberlain,
And he wept and mourned again and again,
As if his own son had been slain:

And round us ever there crowded fast
Great men with faces all aghast:

And who so bold that might tell the thing
Which now they knew to their lord the King?
Much woe I learnt in their communing.

The King had watched with a heart sore stirred
For two whole days, and this was the third:

And still to all his court would he say,
"What keeps my son so long away?"

And they said: "The ports lie far and wide
That skirt the swell of the English tide;

" And England's cliffs are not more white
Than her women are, and scarce so light
Her skies as their eyes are blue and bright;

" And in some port that he reached from France
The Prince has lingered for his pleasaùnce."

But once the King asked: " What distant cry
Was that we heard 'twixt the sea and sky?"

And one said: " With suchlike shouts, pardie !
Do the fishers fling their nets at sea."

And one: " Who knows not the shrieking quest
When the sea-mew misses its young from the nest?"

'Twas thus till now they had soothed his dread,
Albeit they knew not what they said:

But who should speak to-day of the thing
That all knew there except the King?

Then pondering much they found a way,
And met round the King's high seat that day:

And the King sat with a heart sore stirred,
And seldom he spoke and seldom heard.

'Twas then through the hall the King was 'ware
Of a little boy with golden hair,

As bright as the golden poppy is
That the beach breeds for the surf to kiss:

Yet pale his cheek as the thorn in Spring,
And his garb black like the raven's wing.

Nothing heard but his foot through the hall,
For now the lords were silent all.

And the King wondered, and said, " Alack !
Who sends me a fair boy dressed in black ?

" Why, sweet heart, do you pace through the hall
As though my court were a funeral ? "

Then lowly knelt the child at the dais,
And looked up weeping in the King's face.

" O wherefore black, O King, ye may say,
For white is the hue of death to-day.

" Your son and all his fellowship
Lie low in the sea with the White Ship."

King Henry fell as a man struck dead ;
And speechless still he stared from his bed
When to him next day my rede I read.[1]

There's many an hour must needs beguile
A King's high heart that he should smile, —

Full many a lordly hour, full fain
Of his realm's rule and pride of his reign : —

But this King never smiled again.

[1] tale I told.

By none but me can the tale be told,
The butcher of Rouen, poor Berold.
 (*Lands are swayed by a King on a throne.*)
'Twas a royal train put forth to sea,
Yet the tale can be told by none but me.
 (*The sea hath no King but God alone.*)

KING STEPHEN

JOHN KEATS

MATILDA'S rival was Stephen of Blois, the son of the Conqueror's daughter Adela. Distrusting a woman's ability to govern so turbulent a kingdom, the citizens of London declared for Stephen and he was crowned at Westminster (1135). But Stephen, though a man of great personal daring, possessed little stability or force of character. He allowed the barons to oppress the people and failed to enforce the laws. When Matilda brought an army from France to claim her rights, she was gladly received by all law-abiding citizens. In the battle of Lincoln (1140), Stephen was taken prisoner and Matilda was immediately elected queen; but Stephen's partisans succeeded in setting him free and in driving Matilda from the realm. Stephen, however, could not restore order, and the land was devastated by civil war, till Matilda's son, Henry Plantagenet, came in person to England and forced Stephen to recognize him as successor to the throne.

ACT I

SCENE I. *Field of Battle.*

(*Alarum. Enter King Stephen, Knights, and Soldiers.*)

Stephen. If shame can on a soldier's vein-swoll'n front

Spread deeper crimson than the battle's toil,
Blush in your casing helmets! for see, see!
Yonder my chivalry, my pride of war,
Wrench'd with an iron hand from firm array,
Are routed loose about the plashy meads,
Of honor forfeit.   O, that my known voice
Could reach your dastard ears, and fright you more!
Fly, cowards, fly!   Glocester is at your backs!
Throw your slack bridles o'er the flurried manes,
Ply well the rowell with faint trembling heels,
Scampering to death at last!
   1st Knight.   The enemy
Bears his flaunt standard close upon their rear.
   2d Knight.   Sure of a bloody prey, seeing the fens
Will swamp them girth-deep.
   Stephen.   Over head and ears,
No matter!   'Tis a gallant enemy;
How like a comet he goes streaming on.
But we must plague him in the flank, — hey, friends?
We are well breathed, — follow!

SCENE II.   *Another part of the Field.*

(*Trumpets sounding a Victory.   Enter Glocester,
Knights, and Forces.*)

   Glocester.   Now may we lift our bruisèd visors up,
And take the flattering freshness of the air,
While the wide din of battle dies away
Into times past, yet to be echoed sure
In the silent pages of our chroniclers.

    1*st Knight.* Will Stephen's death be mark'd there,
      my good lord,
Or that we gave him lodging in yon towers?
    Glocester. Fain would I know the great usurper's
      fate.   (*Enter two Captains severally.*)
    1*st Captain.* My lord!
    2*d Captain.*   Most noble Earl!
    1*st Captain.* The King —
    2*d Captain.*   The Empress greets —
    Glocester. What of the King?
    1*st Captain.*   He sole and lone maintains
A hopeless bustle 'mid our swarming arms,
And with a nimble savageness attacks,
Escapes, makes fiercer onset, then anew
Eludes death, giving death to most that dare
Trespass within the circuit of his sword!
He must by this have fallen.   Baldwin is taken;
And for the Duke of Bretagne, like a stag
He flies, for the Welsh beagles to hunt down.
God save the Empress!
    Glocester.   Now our dreaded Queen:
What message from her highness?
    2*d Captain.*   Royal Maud
From the throng'd towers of Lincoln hath look'd down,
Like Pallas from the walls of Ilion,
And seen her enemies havock'd at her feet.
She greets most noble Glocester from her heart,
Entreating him, his captains, and brave knights,
To grace a banquet.   The high city gates
Are envious which shall see your triumph pass;
The streets are full of music.

BECKET

Lord Tennyson

HENRY II. was not only a valiant soldier but an able king. The long struggle for the crown had reduced England to a state of anarchy. Henry came to the throne pledged to restore order. He met a serious obstacle in the claim of the church that a priest might not be punished for crime by the civil authorities. Thomas Becket, chancellor of the realm and Henry's closest friend, was appointed Archbishop of Canterbury in the expectation that he would aid in bringing the clergy under the royal jurisdiction. Becket, however, stood by "the honor of his order," and refused to give his official sanction to the document defining the power of the king's courts respecting the clergy. The controversy ripened into open quarrel. Becket fled to the Continent, but was lured back to England by the hope of reconciliation. On December 29, 1170, he was foully murdered in Canterbury Cathedral by four knights, who were impelled to the deed by some angry words of the king. Henry was forced to do penance for his part in the crime, and Becket was canonized as a saint and martyr. Yet the king was right in his belief that there could be no true justice in England till all men were equal before the law.

ACT I

SCENE I. *Becket's House in London. Chamber barely furnished. Becket unrobing. Herbert of Bosham and Servant.*

Becket. Am I the man ? That rang
Within my head last night, and when I slept
Methought I stood in Canterbury Minster,
And spake to the Lord God, and said, "O Lord,
I have been a lover of wines, and delicate meats,
And secular splendors, and a favorer
Of players, and a courtier, and a feeder
Of dogs and hawks, and apes, and lions, and lynxes.

Am *I* the man ? "　And the Lord answer'd me,
" Thou art the man, and all the more the man."
And then I asked again, "O Lord my God,
Henry the King hath been my friend, my brother,
And mine uplifter in this world, and chosen me
For this thy great archbishoprick, believing
That I should go against the Church with him,
And I shall go against him with the Church,
And I have said no word of this to him :
Am *I* the man ? "　And the Lord answer'd me,
" Thou art the man, and all the more the man."
And thereupon, methought, He drew toward me,
And smote me down upon the Minster floor.
I fell.

SCENE III.　*Hall in Northampton Castle.　Arch-*
bishops, bishops, and barons assembled in council.

(*Enter King Henry.*)

　Henry.　Where's Thomas ? hath he signed ? show
　　me the papers !
Sign'd and not seal'd !　How's that ?
　John of Oxford.　　　　　　　He would not seal.
And when he sign'd, his face was stormy-red —
Shame, wrath, I know not what.　He sat down there
And dropt it in his hands, and then a paleness,
Like the wan twilight after sunset, crept
Up even to the tonsure, and he groan'd,
" False to myself !　It is the will of God ! "
　Henry.　God's will be what it will, the man shall seal,
Or I will seal his doom.　My burgher's son —

Nay, if I cannot break him as the prelate,
I'll crush him as the subject.   Send for him back.
                                                    (*Sits on his throne.*)
Barons and bishops of our realm of England,
After the nineteen winters of King Stephen —
A reign which was no reign, when none could sit
By his own hearth in peace ; when murder common
As nature's death, like Egypt's plague, had fill'd
All things with blood ; when every doorway blush'd,
Dash'd red with that unhallow'd passover ;
When every baron ground his blade in blood ;
The household dough was kneaded up with blood ;
The millwheel turn'd in blood ; the wholesome plough
Lay rusting in the furrow's yellow weeds,
Till famine dwarft the race — I came, your King !
Nor dwelt alone, like a soft lord of the East,
In mine own hall, and sucking thro' fools' ears
The flatteries of corruption — went abroad
Thro' all my counties, spied my people's ways ;
Yea, heard the churl against the baron — yea,
And did him justice ; sat in mine own courts
Judging my judges, that had found a King
Who ranged confusions, made the twilight day,
And struck a shape from out the vague, and law
From madness.   And the event — our fallows till'd,
Much corn, repeopled towns, a realm again.
So far my course, albeit not glassy-smooth,
Had prosper'd in the main, but suddenly
Jarr'd on this rock.   A cleric violated
The daughter of his host, and murder'd him.

Bishops — York, London, Chichester, Westminster —
Ye haled this tonsured devil into your courts;
But since your canon will not let you take
Life for a life, ye but degraded him
Where I had hang'd him. What doth hard murder care
For degradation? and that made me muse,
Being bounden by my coronation oath
To do men justice. Look to it, your own selves!
Say that a cleric murder'd an archbishop,
What could ye do? Degrade, imprison him —
Not death for death.

   John of Oxford.   But I, my liege, could swear
To death for death.

   Henry.   And, looking thro' my reign,
I found a hundred ghastly murders done
By men, the scum and offal of the Church;
Then, glancing thro' the story of this realm,
I came on certain wholesome usages,
Lost in desuetude, of my grandsire's day,
Good royal customs — had them written fair
For John of Oxford here to read to you.

ACT II

SCENE II. *Montmirail. "The Meeting of the Kings."
John of Oxford and Henry. Crowd in the distance.*

   Henry.   The friends we were!
Co-mates we were, and had our sport together,
Co-kings we were, and made the laws together.
The world had never seen the like before.
You are too cold to know the fashion of it.

Well, well, we will be gentle with him, gracious —
Most gracious.
                    (*Enter Becket*).
                Only that the rift he made
May close between us, here I am wholly king,
The word should come from him.
    Becket (*kneeling*).   Then, my dear liege,
I here deliver all this controversy
Into your royal hands.
    Henry.   Ah, Thomas, Thomas,
Thou art thyself again, Thomas again.
    Becket (*rising*). Saving God's honor!

LAMENT OF RICHARD DURING HIS IMPRISONMENT

TRANSLATED FROM THE PROVENÇAL BY W. E. AYTOUN

RICHARD I., the Lion Heart, son and successor of Henry II., was hardly an English king. During the ten years of his reign (1189–1199), he passed but five months in England. He was a prince of warlike and adventurous spirit, and spent his best energies and all the treasure he could wring from his unfortunate subjects on a crusade for the deliverance of Jerusalem. Returning from this fruitless enterprise, he was wrecked on the Adriatic coast, taken prisoner by the Duke of Austria, and held for ransom. The sum of money demanded was raised with great difficulty, and Richard was released after two years of captivity. The tradition that he composed this prison-song during his confinement in the Austrian castle of Durrenstein has no improbability in it, for Richard was an accomplished lyrist.

I

If one in prison may not tell his wrong
  Without derision or the chance of blame,

For his own comfort let him speak in song.
Friends have I store, and yet they leave me long!
　　If ransom comes not, let them look for shame.
　　　　Two years — and still not free!

II

For well they know, my barons and my men,
Of England, Normandy, Poitou, Guienne,
　　That not the poorest should in chains be set
If all my wealth could buy him back again.
　　I will not call them false or treacherous — yet
　　　　Two years — and still not free!

III

The captive hath nor friends nor kindred left,
　　For gold is dearer than the dearest tie.
Alas! I feel myself of all bereft;
　　And if within this cell I chance to die,
　　Shame be to them who let their monarch lie
　　　　So long, nor set him free.

IV

'Tis little wonder if I grieve and pine,
When he, my lord, invades these lands of mine;
　　But if he thought upon the sacrament
We took together at the sacred shrine
　　I would not be this day in prison pent,
　　　　But ranging wide and free.

V

O ye of Anjou and of stout Touraine!
  Brave bachelors and knights of warlike deed,
Did you but know the place where I remain,
  Would ye not aid your sovereign in his need?
Would ye not rescue him? — Alas, in vain!
    Ye cannot set me free!

VI

And you, companions, whom I loved so well
  Of Pensavin and Chail, O speak for me!
And let your songs thus much of Richard tell,
That, though a prisoner in a foreign cell;
  False was he never yet, and shall not be,
    Whether in chains or free.

KING RICHARD IN SHERWOOD FOREST

Lord Tennyson

(From "The Foresters")

Robin Hood and Maid Marian, Friar Tuck and George a Green, Will Scarlett, Midge the Miller's Son, Little John, and the rest are legendary characters loved and sung from the fourteenth century to modern times. The charm of these light-hearted highwaymen was felt by Shakespeare himself: "They say he is already in the forest of Arden, and a many merry men with him: and there they live like the old Robin Hood of England; they say many young gentlemen flock to him every day, and fleet the time carelessly, as they did in the golden world." — ("As You Like It," I, i.) Tennyson adopts the tradition that the generous outlaws dwelt in Sherwood Forest in Cumberlandshire, and that their leader, Robin Hood, was the banished Earl of Huntingdon. The plot of "The Foresters" turns upon the sudden return of Richard from his Austrian captivity and the consequent collapse of the intrigues conducted by his crafty and cruel brother John.

ACT II

Scene I. *A broad forest glade, woodman's hut at one side with half-door; Foresters are looking to their bows and arrows, or polishing their swords.*

Foresters sing (as they disperse to their work).

> There is no land like England
>> Where'er the light of day be;
> There are no hearts like English hearts
>> Such hearts of oak as they be.
> There is no land like England
>> Where'er the light of day be;
> There are no men like Englishmen
>> So tall and bold as they be.

(*Full Chorus.*)   And these will strike for England
          And man and maid be free
          To foil and spoil the tyrant
          Beneath the greenwood tree.

> There is no land like England
>> Where'er the light of day be;
> There are no wives like English wives
>> So fair and chaste as they be.
> There is no land like England
>> Where'er the light of day be;
> There are no maids like English maids
>> So beautiful as they be.

(*Full Chorus.*)   And these shall wed with freemen,
          And all their sons be free,
          To sing the songs of England
          Beneath the greenwood tree.

Robin (*alone*). My lonely hour !
The king of day hath stept from off his throne,
Flung by the golden mantle of the cloud,
And sets, a naked fire.   The King of England
Perchance this day may sink as gloriously,
Red with his own and enemy's blood — but no !
We hear he is in prison.   It is my birthday.
I have reign'd one year in the wild wood.   My mother,
For whose sake, and the blessed Queen of Heaven,
I reverence all women, bade me, dying,
Whene'er this day should come about, to carve
One lone hour from it, so to meditate
Upon my greater nearness to the birthday
Of the after-life, when all the sheeted dead
Are shaken from their stillness in the grave
By the last trumpet.
                              Am I worse or better ?
I am outlaw'd.   I am none the worse for that.
I held for Richard, and I hated John.
I am a thief, ay, and a king of thieves.
Ay ! but we rob the robber, wrong the wronger,
And what we wring from them we give the poor.
I am none the worse for that, and all the better
For this free forest-life, for while I sat
Among my thralls in my baronial hall
The groining hid the heavens ; but since I breathed,
A houseless head beneath the sun and stars,
The soul of the woods hath stricken thro' my blood,
The love of freedom, the desire of God,
The hope of larger life hereafter, more

Tenfold than under roof. (*Horn blown.*)
　　　　　　　　　　　True, were I taken
They would prick out my sight.　A price is set
On this poor head ; but I believe there lives
No man who truly loves and truly rules
His following, but can keep his followers true.
I am one with mine.　Traitors are rarely bred
Save under traitor kings.　Our vice-king John,
True king of vice — true play on words — our John
By his Norman arrogance and dissoluteness,
Hath made *me* king of all the discontent
Of England up thro' all the forest land
North to the Tyne : being outlaw'd in a land
Where law lies dead, we make ourselves the law.

ACT IV

SCENE I.　*A forest bower, cavern in background.　Sun-*
rise.

King Richard. What shouts are these that ring
along the wood ?

Friar Tuck (*coming forward*).　Hail, knight, and
　　help us.　Here is one would clutch
Our pretty Marian for his paramour,
This other, willy-nilly, for his bride.

King Richard.　Damsel, is this the truth ?

Marian.　Ay, noble knight.

Friar Tuck.　Ay, and she will not marry till
Richard come.

King Richard (*raising his vizor*).　I am here, and
　　I am he.

Prince John (*lowering his, and whispering to his men*). It is not he — his face — tho' very like —

No, no! we have certain news he died in prison.
Make at him, all of you, a traitor coming
In Richard's name — it is not he — not he.

       (*The men stand amazed.*)

Friar Tuck (*going back to the bush*). Robin, shall we not move?

Robin. It is the King
Who bears all down. Let him alone awhile.
He loves the chivalry of his single arm.
Wait till he blow the horn.

Friar Tuck (*coming back*). If thou be king,
Be not a fool! Why blowest thou not the horn?

  King Richard. I that have turn'd their Moslem crescent pale —

I blow the horn against this rascal rout!

 (*Friar Tuck plucks the horn from him and blows. Richard dashes alone against the Sheriff and John's men, and is almost borne down, when Robin and his men rush in and rescue him.*)

 King Richard (*to Robin Hood*). Thou hast saved my head at the peril of thine own.

 Prince John. A horse! a horse! I must away at once;

I cannot meet his eyes. I go to Nottingham.
Sheriff, thou wilt find me at Nottingham.   [*Exit.*

 Sheriff. If anywhere, I shall find thee in hell.
What! go to slay his brother, and make *me*

The monkey that should roast his chestnuts for him!

King Richard. I fear to ask who left us even
now.

Robin. I grieve to say it was thy father's son.
Shall I not after him and bring him back?

King Richard. No, let him be. Sheriff of Notting-
ham. (*Sheriff kneels.*)

I have been away from England all these years,
Heading the holy war against the Moslem,
While thou and others in our kingless realms
Were fighting underhand unholy wars
Against your lawful king.

Sheriff. My liege, Prince John —

King Richard. Say thou no word against my
brother John.

Sheriff. Why then, my liege, I have no word to
say.

King Richard (*to Robin*). My good friend Robin,
Earl of Huntingdon,

For Earl thou art again, hast thou no fetters
For those of thine own band who would betray thee?

Robin. I have; but these were never worn as yet,
I never found one traitor in my band.

*   *   *   *   *   *   *

Our forest games are ended, our free life,
And we must hence to the King's court. I trust
We shall return to the wood. Meanwhile, farewell
Old friends, old patriarch oaks. A thousand winters
Will strip you bare as death, a thousand summers
Robe you life-green again. *You* seem, as it were,

Immortal, and we mortal.   How few Junes
Will heat our pulses quicker !   How few frosts
Will chill the hearts that beat for Robin Hood !
   Marian.   And yet I think these oaks at dawn and
     even,
Or in the balmy breathings of the night,
Will whisper evermore of Robin Hood.
We leave but happy memories to the forest.
We dealt in the wild justice of the woods.
All those poor serfs whom we have served will bless
     us,
All those pale mouths which we have fed will praise
     us —
All widows we have holpen pray for us,
Our Lady's blessed shrines throughout the land
Be all the richer for us.   You, good friar,
You Much, you Scarlet, you dear Little John,
Your names will cling like ivy to the wood.
And here perhaps a hundred years away
Some hunter in day-dreams or half asleep
Will hear our arrows whizzing overhead,
And catch the winding of a phantom horn.
   Robin.   And surely these old oaks will murmur
     thee
Marian along with Robin.   I am most happy —
Art thou not mine ? — and happy that our King
Is here again, never I trust to roam
So far again, but dwell among his own.
Strike up a stave, my masters, all is well.
       Song while they dance a Country Dance.

Now the king is home again, and nevermore to roam
  again,
Now the king is home again, the king will have his
  own again,
Home again, home again, and each will have his
  own again,
All the birds in merry Sherwood sing and sing him
  home again.

HOW ROBIN HOOD RESCUED THE WIDOW'S THREE SONS

ROBIN HOOD and his followers were bandits and outlaws, but the people loved them because they defied the hateful forest laws and made light of the sheriff. The king's officers were responsible for the maintenance of order, but in these lawless times they often used their power for their own advantage, imposing heavy fines and penalties on the poor and extorting bribes from the rich. The following is one of the oldest and rudest of the many Robin Hood ballads.

There are twelve months in all the year,
  As I hear many say,
But the merriest month in all the year
  Is the merry month of May.

Now Robin Hood is to Nottingham gone,
  With a link a down and a day,
And there he met a silly old woman,
  Was weeping on the way.

"What news? what news, thou silly old woman?
  What news hast thou for me?"
Said she, "There's my three sons in Nottingham town
  To-day condemned to die."

" O, have they parishes burnt ? " he said,
   " Or have they ministers slain ?
Or have they robbed any virgin ?
   Or other men's wives have ta'en ? "

" They have no parishes burnt, good sir,
   Nor yet have ministers slain,
Nor have they robbed any virgin,
   Nor other men's wives have ta'en."

" O, what have they done ? " said Robin Hood,
   " I pray thee tell to me."
" It's for slaying of the king's fallow-deer,
   Bearing their long bows with thee."

" Dost thou not mind, old woman," he said,
   " How thou madest me sup and dine ?
By the truth of my body," quoth bold Robin Hood,
   " You could not tell it in better time."

Now Robin Hood is to Nottingham gone,
   With a link a down and a day,
And there he met with a silly [1] old palmer,
   Was walking along the highway.

" What news ? what news, thou silly old man ?
   What news, I do thee pray ? "
Said he, " Three squires in Nottingham town
   Are condemned to die this day."

" Come change thy apparel with me, old man,
   Come change thy apparel for mine ;
Here is forty shillings in good silver,
   Go drink it in beer or wine."

---

[1] simple.

" O, thine apparel is good," he said,
  " And mine is ragged and torn ;
Wherever you go, wherever you ride,
  Laugh ne'er an old man to scorn."

" Come change thy apparel with me, old churl,
  Come change thy apparel for mine ;
Here are twenty pieces of good broad gold,
  Go feast thy brethren with wine."

Then he put on the old man's hat,
  It stood full high on the crown :
" The first bold bargain that I come at,
  It shall make thee come down."

Then he put on the old man's cloak,
  Was patched black, blue, and red ;
He thought it no shame all the day long,
  To wear the bags of bread.

Then he put on the old man's breeks,[1]
  Was patched from leg to side :
" By the truth of my body," bold Robin can say,
  " This man loved little pride."

Then he put on the old man's hose,
  Were patched from knee to wrist :[2]
" By the truth of my body," said bold Robin Hood,
  " I'd laugh if I had any list." [3]

Then he put on the old man's shoes,
  Were patched both beneath and aboon ;

[1] breeches.   [2] instep.   [3] inclination.

Then Robin Hood swore a solemn oath,
   "It's good habit that makes a man."

Now Robin Hood is to Nottingham gone,
   With a link a down and a down,
And there he met with the proud sheriff,
   Was walking along the town.

"O Christ you save, O sheriff!" he said;
   "O Christ you save and see;[1]
And what will you give to a silly old man
   To-day will your hangman be?"

"Some suits, some suits," the sheriff he said,
   "Some suits I'll give to thee;
Some suits, some suits, and pence thirteen,
   To-day's a hangman's fee."

Then Robin he turns him round about,
   And jumps from stock to stone:
"By the truth of my body," the sheriff he said,
   "That's well jumpt, thou nimble old man."

"I was ne'er a hangman in all my life,
   Nor yet intends to trade;
But curst be he," said bold Robin,
   "That first a hangman was made!

"I've a bag for meal, and a bag for malt,
   And a bag for barley and corn;
A bag for bread, and a bag for beef,
   And a bag for my little small horn.

[1] keep.

"I have a horn in my pocket,
　I got it from Robin Hood,
And still when I set it to my mouth,
　For thee it blows little good."

"O, wind thy horn, thou proud fellow,
　Of thee I have no doubt.[1]
I wish that thou give such a blast,
　Till both thy eyes fall out."

The first loud blast that he did blow,
　He blew both loud and shrill;
A hundred and fifty of Robin Hood's men
　Came riding over the hill.

The next loud blast that he did give,
　He blew both loud and amain,
And quickly sixty of Robin Hood's men
　Came shining over the plain.

"O, who are these," the sheriff he said,
　"Come tripping over the lee?"
"They're my attendants," brave Robin did say;
　"They'll pay a visit to thee."

They took the gallows from the slack,[2]
　They set it in the glen,
They hanged the proud sheriff on that,
　Released their own three men.

------

[1] fear.　　　　　[2] hillside.

KING JOHN

WILLIAM SHAKESPEARE

ARTHUR, Duke of Brittany, was son of Geoffrey, the third son of Henry II., and therefore had a better title to the throne than the fourth son, John. John succeeded in getting himself crowned king of England, but when he ventured to assert his claim to Normandy, Arthur, then a boy of sixteen years, took up arms to defend his inheritance. He was laying siege to a fortress in Poictou, where his grandmother Eleanor lay intrenched, when his troops were surprised and cut to pieces by John, and he himself was taken prisoner. He was murdered at Rouen, whether at the hands of his uncle or merely by his uncle's order, no man knows. Philip Augustus, king of France, undertook to punish the crime, and he was aided by the English barons, who had wrongs of their own to avenge. They had forced John to sign the Great Charter, promising to govern justly and in accordance with English custom. When he broke his pledge, they offered the crown to Louis, the Dauphin. He crossed the Channel with a French army, and the barons flocked to his standard. Only John's sudden death prevented his deposition.

ACT III

SCENE III. PLAINS NEAR ANGIERS.

(*Enter King John, Elinor, Arthur, Faulconbridge, Hubert, and Lords.*)

King John (*to Elinor*). So shall it be; your grace
    shall stay behind
So strongly guarded. — (*To Arthur.*) Cousin, look not
    sad :
Thy grandam loves thee; and thy uncle will
As dear be to thee as thy father was.
    Arthur. O, this will make my mother die with grief !
    King John (*to Faulconbridge*). Cousin, away for
    England ! haste before ;

And, ere our coming, see thou shake the bags
Of hoarding abbots.   Set at liberty
Imprison'd angels; the fat ribs of peace
Must by the hungry now be fed upon.
Use our commission in his [1] utmost force.
    Faulconbridge. Bell, book, and candle shall not
        drive me back,
When gold and silver becks me to come on.
I leave your highness. — Grandam, I will pray,
If ever I remember to be holy,
For your fair safety ; so, I kiss your hand.
    Elinor. Farewell, gentle cousin.
    King John.   Coz, farewell.   [*Exit Faulconbridge.*
    Elinor. Come hither, little kinsman ; hark, a word.
    King John. Come hither, Hubert. O my gentle
        Hubert,
We owe thee much ! within this wall of flesh
There is a soul counts thee her creditor,
And with advantage means to pay thy love;
And, my good friend, thy voluntary oath
Lives in this bosom, dearly cherishèd.
Give me thy hand.   I had a thing to say,
But I will fit it with some better time.
By heaven, Hubert, I am almost ashamed
To say what good respect I have of thee.
    Hubert. I am much bounden [2] to your majesty.
    King John. Good friend, thou hast no cause to say
        so yet.
But thou shalt have ; and creep time ne'er so slow,
          [1] its.   [2] obliged.

Yet it shall come for me to do thee good.
I had a thing to say, but let it go:
The sun is in the heaven, and the proud day,
Attended with the pleasures of the world,
Is all too wanton and too full of gawds
To give me audience.   If the midnight bell
Did, with his iron tongue and brazen mouth,
Sound on into the drowsy race of night;
If this same were a churchyard where we stand,
And thou possessèd with a thousand wrongs,
Or if that surly spirit, melancholy,
Had baked thy blood and made it heavy-thick,
Which else runs tickling up and down the veins,
Making that idiot, laughter, keep men's eyes
And strain their cheeks to idle merriment,
A passion hateful to my purposes;
Or if that thou couldst see me without eyes,
Hear me without thine ears, and make reply
Without a tongue, using conceit [1] alone,
Without eyes, ears, and harmful sound of words;
Then, in despite of brooded [2] watchful day,
I would into thy bosom pour my thoughts:
But, ah, I will not! yet I love thee well;
And, by my troth, I think thou lov'st me well.

Hubert.   So well, that what you bid me undertake,
Though that my death were adjunct to my act,
By heaven, I would do it.

King John.   Do not I know thou would'st?
Good Hubert, Hubert, Hubert, throw thine eye

---

[1] thought.   [2] brooding.

On yon young boy : I'll tell thee what, my friend,
He is a very serpent in my way ;
And wheresoe'er this foot of mine doth tread,
He lies before me : dost thou understand me ?
Thou art his keeper.
    Hubert.   And I'll keep him so
That he shall not offend your majesty.
    King John.   Death.
    Hubert. My lord ?
    King John.   A grave.
    Hubert.   He shall not live.
    King John.   Enough.
I could be merry now.   Hubert, I love thee ;
Well, I'll not say what I intend for thee :
Remember.   Madam, fare you well ;
I'll send those powers [1] o'er to your majesty.
    Elinor. My blessing go with thee !
    King John.   For England, cousin, go :
Hubert shall be your man, attend on you
With all true duty.   On toward Calais, ho !
                        [Exeunt.

ACT IV

Scene I. *A Room in a Castle.*
(*Enter Hubert and Executioners.*)

    Hubert. Heat me these irons hot ; and look thou
      stand
Within the arras : when I strike my foot
Upon the bosom of the ground, rush forth,

             [1] that army.

And bind the boy which you shall find with me
Fast to the chair : be heedful : hence, and watch.

    First Exec. I hope your warrant will bear out the
      deed.

    Hubert. Uncleanly[1] scruples ! fear not you : look
      to't.

                  [Exeunt Executioners.

Young lad, come forth ; I have to say with you.

            (*Enter Arthur.*)

    Arthur. Good morrow, Hubert.

    Hubert.   Good morrow, little prince.

    Arthur. As little prince, having so great a title
To be more prince, as may be. You are sad.

    Hubert. Indeed, I have been merrier.

    Arthur.   Mercy on me !
Methinks no body should be sad but I :
Yet, I remember, when I was in France,
Young gentlemen would be as sad as night,
Only for wantonness. By my christendom,
So I were out of prison and kept sheep,
I should be as merry as the day is long ;
And so I would be here, but that I doubt
My uncle practises more harm to me :
He is afraid of me and I of him :
Is it my fault that I was Geffrey's son ?
No, indeed, is't not ; and I would to heaven
I were your son, so you would love me, Hubert.

    Hubert (*aside*). If I talk to him, with his innocent
      prate [2]

---

  [1] unbecoming.   [2] prattle.

He will awake my mercy which lies dead:
Therefore I will be sudden and despatch.

   Arthur. Are you sick, Hubert? you look pale
     to-day:
In sooth, I would you were a little sick,
That I might sit all night and watch with you:
I warrant I love you more than you do me.

   Hubert (*aside*). His words do take possession of
     my bosom.
Read here, young Arthur. (*Showing a paper.*)

             (*Aside*). How now, foolish rheum![1]
Turning dispiteous[2] torture out of door!
I must be brief, lest resolution drop
Out at mine eyes in tender womanish tears.
Can you not read it? is it not fair writ?

   Arthur. Too fairly, Hubert, for so foul effect:[3]
Must you with hot irons burn out both mine eyes?

   Hubert. Young boy, I must.

   Arthur.   And will you?

   Hubert.   And I will.

   Arthur. Have you the heart? When your head did
     but ache,
I knit my handkercher about your brows,
The best I had, a princess wrought it me,
And I did never ask it you again;
And with my hand at midnight held your head,
And like the watchful minutes to the hour,
Still and anon cheer'd up the heavy time,

---

      [1] tears.   [2] pitiless.   [3] import.

Saying, "What lack you?" and "Where lies your
  grief?"
Or "What good love may I perform for you?"
Many a poor man's son would have lien still
And ne'er have spoke a loving word to you;
But you at your sick service had a prince.
Nay, you may think my love was crafty love,
And call it cunning: do, and if you will:
If heaven be pleased that you must use me ill,
Why then you must. Will you put out mine eyes?
These eyes that never did nor never shall
So much as frown on you.

    Hubert.   I have sworn to do it;
And with hot irons must I burn them out.

    Arthur. Ah, none but in this iron age would do it!
The iron of itself, though heat red-hot,
Approaching near these eyes, would drink my tears
And quench his fiery indignation
Even in the matter of mine innocence;
Nay, after that, consume away in rust,
But for containing fire to harm mine eye.
Are you more stubborn-hard than hammer'd iron?
An if an angel should have come to me
And told me Hubert should put out mine eyes
I would not have believed him, — no tongue but
  Hubert's.

    Hubert. Come forth. (*Stamps.*)

    Reënter Executioners, with a cord, irons, etc.

                  Do as I bid you do.

Arthur. O, save me, Hubert, save me! my eyes are
    out
Even with the fierce looks of these bloody men.
    Hubert. Give me the iron, I say, and bind him here.
    Arthur. Alas, what need you be so boisterous-
        rough?
I will not struggle, I will stand stone-still.
For heaven sake, Hubert, let me not be bound!
Nay, hear me, Hubert, drive these men away,
And I will sit as quiet as a lamb;
I will not stir, nor wince, nor speak a word,
Nor look upon the iron angerly.
Thrust but these men away, and I'll forgive you,
Whatever torment you do put me to.
    Hubert. Go, stand within; let me alone with him.
    First Exec. I am best pleased to be from such a
        deed.   [*Exeunt Executioners.*
    Arthur. Alas, I then have chid away my friend!
He hath a stern look, but a gentle heart:
Let him come back, that his compassion may
Give life to yours.
    Hubert.   Come, boy, prepare yourself.
    Arthur. Is there no remedy?
    Hubert.   None, but to lose your eyes.
    Arthur. O heaven, that there were but a mote in
        yours,
A grain, a dust, a gnat, a wandering hair,
Any annoyance in that precious sense!
Then, feeling what small things are boisterous there,
Your vile intent must needs seem horrible.

Hubert. Is this your promise? go to, hold your
    tongue.

Arthur. Hubert, the utterance of a brace of tongues
Must needs want pleading for a pair of eyes:
Let me not hold my tongue, let me not, Hubert;
Or, Hubert, if you will, cut out my tongue,
So I may keep mine eyes: O, spare mine eyes,
Though to no use but still to look on you!
Lo, by my troth, the instrument is cold
And would not harm me.

Hubert.   I can heat it, boy.

Arthur. No, in good sooth; the fire is dead with
    grief,
Being create for comfort, to be used
In undeserved extremes: see else yourself;
There is no malice in this burning coal;
The breath of heaven hath blown his spirit out
And strew'd repentant ashes on his head.

Hubert. But with my breath I can revive it, boy.

Arthur. And if you do, you will but make it blush
And glow with shame of your proceedings, Hubert:
Nay, it perchance will sparkle in your eyes;
And like a dog that is compell'd to fight,
Snatch at his master that doth tarre [1] him on.
All things that you should use to do me wrong
Deny their office: only you do lack
That mercy which fierce fire and iron extends,
Creatures of note for mercy-lacking uses.

Hubert. Well, see to live; I will not touch thine eye

---

[1] urge.

For all the treasure that thine uncle owes: [1]
Yet am I sworn and I did purpose, boy,
With this same very iron to burn them out.

    Arthur. O, now you look like Hubert! all this
      while
You were disguised.

    Hubert.   Peace; no more. Adieu.
Your uncle must not know but you are dead;
I'll fill these doggèd spies with false reports:
And, pretty child, sleep doubtless [2] and secure,
That Hubert, for the wealth of all the world,
Will not offend thee.

    Arthur.   O heaven! I thank you, Hubert.

    Hubert. Silence; no more: go closely [3] in with me:
Much danger do I undergo for thee.

                       [Exeunt.

ACT V

SCENE VII. *The Orchard at Swinstead Abbey.*

    (*Enter Prince Henry, Salisbury, and Bigot.*)

    Prince Henry. It is too late: the life of all his
      blood
Is touch'd corruptibly, and his pure brain,
Which some suppose the soul's frail dwelling-house,
Doth by the idle comments that it makes
Foretell the ending of mortality.

            (*Enter Pembroke.*)

    Pembroke. His highness yet doth speak, and holds
      belief

      [1] owns.   [2] fearless.   [3] secretly.

That, being brought into the open air,
It would allay the burning quality
Of that fell poison which assaileth him.
  Prince Henry. Let him be brought into the orchard
    here.
Doth he still rage?   *[Exit Bigot.*
  Pembroke.   He is more patient
Than when you left him; even now he sung.
  Prince Henry. O vanity of sickness! fierce ex-
    tremes
In their continuance will not feel themselves.
Death, having prey'd upon the outward parts,
Leaves them insensible, and his siege is now
Against the mind, the which he pricks and wounds
With many legions of strange fantasies,
Which, in their throng and press to that last hold,
Confound themselves.   'Tis strange that death should
    sing.
I am the cygnet to this pale faint swan,
Who chants a doleful hymn to his own death,
And from the organ-pipe of frailty sings
His soul and body to their lasting rest.
  Salisbury. Be of good comfort, prince; for you are
    born
To set a form upon that indigest[1]
Which he hath left so shapeless and so rude.
  (*Enter Attendants, and Bigot, carrying King John in a
    chair.*)

  King John. Ay, marry, now my soul hath elbow-
    room;
                  [1] chaos.

It would not out at windows nor at doors.
There is so hot a summer in my bosom,
That all my bowels crumble up to dust:
I am a scribbled form, drawn with a pen
Upon a parchment, and against this fire
Do I shrink up.

   Prince Henry. How fares your majesty?
   King John. Poison'd, — ill   fare — dead, forsook,
     cast off;
And none of you will bid the winter come
And thrust his icy fingers in my maw,
Nor let my kingdom's rivers take their course
Through my burn'd bosom, nor entreat the north
To make his bleak winds kiss my parchèd lips
And comfort me with cold.   I do not ask you much,
I beg cold comfort; and you are so strait
And so ingrateful, you deny me that.

   Prince Henry. O that there were some virtue in
     my tears,
That might relieve you!
   King John.   The salt in them is hot.
Within me is a hell; and there the poison
Is as a fiend confined to tyrannize
On unreprievable condemnèd blood.

(Enter Faulconbridge.)

   Faulconbridge. O, I am scalded with my violent
     motion
And spleen[1] of speed to see your majesty!

[1] passion.

King John. O cousin, thou art come to set[1] mine
    eye;
The tackle of my heart is crack'd and burn'd
And all the shrouds wherewith my life should sail
Are turnèd to one thread, one little hair;
My heart hath one poor string to stay it by,
Which holds but till thy news be utterèd;
And then all this thou seest is but a clod
And module[2] of confounded royalty.
    Faulconbridge. The Dauphin is preparing hither-
    ward,
Where heaven He knows how we shall answer him;
For in a night the best part of my power,
As I upon advantage did remove,
Were in the Washes all unwarily
Devoured by the unexpected flood. (*The King dies.*)
    Salisbury. You breathe these dead news in as dead
    an ear.
My liege! my lord! But now a king, now thus.
    Prince Henry. Even so must I run on, and even so
    stop.
What surety of the world, what hope, what stay,
When this was now a king, and now is clay?

    *   *   *   *   *   *   *

    Faulconbridge. O, let us pay the time but needful
    woe,
Since it hath been beforehand with our griefs.
This England never did, nor never shall,
Lie at the proud foot of a conqueror,

            [1] close.   [2] image.

But when it first did help to wound itself.
Now these her princes are come home again,
Come the three corners of the world in arms,
And we shall shock them.　Nought shall make us
　　rue,
If England to itself do rest but true.

SIMON DE MONTFORT, EARL OF LEICESTER

James Lincoln

Henry III. was a weak and pleasure-loving king.　In his coronation oath he had sworn to abandon the evil practices of John's reign, but he broke his pledge, defied the law, and plundered the poor without mercy.　The barons rose against Henry as they had risen against John, and forced him to abide by the Charter.　The revolt was led by Simon de Montfort.　This greatest of English patriots was a Frenchman by birth, but he stood high in favor with Henry, who bestowed on him the earldom of Leicester.　Earl Simon's steadfast loyalty to right and justice brought him into frequent conflict with the king.　Thrice he was banished from the realm, and twice he levied an army to meet the royal troops sent against him.　In the battle of Lewes (1264) King Henry and Prince Edward were taken prisoners.　In the battle of Evesham (1265) De Montfort was killed and his following cut to pieces.　But the final victory was with the champion of the nation's rights.　When Prince Edward came to the throne, he governed in accordance with the principles maintained by Simon de Montfort.

Born and bred in a castle of France,
　He wore an English sword.
He was Henry's pearl, made belted earl
　And seated high at board,
Till the King's own sister loved his glance
　And had him for wedded lord.

'Twas the Earl of Leicester took the vows
   For his godchild, England's prince ;
But the grace of a king is a brittle thing,
   And evil tongues convince
More than the flush on lifted brows
   And the look that will not wince.

The Earl and his Countess fled beyond
   Our ribbon of sea and spray.
His enemies laughed and his own wine quaffed
   To the set of the Frenchman's day ;
But the loves of youth knit a silken bond
   That may hold where chains give way.

So the King, at pinch, found a noble friend,
   Where he well had earned a foe,
And on English earth, in Kenilworth,
   Montfort made splendid show
For many a joyous year, whose end
   Thank God he could not know.

Weak and wilful was Henry Third,
   And the Earl had a haughty heart.
Again it came to the quarrel-flame,
   And their hands were rent apart,
And again, like the song of a far-off bird,
   Did memory soothe the smart.

But when all the land was murmuring
   Against the royal greed,
For the reign went still from ill to ill,
   A garden choked with weed,

The barons rose against the King,
    De Montfort in the lead.

This King had ever a craven mind.
    The lightning in the skies
Affrayed him sore, but he dreaded more
    The flash of Earl Simon's eyes;
And the loves of youth went down the wind
    Of a royal captive's sighs.

" Key of England " and " Mountain Strong,"
    De Montfort's fame waxed bright.
" I will die under ban, a landless man,
    Ere I forsake the right."
And the people lauded him in song
    For Freedom's Redcross Knight.

The people loved the proud French lord,
    But the Prince, his godchild, whom
He had taught to war, was his conqueror
    With a host that scarce gave room
For the last grand swing of a hero's sword
    In Evesham's battle-gloom.

Now call him Montfort the Englishman,
    Who died for England's sake,
Who had fenced her cause with mightier laws
    Than ever a king should break,
And fell on sleep, as the weary can,
    When Freedom was awake.

THE DEATH OF WALLACE

ROBERT SOUTHEY

EDWARD I. was an able king. He did much for justice and good government in England, and he undertook to bring all of Great Britain under his rule. Wales was annexed after spirited but brief resistance, but Scotland proved more difficult of conquest. Edward took advantage of a dispute as to the succession to possess himself of the government. The Scotch, however, resented English dominion. Under the lead of William Wallace, they rose in revolt and won a signal victory at Stirling Bridge (1297). Demoralized by jealous wrangles among its leaders, the Scotch army was defeated at Falkirk in the following year. Wallace escaped, but a price was set on his head. He was betrayed, taken prisoner, and carried to London, where, after being dragged through the streets as a show for the angry populace (1305), he suffered the common fate of traitors.

Joy, joy in London now!
He goes, the rebel Wallace goes to death;
At length the traitor meets the traitor's doom.
Joy, joy in London now!

He on a sledge is drawn,
His strong right arm unweapon'd and in chains,
And garlanded around his helmless head
The laurel wreath of scorn.

They throng to view him now
Who in the field had fled before his sword,
Who at the name of Wallace once grew pale
And falter'd out a prayer.

Yes! they can meet his eye,
That only beams with patient courage now;

Yes! they can look upon those manly limbs,
　　Defenceless now and bound.

And that eye did not shrink
As he beheld the pomp of infamy;
Not one ungovern'd feeling shook those limbs,
　　When the last moment came.

He called to mind his deeds
Done for his country in the embattled field;
He thought of that good cause for which he died,
　　And it was joy in death.

THE BATTLE OF BANNOCKBURN

Bruce's Address to his Men

Robert Burns

Robert Bruce fought on the English side at Falkirk, but his heart
was with the Scots. In 1306 he declared himself for the indepen-
dence of Scotland, and was chosen king. He had a good chance of
success, for Edward I. died in 1307. His successor, Edward II., was
a weak and foolish prince, who wasted in self-indulgence the money
that should have been spent for the conquest of Scotland. The
patriotism and courage of Bruce inspired all true Scots, nobles and
peasants alike, to fight for their country. He led a devoted and well-
disciplined army to meet the English at Bannockburn.

Scots, wha hae wi' Wallace bled,
Scots, wham Bruce has often led;
Welcome to your gory bed,
　　Or to glorious victory!

Now's the day, and now's the hour;
See the front o' battle lour;

See approach proud Edward's power —
  Edward! chains and slavery!

Wha will be a traitor knave?
Wha can fill a coward's grave?
Wha sae base as be a slave?
  Traitor! coward! turn and flee!

Wha for Scotland's king and law
Freedom's sword will strongly draw,
Freeman stand, or freeman fa'?
  Caledonian! on wi' me!

By oppression's woes and pains!
By your sons in servile chains!
We will drain our dearest veins,
  But they shall be — shall be free!

Lay the proud usurpers low!
Tyrants fall in every foe!
Liberty's in every blow!
  Forward! let us do or die!

BANNOCKBURN

Sir Walter Scott

(From "The Lord of the Isles," Canto VI)

THE victory of Bannockburn gave Stirling to Robert Bruce and secured the independence of Scotland. His success was due to the excellent discipline of the Scotch foot soldiers, who stood unmoved in solid squares until the English archers were scattered by a sudden rush of cavalry. Edward's mounted knights fell into the pitfalls the Scotch had dug in the plain and were rendered useless. The appearance of a body of camp-followers whom the English took to be reënforcements converted their discomfiture into rout. Hundreds of English lords and gentlemen were left dead upon the field. King Edward himself barely escaped with a small body-guard to Bamborough.

O gay, yet fearful to behold,
Flashing with steel and rough with gold,
        And bristled o'er with bills and spears,
With plumes and pennons waving fair,
Was that bright battle-front! for there
        Rode England's King and peers :
And who, that saw that monarch ride,
His kingdom battled by his side,
Could then his direful doom foretell! —
Fair was his seat in knightly selle,[1]
And in his sprightly eye was set
Some spark of the Plantagenet.
Though light and wandering was his glance,
It flashed at sight of shield and lance.

    *   *   *   *   *   *   *

Now onward, and in open view,
The countless ranks of England drew,
Dark rolling like the ocean-tide,
When the rough west hath chafed his pride,
And his deep roar sends challenge wide
        To all that bars his way !
In front the gallant archers trode,
The men-at-arms behind them rode,
And midmost of the phalanx broad
        The Monarch held his sway.

[1] saddle.

Beside him many a war-horse fumes,
Around him waves a sea of plumes,
Where many a knight in battle known,
And some who spurs had first braced on,
And deemed that fight should see them won,
    King Edward's hests obey.
De Argentine attends his side,
With stout De Valence, Pembroke's pride,
Selected champions from the train,
To wait upon his bridle-rein.
Upon the Scottish foe he gazed —
— At once, before his sight amazed,
    Sunk banner, spear, and shield;
Each weapon-point is downward sent,
Each warrior to the ground is bent.
    "The rebels, Argentine, repent!
    For pardon they have kneeled." —
"Aye! — but they bend to other powers,
And other pardons sue than ours!
See where yon bare-foot Abbot stands,
And blesses them with lifted hands!
These men will die or win the field." —
— "Then prove we if they die or win!
Bid Gloster's Earl the fight begin."

Earl Gilbert waved his truncheon high,
    Just as the Northern ranks arose,
Signal for England's archery
    To halt and bend their bows.
Then stepped each yeoman forth apace,

Glanced at the intervening space,
    And raised his left hand high;
To the right ear the cords they bring —
— At once ten thousand bow-strings ring,
    Ten thousand arrows fly!
Nor paused on the devoted Scot
The ceaseless fury of their shot;
    As fiercely and as fast,
Forth whistling came the gray-goose wing
As the wild hailstones pelt and ring
    Adown December's blast.
Nor mountain targe of tough bull-hide,
Nor lowland mail, that storm may bide;
Woe, woe to Scotland's bannered pride,
    If the fell shower may last!
Upon the right, behind the wood,
Each by his steed dismounted, stood
    The Scottish chivalry; —
— With foot in stirrup, hand on mane,
Fierce Edward Bruce can scarce restrain
His own keen heart, his eager train,
Until the archers gained the plain;
    Then, "Mount, ye gallants free!"
He cried; and vaulting from the ground,
His saddle every horseman found.
On high their glittering crests they toss,
As springs the wild-fire from the moss;
The shield hangs down on every breast,
Each ready lance is in the rest,
    And loud shouts Edward Bruce, —

" Forth, Marshall, on the peasant foe!
We'll tame the terrors of their bow,
   And cut the bow-string loose! "

Then spurs were dashed in chargers' flanks,
They rushed among the archer ranks.
No spears were there the shock to let,
No stakes to turn the charge were set,
And how shall yeoman's armor slight
Stand the long lance and mace of might?
Or what may their short swords avail,
'Gainst barbèd horse and shirt of mail?
Amid their ranks the chargers sprung,
High o'er their heads the weapons swung,
And shriek and groan and vengeful shout
Give note of triumph and of rout!
Awhile, with stubborn hardihood,
Their English hearts the strife made good.
Borne down at length on every side,
Compelled to flight, they scatter wide.

*   *   *   *   *   *   *

The tug of strife to flag begins,
Though neither loses yet nor wins.
High rides the sun, thick rolls the dust,
And feebler speeds the blow and thrust.
Douglas leans on his war-sword now,
And Randolph wipes his bloody brow;
Nor less had toiled each Southern knight,
From morn till mid-day in the fight.
Strong Egremont for air must gasp,

Beauchamp undoes his vizor-clasp,
And Montague must quit his spear,
And sinks thy falchion, bold De Vere!
The blows of Berkley fall less fast,
And gallant Pembroke's bugle-blast
        Hath lost its lively tone;
Sinks, Argentine, thy battle-word,
And Percy's shout was fainter heard,
        " My merry-men, fight on!"

Bruce, with the pilot's wary eye,
The slackening of the storm could spy.
        " One effort more, and Scotland's free!
        Lord of the Isles, my trust in thee
        Is firm as Ailsa Rock;
Rush on with Highland sword and targe,
I, with my Carrick spearmen, charge;
        Now, forward to the shock!"
At once the spears were forward thrown,
Against the sun the broadswords shone;
The pibroch lent its maddening tone,
And loud King Robert's voice was known
" Carrick, press on — they fail, they fail!
Press on, brave sons of Innisgail,
        The foe is fainting fast!
Each strike for parent, child, and wife,
For Scotland, liberty, and life, —
        The battle cannot last!"

  *   *   *   *   *   *   *

The multitude that watched afar,

Rejected from the ranks of war,
Had not unmoved beheld the fight,
When strove the Bruce for Scotland's right;
Each heart had caught the patriot spark,
Old man and stripling, priest and clerk,
Bondsman and serf; even female hand
Stretched to the hatchet or the brand.

* * * * * *

"To us, as to our lords, are given
A native earth, a promised heaven;
To us, as to our lords, belongs
The vengeance for our nation's wrongs;
The choice, 'twixt death or freedom, warms
Our breasts as theirs — To arms, to arms!"
To arms they flew, — axe, club, or spear, —
And mimic ensigns high they rear,
And, like a bannered host afar,
Bear down on England's wearied war.

Already scattered o'er the plain,
Reproof, command, and counsel vain,
The rearward squadrons fled amain,
 Or made but doubtful stay: —
But when they marked the seeming show
Of fresh and fierce and marshalled foe,
 The boldest broke array.
O give their hapless prince his due!
In vain the royal Edward threw
 His person 'mid the spears,
Cried "Fight!" to terror and despair,

Menaced, and wept, and tore his hair,
   And cursed their caitiff fears;
Till Pembroke turned his bridle rein,
And forced him from the fatal plain.
      With them rode Argentine, until
      They gained the summit of the hill,
But quitted there the train : —

    *   *   *   *   *   *   *

" Speed hence, my Liege, for on your trace
The fiery Douglas takes the chase,
   I know his banner well.
God send my Sovereign joy and bliss,
And many a happier field than this ! —
Once more, my Liege, farewell."

KING EDWARD THE SECOND

CHRISTOPHER MARLOWE

THE deposition of the second Edward was due to his foolish fondness for favorites. The first of these, Piers Gaveston, a French adventurer, had been banished by Edward I. Immediately on his accession to the throne, Edward II. recalled his " Brother Peter " and lavished estates and great offices upon him. The haughty and insolent ways of Gaveston rendered him hateful to the English lords, and they sought to drive him from the kingdom. Failing in this, they put him to death. The king consoled himself with a new favorite, Hugh Despenser, English born, but quite as unpopular as the Frenchman. The exasperated barons rose in revolt against their unworthy sovereign. They found an ally in Queen Isabel who, neglected by her husband, schemed to place her son upon the throne. Edward and Despenser were taken prisoners, the favorite was put to death, the king deposed (1327), and the young prince proclaimed as

Edward III. The fate of Edward II. is uncertain, but it seems most probable that he was secretly and brutally murdered by order of Mortimer.

ACT I

SCENE I. *A Street in London. Enter Gaveston, reading a letter.*

Gav. " *My father is deceas'd! Come, Gaveston,*
And share the kingdom with thy dearest friend."
Ah! words that make me surfeit with delight!
What greater bliss can hap to Gaveston
Than live and be the favourite of a king!
Sweet prince, I come! these, these thy amorous lines
Might have enforc'd me to have swum from France,
And, like Leander, gasp'd upon the sand,
So thou wouldst smile, and take me in thine arms.
The sight of London to my exil'd eyes
Is as Elysium to a new-come soul;
Not that I love the city, or the men,
But that it harbours him I hold so dear, —
The king, upon whose bosom let me lie,
And with the world be still at enmity.
What need the Arctic people love starlight,
To whom the sun shines both by day and night?
Farewell base stooping to the lordly peers!
My knee shall bow to none but to the king.
As for the multitude, that are but sparks,
Raked up in embers of their poverty, —
Tanti; I'll fawn first on the wind
That glanceth at my lips, and flieth away.

* * * * * * *

(*Enter King Edward, Lancaster, the Elder Mortimer,*
Young Mortimer, Kent, Warwick, and Attendants.)

  K. Edw. Lancaster!

  Lan. My Lord.

  Gav. That Earl of Lancaster do I abhor. (*Aside.*)

  K. Edw. Will you not grant me this?   In spite of
    them

I'll have my will; and these two Mortimers,

That cross me thus, shall know I am displeased.

                                    (*Aside.*)

  E. Mor. If you love us, my lord, hate Gaveston.

  Gav. That villain Mortimer!   I'll be his death.

                                    (*Aside.*)

  Y. Mor. Mine uncle here, this earl, and I myself,

Were sworn to your father at his death,

That he should ne'er return into the realm:

And know, my lord, ere I will break my oath,

This sword of mine, that should offend your foes,

Shall sleep within the scabbard at thy need,

And underneath thy banners march who will,

For Mortimer will hang his armour up.

  Gav. Mort Dieu!   (*Aside.*)

  K. Edw. Well, Mortimer, I'll make thee rue these
    words.

Beseems it thee to contradict thy king?

Frown'st thou thereat, aspiring Lancaster?

The sword shall plane the furrows of thy brows,

And hew these knees that now are grown so stiff.

I will have Gaveston; and you shall know

What danger 'tis to stand against your king.

Gav. Well done, Ned! (*Aside.*)

Lan. My lord, why do you thus incense your
peers,
That naturally would love and honour you
But for that base and obscure Gaveston?
Four earldoms have I, besides Lancaster —
Derby, Salisbury, Lincoln, Leicester;
These will I sell, to give my soldiers pay,
Ere Gaveston shall stay within the realm;
Therefore, if he be come, expel him straight.

Kent. Barons and earls, your pride hath made me
mute;
But now I'll speak, and to the proof, I hope.
I do remember, in my father's days,
Lord Percy of the north, being highly moved,
Braved Moubery in presence of the king;
For which, had not his highness lov'd him well,
He should have lost his head; but with his look
The undaunted spirit of Percy was appeas'd,
And Moubery and he were reconcil'd:
Yet dare you brave the king unto his face. —
Brother, revenge it, and let these their heads
Preach upon poles, for trespass of their tongues.

War. O, our heads!

K. Edw. Ay, yours; and therefore I would wish
you grant —

War. Bridle thy anger, gentle Mortimer.

Y. Mor. I cannot, nor I will not; I must speak. —
Cousin, our hands I hope shall fence our heads,
And strike off his that makes you threaten us. —

Come, uncle, let us leave the brain-sick king,
And henceforth parley with our naked swords.

   E. Mor. Wiltshire hath men enough to save our
     heads.

   War. All Warwickshire will love him for my sake.

   Lan. And northward Gaveston hath many
     friends. —

Adieu, my lord; and either change your mind,
Or look to see the throne, where you should sit,
To float in blood; and at thy wanton head
The glozing head of thy base minion thrown.

    [*Exeunt all except King Edward, Kent, Gaveston,
     and Attendants.*

   K. Edw. I cannot brook these haughty menaces;
Am I a king, and must be overrul'd? —
Brother, display my ensigns in the field;
I'll bandy with the barons and the earls,
And either die or live with Gaveston.

   Gav. I can no longer keep me from my lord.

                   (*Comes forward.*)

   K. Edw. What, Gaveston! welcome! Kiss not my
     hand;

Embrace me, Gaveston, as I do thee.
Why shouldst thou kneel? know'st thou not who I
     am?
Thy friend, thyself, another Gaveston!
Not Hylas was more mourned of Hercules,
Than thou hast been of me since thy exile.

   Gav. And since I went from hence, no soul in hell
Hath felt more torment than poor Gaveston.

K. Edw. I know it. — Brother, welcome home my
    friend. —
Now let the treacherous Mortimers conspire,
And that high-minded Earl of Lancaster:
I have my wish, in that I joy thy sight;
And sooner shall the sea o'erwhelm my land,
Than bear the ship that shall transport thee hence.
I here create thee Lord High Chamberlain,
Chief Secretary to the State and me,
Earl of Cornwall, King and Lord of Man.
    Gav. My lord, these titles far exceed my worth.
    Kent. Brother, the least of these may well suffice
For one of greater birth than Gaveston.
    K. Edw. Cease, brother; for I cannot brook these
    words. —
Thy worth, sweet friend, is far above my gifts,
Therefore, to equal it, receive my heart.
If for these dignities thou be envied,
I'll give thee more; for, but to honour thee,
Is Edward pleas'd with kingly regiment.[1]
Fear'st thou thy person? thou shalt have a guard:
Wantest thou gold? go to my treasury:
Wouldst thou be lov'd and fear'd? receive my seal,
Save or condemn, and in our name command
Whatso thy mind affects, or fancy likes.
    Gav. It shall suffice me to enjoy your love,
Which whiles I have, I think myself as great
As Cæsar riding in the Roman street,
With captive kings at his triumphal car.

[1] rule.

ACT V

SCENE I. *Killingworth Castle.   Enter King Edward, Leicester, the Bishop of Winchester, and Trussel.*

B. of Win. Your grace mistakes; it is for England's good,
And princely Edward's right we crave the crown.
K. Edw. No, 'tis for Mortimer, not Edward's head;
For he's a lamb, encompassèd by wolves,
Which in a moment will abridge his life.
But if proud Mortimer do wear this crown,
Heavens turn it to a blaze of quenchless fire!
Or, like the snaky wreath of Tisiphon,
Engirt the temples of his hateful head;
So shall not England's vine be perishèd,
But Edward's name survive, though Edward dies.
Leices. My lord, why waste you thus the time away?
They stay your answer; will you yield your crown?
K. Edw. Ah, Leicester, weigh how hardly I can brook
To lose my crown and kingdom without cause;
To give ambitious Mortimer my right,
That like a mountain overwhelms my bliss,
In which extreme my mind here murdered is.
But what the heavens appoint, I must obey:
Here, take my crown; the life of Edward too;
                                    (*Taking off the crown.*)

Two kings in England cannot reign at once.
But stay awhile: let me be king till night,
That I may gaze upon this glittering crown;
So shall my eyes receive their last content,
My head, the latest honour due to it,
And jointly both yield up their wishèd right.
Continue ever, thou celestial sun;
Let never silent night possess this clime:
Stand still, you watches of the element;
All times and seasons, rest you at a stay,
That Edward may be still fair England's king!
But day's bright beam doth vanish fast away,
And needs I must resign my wishèd crown.
Inhuman creatures, nursed with tiger's milk,
Why gape you for your sovereign's overthrow?
My diadem, I mean, and guiltless life.
See, monsters, see! I'll wear my crown again.

(He puts on the crown.)

What, fear you not the fury of your king? —
But, hapless Edward, thou art fondly [1] led;
They pass not for [2] thy frowns as late they did,
But seek to make a new-elected king;
Which fills my mind with strange despairing thoughts,
Which thoughts are martyrèd with endless torments;
And in this torment comfort find I none,
But that I feel the crown upon my head;
And therefore let me wear it yet awhile.

> *Trus.* My lord, the parliament must have present
> news;

---

[1] foolishly. [2] regard not.

And therefore say, will you resign or no ?

(*The King rageth.*)

K. Edw. I'll not resign, but whilst I live be king.
Traitors, begone, and join you with Mortimer !
Elect, conspire, install, do what you will :
Their blood and yours shall seal these treacheries !

> *B. of Win.* This answer we'll return, and so fare-
> well.   (*Going with Trussel.*)
> *Leices.* Call them again, my lord, and speak them
> fair ;

For if they go, the prince shall lose his right.

> *K. Edw.* Call thou them back ; I have no power
> to speak.
> *Leices.* My lord, the king is willing to resign.
> *B. of Win.* If he be not, let him choose.
> *K. Edw.* O would I might ! but heavens and earth
> conspire

To make me miserable.   Here, receive my crown.
Receive it ? no, these innocent hands of mine
Shall not be guilty of so foul a crime :
He of you all that most desires my blood,
And will be call'd the murderer of a king,
Take it.   What, are you mov'd ? pity you me ?
Then send for unrelenting Mortimer,
And Isabel, whose eyes, being turn'd to steel,
Will sooner sparkle fire than shed a tear.
Yet stay ; for rather than I'll look on them,
Here, here !   (*Gives the crown.*)

Now, sweet God of heaven,

Make me despise this transitory pomp,

And sit for aye enthronizèd in heaven!
Come, death, and with thy fingers close my eyes,
Or if I live, let me forget myself!

B. of Win. My lord —

K. Edw. Call me not lord; away, out of my sight!
Ah, pardon me! grief makes me lunatic.
Let not that Mortimer protect my son;
More safety there is in a tiger's jaws
Than his embracements. Bear this to the queen,
Wet with my tears, and dried again with sighs;

(Gives a handkerchief.)

If with the sight thereof she be not mov'd,
Return it back and dip it in my blood.
Commend me to my son, and bid him rule
Better than I: yet how have I transgress'd
Unless it be with too much clemency?

Trus. And thus most humbly do we take our leave.
[*Exeunt the Bishop of Winchester and Trussel
with the crown.*

K. Edw. Farewell; I know the next news that
they bring
Will be my death; and welcome shall it be;
To wretched men, death is felicity.

SCENE II. *The Royal Palace, London. Enter Queen
Isabella and Young Mortimer.*

(*Enter Messenger.*)

Q. Isab. How fares my lord the king?
Mess. In health, madam, but full of pensiveness.

Q. Isab. Alas, poor soul, would I could ease his grief!

(*Enter the Bishop of Winchester with the crown.*)

Thanks, gentle Winchester. (*To the Messenger.*)
                Sirrah, begone. [*Exit Messenger.*

B. of Win. The king hath willingly resign'd his crown.

Q. Isab. Oh happy news! send for the prince, my son.

B. of Win. Further, or this letter was seal'd, Lord Berkeley came,

So that he now is gone from Killingworth;
And we have heard that Edmund laid a plot
To set his brother free; no more but so.
The lord of Berkeley is so pitiful
As Leicester that had charge of him before.

Q. Isab. Then let some other be his guardian.

Y. Mort. Let me alone; here is the privy seal. —
                [*Exit the Bishop of Winchester.*

Who's there? — Call hither Gurney and Matrevis. —
                (*To Attendants within.*)

To dash the heavy-headed Edmund's drift,
Berkeley shall be discharg'd, the king remov'd,
And none but we shall know where he lieth.

Q. Isab. But, Mortimer, as long as he survives,
What safety rests for us, or for my son?

Y. Mort. Speak, shall he presently [1] be despatch'd and die?

---

[1] immediately.

Q. Isab. I would he were, so 'twere not by my
   means.

   (*Enter Matrevis and Gurney.*)

Y. Mort. Enough. —
Matrevis, write a letter presently [1]
Unto the lord of Berkeley from ourself
That he resign the king to thee and Gurney;
And when 'tis done, we will subscribe our name.

Mat. It shall be done, my lord. (*Writes.*)

Y. Mort. Gurney, —

Gur. My lord?

Y. Mort. As thou intend'st to rise by Mortimer,
Who now makes Fortune's wheel turn as he please,
Seek all the means thou canst to make him droop,
And neither give him kind word nor good look.

Gur. I warrant you, my lord.

Y. Mort. And this above the rest: because we hear
That Edmund casts to work his liberty,
Remove him still from place to place by night,
Till at the last he come to Killingworth,
And then from thence to Berkeley back again;
And by the way, to make him fret the more,
Speak curstly [2] to him; and in any case
Let no man comfort him, if he chance to weep,
But amplify his grief with bitter words.

Mat. Fear not, my lord; we'll do as you command.

Y. Mort. So now away! post thitherwards amain.

Q. Isab. Whither goes this letter? to my lord the
   king?

[1] immediately.   [2] sharply.

Commend me humbly to his majesty,
And tell him that I labour all in vain
To ease his grief and work his liberty;
And bear him this as witness of my love.

                                        (*Gives a ring.*)

  Mat. I will, madam.   [*Exit with Gurney.*

  Y. Mort. Finely dissembled! Do so still, sweet
    queen.

Here comes the young prince with the Earl of Kent.

  Q. Isab. Something he whispers in his childish ears.

  Y. Mort. If he have such access unto the prince,
Our plots and stratagems will soon be dash'd.

  Q. Isab. Use Edmund friendly, as if all were well.

(*Enter Prince Edward, and Kent talking with him.*)

  Y. Mort. How fares my honourable lord of Kent?

  Kent. In health, sweet Mortimer.—How fares your
    grace?

  Q. Isab. Well, if my lord your brother were en-
    larg'd.

  Kent. I hear of late he hath depos'd himself.

  Q. Isab. The more my grief.

  Y. Mort. And mine.

  Kent. Ah, they do dissemble!   (*Aside.*)

  Q. Isab. Sweet son, come hither; I must talk with
    thee.

  Y. Mort. You, being his uncle and the next of
    blood,
Do look to be protector o'er the prince.

  Kent. Not I, my lord; who should protect the son,
But she that gave him life? I mean the queen.

P. Edw. Mother, persuade me not to wear the
  crown :
Let him be king ; I am too young to reign.

  Q. Isab. But be content, seeing 'tis his highness'
  pleasure.

  P. Edw. Let me but see him first, and then I will.

  Kent. Ay, do, sweet nephew.

  Q. Isab. Brother, you know it is impossible.

  P. Edw. Why, is he dead ?

  Q. Isab. No, God forbid.

  Kent. I would those words proceeded from your
  heart !

  Y. Mort. Inconstant Edmund, dost thou favour him,
That wast a cause of his imprisonment ?

  Kent. The more cause have I now to make amends.

  Y. Mort. (*aside to Queen Isab.*) I tell thee, 'tis not
  meet that one so false
Should come about the person of a prince. —
My lord, he hath betray'd the king his brother,
And therefore trust him not.

  P. Edw. But he repents, and sorrows for it now.

  Q. Isab. Come, son, and go with this gentle lord
  and me.

  P. Edw. With you I will, but not with Mortimer.

  Y. Mort. Why, youngling, 'sdain'st [1] thou so of
  Mortimer ?
Then I will carry thee by force away.

  P. Edw. Help, Uncle Kent ! Mortimer will wrong
  me.

[1] disdainest.

Q. Isab. Brother Edmund, strive not; we are his
    friends;

Isabel is nearer than the Earl of Kent.

    Kent. Sister, Edward is my charge; redeem him.

    Q. Isab. Edward is my son, and I will keep
    him.

    Kent. Mortimer shall know that he hath wrongèd
    me! —

Hence will I haste to Killingworth Castle

And rescue agèd Edward from his foes,

To be reveng'd on Mortimer and thee.   (*Aside.*)

    [*Exeunt on one side Queen Isabella, Prince Ed-
    ward, and Young Mortimer; on the other, Kent.*

SCENE III. *Near Killingworth Castle. Enter Matrevis
    and Gurney and Soldiers, with King Edward.*

    Mat. My lord, be not pensive, we are your friends;

Men are ordained to live in misery,

Therefore come; dalliance dangereth our lives.

    K. Edw. Friends, whither must unhappy Edward
    go?

Will hateful Mortimer appoint no rest?

Must I be vexèd like the nightly bird,

Whose sight is loathsome to all wingèd fowls?

When will the fury of his mind assuage?

When will his heart be satisfied with blood?

If mine will serve, unbowel straight this breast,

And give my heart to Isabel and him:

It is the chiefest mark they level[1] at.

---

[1] aim.

Gur. Not so, my liege; the queen hath given this charge
To keep your grace in safety;
Your passions make your dolours to increase.

K. Edw. This usage makes my misery increase.
But can my air of life continue long
When all my senses are annoy'd with stench?
Within a dungeon England's king is kept,
Where I am starv'd for want of sustenance;
My daily diet is heart-breaking sobs,
That almost rents [1] the closet of my heart;
Thus lives old Edward not reliev'd by any,
And so must die, though pitièd by many.
O, water, gentle friends, to cool my thirst,
And clear my body from foul excrements!

Mat. Here's channel [2] water, as our charge is given:
Sit down, for we'll be barbers to your grace.

K. Edw. Traitors, away! what, will you murder me,
Or choke your sovereign with puddle water?

Gur. No; but wash your face, and shave away your beard,
Lest you be known, and so be rescuèd.

Mat. Why strive you thus? your labour is in vain!

K. Edw. The wren may strive against the lion's strength,
But all in vain: so vainly do I strive
To seek for mercy at a tyrant's hand.

(*They wash him with puddle water, and shave off his beard.*)

---

[1] rend. [2] gutter.

Immortal powers, that know the painful cares
That wait upon my poor distressèd soul,
O level all your looks upon these daring men,
That wrong their liege and sovereign, England's king!
O Gaveston, 'tis for thee that I am wrong'd,
For me, both thou and both the Spencers died!
And for your sakes a thousand wrongs I'll take.
The Spencers' ghosts, wherever they remain,
Wish well to mine; then, tush, for them I'll die.

  Mat. 'Twixt theirs and yours shall be no enmity.
Come, come away! now put the torches out:
We'll enter in by darkness to Killingworth.

KING EDWARD THE THIRD

YOUNG, ambitious, and assured of the support of the great nobles, Edward III. was eager for valiant deeds. The French succession was in dispute, and Edward, the only surviving grandson of Philip the Fair, laid claim to the crown. In the first years of the long war that followed, the English were brilliantly successful. At the battle of Cressy (1346), the French forces were driven from the field, and the Black Prince won his spurs.

ACT III

SCENE V. *During the Battle of Cressy.*

(*Drums. Enter King Edward and Audley.*)

  K. Edw. Lord Audley, whiles our son is in the
      chase,
Withdraw your powers [1] unto this little hill,
And here a season let us breathe ourselves.

[1] forces.

Aud. I will, my lord.   [*Exit. Retreat.*

K. Edw. Just dooming Heaven, whose secret providence

To our gross judgment is inscrutable,

How are we bound to praise thy wondrous works,

That hast this day giv'n way unto the right

And made the wicked stumble at themselves!

(*Enter Artois, hastily.*)

Art. Rescue, King Edward! rescue for thy son!

K. Edw. Rescue, Artois? what, is he prisoner?

Or by violence fell beside his horse?

Art. Neither, my lord; but narrowly beset

With turning Frenchmen whom he did pursue,

As 'tis impossible that he should 'scape

Except your highness presently descend.

K. Edw. Tut, let him fight; we gave him arms to-day,

And he is labouring for a knighthood, man.

(*Enter Derby, hastily.*)

Der. The prince, my lord, the prince! O, succour him;

He's close encompass'd with a world of odds!

K. Edw. Then will he win a world of honour too

If he by valour can redeem him thence:

If not, what remedy? we have more sons

Than one, to comfort our declining age.

(*Reënter Audley, hastily.*)

Aud. Renownèd Edward, give me leave, I pray,

To lead my soldiers where I may relieve

Your grace's son, in danger to be slain.
The snares of French, like emmets on a bank,
Muster about him; whilst he, lion-like,
Entangled in the net of their assaults,
Franticly rends and bites the woven toil:
But all in vain, he cannot free himself.

   K. Edw. Audley, content; I will not have a man,
On pain of death, sent forth to succour him:
This is the day ordain'd by destiny
To season his courage with those grievous thoughts,
That, if he breathe out Nestor's years on earth,
Will make him savour still of this exploit.

   Der. Ah, but he shall not live to see those days.

   K. Edw. Why, then his epitaph is lasting praise.

   Aud. Yet, good my lord, 'tis too much wilfulness,
To let his blood be spilt that may be sav'd.

   K. Edw. Exclaim no more; for none of you can
      tell
Whether a borrow'd aid will serve or no.
Perhaps, he is already slain or ta'en:
And dare [1] a falcon when she's in her flight,
And ever after she'll be haggard-like: [2]
Let Edward be deliver'd by our hands,
And still in danger he'll expect the like;
But if himself himself redeem from thence,
He will have vanquish'd, cheerful, death and fear,
And ever after dread their force no more
Than if they were but babes or captive slaves.

   Aud. O cruel father! — Farewell, Edward, then!

      [1] balk.   [2] wild, untrusty.

Der. Farewell, sweet prince, the hope of chivalry!

Art. O, would my life might ransom him from death!

K. Edw. But, soft; methinks I hear

(Retreat sounded.)

The dismal charge of trumpets' loud retreat:
All are not slain, I hope, that went with him;
Some will return with tidings, good or bad.

(*Enter Prince Edward in triumph, bearing in his hand his shivered lance; his sword, and battered armour, borne before him, and the body of the King of Bohemia, wrapped in the colours. Lords run and embrace him.*)

Aud. O joyful sight! victorious Edward lives!

Der. Welcome, brave prince!

K. Edw.   Welcome, Plantagenet!

(Embracing him.)

Pr. Edw. First having done my duty, as beseem'd,

(Kneels, and kisses his father's hand.)

Lords, I regreet you all with hearty thanks.
And now, behold, — after my winter's toil,
My painful voyage on the boist'rous sea
Of war's devouring gulfs and steely rocks, —
I bring my fraught unto the wishèd port,
My summer's hope, my travel's sweet reward:
And here with humble duty I present
This sacrifice, this firstfruit of my sword,
Cropp'd and cut down even at the gate of death,
The King of Boheme, father, whom I slew;

Whose thousands had intrench'd me round about,
And lay as thick upon my batter'd crest
As on an anvil with their pond'rous glaives:
Yet marble courage still did underprop;
And when my weary arms with often blows, —
Like the continual-lab'ring woodman's axe
That is enjoin'd to fell a load of oaks, —
Began to falter, straight I would remember
My gifts you gave me and my zealous vow,
And then new courage made me fresh again;
That, in despite, I carv'd my passage forth
And put the multitude to speedy flight.
Lo, thus hath Edward's hand fill'd your request,
And done, I hope, the duty of a knight.

    K. Edw. Ay, well thou hast deserv'd a knighthood,
      Ned!
And, therefore, with thy sword, yet reeking warm
    (*Receiving it from the soldier who bore it and lay-*
      ing it on the kneeling Prince.)
With blood of those that sought to be thy bane,
Arise, Prince Edward, trusty knight at arms:
This day thou hast confounded me with joy
And proved thyself fit heir unto a king.

WAT TYLER

Robert Southey

The French war so brilliantly begun dragged on through the fourteenth century. France could not be forced to accept a foreign king ; while the frequent expeditions across the Channel brought a ruinous drain upon the resources of England. Thousands of peasant soldiers were killed in battle or left to die of wounds or disease, and the burden of taxation was felt even by the very poor. Richard II., the ten-year-old son of the Black Prince, came to the throne on the death of Edward III. He was a brave, handsome lad, who sought his own pleasure and did nothing to remedy the distress of the people. The ruthless exaction of a poll-tax in 1381 exasperated the peasants beyond endurance, and they rose in revolt. The government was not prepared for resistance, and the insurgents got possession of London. The counsellors of the king urged him to quiet the people by promising all they asked. He did so and easily persuaded them to return to their homes, bearing the king's worthless pledges that their grievances should be set right. Some of the leaders, Wat Tyler, John Ball, and others, stayed in London to make sure that the royal word was kept. They were summoned to meet the king at Smithfield, and there, because he dared to speak openly, Wat Tyler was struck down and fatally wounded. John Ball was soon after arrested, tried, and put to death. Thousands of peasants were slain by the king's officers, who were sent into the provinces to quell the insurrection. So the Peasants' Revolt was crushed in blood, but the ideas of Wat Tyler and John Ball have nevertheless prevailed.

ACT I

SCENE I. *A Blacksmith's Shop; Wat Tyler at work within ; a May-pole before the door.*

Hob Carter. Curse on these taxes — one succeeds another —

Our ministers, panders of a king's will,

Drain all our wealth away, waste it in revels,
And lure, or force away our boys, who should be
The props of our old age, to fill their armies,
And feed the crows of France.   Year follows year,
And still we madly prosecute the war ;
Draining our wealth, distressing our poor peasants,
Slaughtering our youths — and all to crown our chiefs
With glory ! — I detest the hell-sprung name.

    Tyler. What matters me who wears the crown of
      France ?
Whether a Richard or a Charles possess it ?
They reap the glory — they enjoy the spoil —
We pay — we bleed ! The sun would shine as cheerly,
The rains of heaven as seasonably fall,
Though neither of these royal pests existed.

    Hob. Nay, as for that we poor men should fare
      better ;
No legal robbers then should force away
The hard-earn'd wages of our honest toil.
The Parliament forever cries *more money,*
The service of the state demands more money ;
Just heaven ! of what service is the state ?

    Tyler. Oh, 'tis of vast importance ! who should
      pay for
The luxuries and riots of the court ?
Who should support the flaunting courtiers' pride,
Pay for their midnight revels, their rich garments,
Did not the state enforce ? — Think ye, my friend,
That I, a humble blacksmith, here at Deptford,
Would part with these six groats — earn'd by hard toil,

All that I have! to massacre the Frenchmen,
Murder as enemies men I never saw!
Did not the state compel me?
(*Tax-gatherers pass by.*)   There they go,
Privileged ruffians!

ACT II

SCENE I. BLACKHEATH. *Tyler, Hob, etc.*

Song.

"When Adam delved and Eve span,
    Who was then the gentleman?"

Jack Straw. The mob are up in London — the
    proud courtiers
Begin to tremble.
Tom Miller.   Ay, ay, 'tis time to tremble:
Who'll plough their fields, who'll do their drudgery
    now,
And work like horses to give them the harvest?
Jack Straw. I only wonder we lay quiet so long.
We had always the same strength; and we deserved
The ills we met with for not using it.
Hob. Why do we fear those animals call'd lords?
What is there in the name to frighten us?
Is not my arm as mighty as a Baron's?

*   *   *   *   *   *   *

Jack Straw.   March we for London.
Tyler. Mark me, my friends — we rise for Liberty —
Jack Straw. Justice shall be our guide: let no man
    dare

To plunder in the tumult.

  Mob. Lead us on. Liberty! Justice!
  [*Exeunt with cries of Liberty! No poll-tax!
    No war!*

SCENE II. *The Tower. King Richard, Archbishop
of Canterbury, Walworth, Philpot.*

  King. What must we do? the danger grows more
    imminent.
The mob increases.
  Philpot.   Every moment brings
Fresh tidings of our peril.
  King.   It were well
To grant them what they ask.
  Archbishop.   Ay, that, my liege,
Were politic. Go boldly forth to meet them,
Grant all they ask — however wild and ruinous —
Meantime, the troops you have already summon'd
Will gather round them. Then my Christian power
Absolves you of your promise.
  Walworth. Were but their ringleaders cut off, the
    rabble
Would soon disperse.
  Philpot.   United in a mass,
There's nothing can resist them — once divide them
And they will fall an easy sacrifice.
  Archbishop. Lull them by promises— bespeak them
    fair.
Go forth, my liege — spare not, if need requires,
A solemn oath to ratify the treaty.

King. I dread their fury.

Archbishop. 'Tis a needless dread,
There is divinity about your person;
It is the sacred privilege of Kings,
Howe'er they act, to render no account
To man. The people have been taught this lesson,
Nor can they soon forget it.

King. I will go —
I will submit to everything they ask;
My day of triumph will arrive at last.

(*Shouts without.*)

(*Enter Messenger.*)

Mess. The mob are at the city gates.

Archbishop. Haste! Haste!
Address them ere too late. I'll remain here,
For they detest me much. (*Shouts again.*)

(*Enter another Messenger.*)

Mess. The Londoners have opened the city gates;
The rebels are admitted.

King. Fear then must give me courage. My lord
mayor,
Come you with me. [*Exeunt. Shouts without.*

ACT III

SCENE II. *Westminster Hall. King, Walworth, Philpot, Sir John Tresilian, etc.*

Walworth. My liege, 'twas wisely ordered, to destroy
The dunghill rabble, but take prisoner

That old seditious priest : his strange wild notions
Of this equality, when well exposed,
Will create ridicule, and shame the people
Of their late tumults.

   Sir John Tr.   Ay, there's nothing like
A fair, free, open trial, where the King
Can choose his jury and appoint his judges.

    King. Walworth, I must thank you for my deliver-
      ance,
'Twas a bold deed to stab him in the parley.
Kneel down, and rise a knight, Sir William Walworth.

               (*Enter Messenger.*)

   Mess. I left them hotly at it. Smithfield smoked
With the rebels' blood ! your troops fought loyally,
There's not a man of them will lend an ear
To pity.

   Walworth. Is John Ball secured ?
   Mess.   They have seized him.

        (*Enter Guards, with John Ball.*)

   1*st Guard.* We've brought the old villain.

   2*d Guard.*   An old mischief maker —
Why there's fifteen hundred of the mob are killed,
All through his preaching.

   Sir John Tr. Prisoner, are you the arch-rebel John
    Ball?

   John Ball. I am John Ball ; but I am not a rebel.
Take ye the name, who, arrogant in strength,
Rebel against the people's sovereignty.

   Sir John Tr. John Ball, you are accused of stirring
    up

The poor deluded people to rebellion;
Not having the fear of God and of the King
Before your eyes; of preaching up strange notions,
Heretical and treasonous; such as saying
That kings have not a right from Heaven to govern;
That all mankind are equal; and that rank
And the distinctions of society,
Ay, and the sacred rights of property,
Are evil and oppressive; plead you guilty
To this most heavy charge?
  John Ball.   If it be guilt,
To preach what you are pleased to call strange
     notions,
That all mankind as brethren must be equal;
That privileged orders of society
Are evil and oppressive; that the right
Of property is a juggle to deceive
The poor whom you oppress; I plead me guilty.
  Sir John Tr. It is against the custom of this
     court
That the prisoner should plead guilty.
  John Ball.   Why then put you
The needless question? Sir Judge, let me save
The vain and empty insult of a trial.
What I have done, that I dare justify.
  Sir John Tr. Did you not tell the mob they were
     oppress'd;
And preach upon the equality of man;
With evil intent thereby to stir them up
To tumult and rebellion?

John Ball.   That I told them
That all mankind are equal, is most true :
Ye came as helpless infants to the world;
Ye feel alike the infirmities of nature;
And at last moulder into common clay.
Why then these vain distinctions ? — bears not the
    earth
Food in abundance ? — must your granaries
O'erflow with plenty, while the poor man starves?
Sir Judge, why sit you there, clad in your furs;
Why are your cellars stored with choicest wines?
Your larders hung with dainties, while your vassal,
As virtuous, and as able too by nature,
Though by your selfish tyranny deprived
Of mind's improvement, shivers in his rags,
And starves amid the plenty he creates?
I have said this is wrong, and I repeat it —
And there will be a time when this great truth
Shall be confess'd — be felt by all mankind.
The electric truth shall run from man to man,
And the blood-cemented pyramid of greatness
Shall fall before the flash.
    Sir John Tr.   Audacious rebel;
How darest thou insult this sacred court,
Blaspheming all the dignities of rank?
How could the Government be carried on
Without the sacred orders of the King
And the nobility?
    John Ball.   Tell me, Sir Judge,
What does the Government avail the peasant?

Would not he plough his field, and sow the corn,
Ay, and in peace enjoy the harvest too?
Would not the sun shine and the dews descend,
Though neither King nor Parliament existed?
Do your court politics ought matter him?
Would he be warring even unto death
With his French neighbours?   Charles and Richard
     contend,
The people fight and suffer : — think ye, Sirs,
If neither country had been cursed with a chief,
The peasants would have quarrell'd?
   King.   This is treason!
The patience of the court has been insulted —
Condemn the foul-mouth'd, contumacious rebel.
   Sir John Tr. John Ball, whereas you are accused
     before us,
Of stirring up the people to rebellion,
And preaching to them strange and dangerous doc-
     trines ;
And whereas your behaviour to the court
Has been most insolent and contumacious ;
Insulting Majesty — and since you have pleaded
Guilty to all these charges ; I condemn you
To death : you shall be hangèd by the neck,
But not till you are dead — your bowels open'd —
Your heart torn out, and burnt before your face —
Your traitorous head be severed from your body —
Your body quarter'd, and exposed upon
The city gates — a terrible example —
And the Lord God have mercy on your soul.

John Ball. Why, be it so. I can smile at your
    vengeance,
For I am arm'd with rectitude of soul.
The truth, which all my life I have divulged,
And am now doom'd in torments to expire for,
Shall still survive. The destined hour must come,
When it shall blaze with sun-surpassing splendour,
And the dark mists of prejudice and falsehood
Fade in its strong effulgence. Flattery's incense
No more shall shadow round the gore-dyed throne;
That altar of oppression, fed with rites,
More savage than the priests of Moloch taught,
Shall be consumed amid the fire of Justice;
The rays of truth shall emanate around
And the whole world be lighted.
King.   Drag him hence:
Away with him to death; order the troops
Now to give quarter, and make prisoners —
Let the blood-reeking sword of war be sheathed,
That the law may take vengeance on the rebels.

KING RICHARD THE SECOND

WILLIAM SHAKESPEARE

THE wayward boy became a passionate and wilful man. He re-
jected the counsel of the great lords and banished them from the king-
dom. His uncle, John of Gaunt, the Duke of Lancaster, had been a
party to the extravagance and corruption attending the French wars.
He knew better than any one else the influences that were ruining
England. But Richard the Redeless, as he was called, turned a deaf
ear to his words of warning. Henry Bolingbroke, Gaunt's son, was

sent into exile and, after the death of John of Gaunt, the Lancastrian estates were confiscated by the king. In 1399, Bolingbroke returned to claim first his inheritance and, later, the kingdom. The leading nobles crowded to his standard, and London sent an army to his aid. Richard, deserted by his most trusted friends, was obliged to yield himself a prisoner and to surrender the crown to his " fair cousin Bolingbroke." The death of the deposed king is variously reported by tradition as due to hard usage, assassination, voluntary starvation.

ACT II

SCENE I. LONDON. *A Room in Ely House.*

(*Gaunt on a couch; the Duke of York and others standing by him*).

   Gaunt. Will the king come, that I may breathe my last
In wholesome counsel to his unstaid youth ?
   York. Vex not yourself, nor strive not with your breath ;
For all in vain comes counsel to his ear.
   Gaunt. O, but they say the tongues of dying men
Enforce attention like deep harmony :
Where words are scarce, they are seldom spent in vain,
For they breathe truth that breathe their words in pain.
He that no more must say is listen'd more
Than they whom youth and ease have taught to glose ;
More are men's ends mark'd than their lives before :
The setting sun, and music at the close,

As the last taste of sweets, is sweetest last,
Writ in remembrance more than things long past :
Though Richard my life's counsel would not hear,
My death's sad tale may yet undeaf his ear.

   York. No; it is stopp'd with other flattering
    sounds,
As praises, of whose taste the wise are fond,
Lascivious metres, to whose venom sound
The open ear of youth doth always listen ;
Report of fashions in proud Italy,
Whose manners still our tardy apish nation
Limps after in base imitation.
Where doth the world thrust forth a vanity —
So it be new, there's no respect how vile —
That is not quickly buzz'd into his ears ?
Then all too late comes counsel to be heard,
Where will doth mutiny with wit's regard.
Direct not him whose way himself will choose :
'Tis breath thou lack'st, and that breath wilt thou
    lose.

   Gaunt. Methinks I am a prophet new inspired
And thus expiring do foretell of him :
His rash fierce blaze of riot cannot last,
For violent fires soon burn out themselves ;
Small showers last long, but sudden storms are
    short ;
He tires betimes that spurs too fast betimes ;
With eager feeding food doth choke the feeder :
Light vanity, insatiate cormorant,
Consuming means, soon preys upon itself.

This royal throne of kings, this sceptred isle,
This earth of majesty, this seat of Mars,
This other Eden, demi-paradise;
This fortress built by Nature for herself
Against infection and the hand of war;
This happy breed of men, this little world,
This precious stone set in the silver sea,
Which serves it in the office of a wall,
Or as a moat defensive to a house,
Against the envy of less happier lands;
This blessèd plot, this earth, this realm, this England,
This nurse, this teeming womb of royal kings,
Fear'd by their breed, and famous by their birth,
Renownèd for their deeds as far from home,
For Christian service and true chivalry,
As is the sepulchre in stubborn Jewry
Of the world's ransom, blessèd Mary's Son;
This land of such dear souls, this dear dear land,
Dear for her reputation through the world,
Is now leas'd out, I die pronouncing it,
Like to a tenement or pelting [1] farm:
England, bound in with the triumphant sea,
Whose rocky shore beats back the envious siege
Of watery Neptune, is now bound in with shame,
With inky blots and rotten parchment bonds:
That England, that was wont to conquer others,
Hath made a shameful conquest of itself.
Ah, would the scandal vanish with my life,
How happy then were my ensuing death!

[1] paltry.

ACT III

SCENE III. WALES. *Before Flint Castle.*

(*Enter, with drums and colours, Bolingbroke and Forces; York, Northumberland, and others. A parle sounded, and answered by another trumpet within. Flourish. Enter on the walls King Richard, the Bishop of Carlisle, Aumerle, Scroop, and Salisbury.*)

Bolingbroke. See, see, King Richard doth himself appear,
As doth the blushing discontented sun
From out the fiery portal of the east,
When he perceives the envious clouds are bent
To dim his glory and to stain the track
Of his bright passage to the occident.

York. Yet looks he like a king: behold, his eye,
As bright as is the eagle's, lightens forth
Controlling majesty: alack, alack, for woe,
That any harm should stain so fair a show!

K. Richard. We are amaz'd; and thus long have we stood

(*To Northumberland.*)

To watch the fearful bending of thy knee,
Because we thought ourself thy lawful king:
And if we be, how dare thy joints forget
To pay their awful duty to our presence?
If we be not, show us the hand of God
That hath dismiss'd us from our stewardship;
For well we know, no hand of blood and bone

Can gripe the sacred handle of our sceptre,
Unless he do profane, steal, or usurp.
And though you think that all, as you have done,
Have torn their souls by turning them from us,
And we are barren and bereft of friends,
Yet know, my master, God omnipotent,
Is mustering in his clouds, on our behalf,
Armies of pestilence; and they shall strike
Your children yet unborn and unbegot,
That lift your vassal hands against my head,
And threat the glory of my precious crown.
Tell Bolingbroke — for yond methinks he stands —
That every stride he makes upon my land
Is dangerous treason : he is come to ope
The purple testament of bleeding war ;
But ere the crown he looks for live in peace,
Ten thousand bloody crowns of mothers' sons
Shall ill become the flower of England's face,
Change the complexion of her maid-pale peace
To scarlet indignation, and bedew
Her pastures' grass with faithful English blood.
    Northumberland. The King of Heaven forbid our
        lord the king
Should so with civil and uncivil arms
Be rush'd upon ! Thy thrice-noble cousin,
Harry Bolingbroke, doth humbly kiss thy hand ;
And by the honourable tomb he swears,
That stands upon your royal grandsire's bones,
And by the royalties of both your bloods,
Currents that spring from one most gracious head,

And by the buried hand of warlike Gaunt,
And by the worth and honour of himself,
Comprising all that may be sworn or said,
His coming hither hath no further scope
Than for his lineal royalties, and to beg
Enfranchisement immediate on his knees:
Which on thy royal party granted once,
His glittering arms he will commend to rust,
His barbèd steeds to stables, and his heart
To faithful service of your majesty.
This swears he, as he is a prince, is just;
And, as I am a gentleman, I credit him.

    K. Richard. Northumberland, say thus the king
      returns: —
His noble cousin is right welcome hither;
And all the number of his fair demands
Shall be accomplish'd without contradiction:
With all the gracious utterance thou hast
Speak to his gentle hearing kind commends.
We do debase ourself, cousin, do we not, (*To Aumerle.*)
To look so poorly, and to speak so fair?
Shall we call back Northumberland, and send
Defiance to the traitor, and so die?

    Aumerle. No, good my lord; let's fight with gentle
      words
Till time lend friends, and friends their helpful swords.

    K. Richard. O God, O God! that e'er this tongue
      of mine,
That laid the sentence of dread banishment
On yond proud man, should take it off again

With words of sooth. O that I were as great
As is my grief, or lesser than my name!
Or that I could forget what I have been!
Or not remember what I must be now!
Swell'st thou, proud heart? I'll give thee scope to
beat,
Since foes have scope to beat both thee and me.

    Aumerle. Northumberland comes back from Bol-
ingbroke.

    K. Richard. What must the king do now? Must
he submit?
The king shall do it. Must he be depos'd?
The king shall be contented. Must he lose
The name of king? O' God's name, let it go.
I'll give my jewels for a set of beads,
My gorgeous palace for a hermitage,
My gay apparel for an alms-man's gown,
My figured goblets for a dish of wood,
My sceptre for a palmer's walking staff,
My subjects for a pair of carvèd saints,
And my large kingdom for a little grave,
A little little grave, an obscure grave;
Or I'll be buried in the king's highway,
Some way of common trade, where subjects' feet
May hourly trample on their sovereign's head;
For on my heart they tread now whilst I live;
And, buried once, why not upon my head?—
Aumerle, thou weep'st, my tender-hearted cousin!
We'll make foul weather with despisèd tears;
Our sighs and they shall lodge [1] the summer corn,

              [1] beat down.

And make a dearth in this revolting land.
Or shall we play the wantons with our woes,
And make some pretty match with shedding tears?
As thus; — to drop them still upon one place,
Till they have fretted us a pair of graves
Within the earth; and, therein laid, — there lies
Two kinsmen digg'd their graves with weeping eyes.
Would not this ill do well? Well, well, I see
I talk but idly, and you mock at me. —
Most mighty prince, my Lord Northumberland,
What says King Bolingbroke? will his majesty
Give Richard leave to live till Richard die?

ACT IV

SCENE I. LONDON. *Westminster Hall. The Lords spiritual on the right side of the throne; the Lords temporal on the left; the Commons below.*

(*Enter Bolingbroke, Aumerle, Surrey, Northumberland, Percy, Fitzwater, another Lord, the Bishop of Carlisle, the Abbot of Westminster, and Attendants. Officers behind with Bagot. Enter York, with King Richard, and Officers bearing the crown, etc.*)

K. Richard. Alack! why am I sent for to a king,
Before I have shook off the regal thoughts
Wherewith I reign'd? I hardly yet have learn'd
To insinuate, flatter, bow, and bend my limbs:
Give sorrow leave awhile to tutor me
To this submission. Yet I well remember
The favours [1] of these men: were they not mine?

[1] countenances.

Did they not sometime cry, " All hail ! " to me ?
So Judas did to Christ : but he, in twelve,
Found truth in all but one ; I, in twelve thousand, none.
God save the king !   Will no man say amen ?
Am I both priest and clerk ?   Well then, amen.
God save the king !   Although I be not he ;
And yet, amen, if heaven do think him me.
To do what service am I sent for hither ?
   York. To do that office of thine own good will
Which tired majesty did make thee offer,
The resignation of thy state and crown
To Henry Bolingbroke.
   K. Richard. Give me the crown.   Here, cousin,
      seize the crown ;
On this side my hand, and on that side thine.
Now is this golden crown like a deep well
That owes [1] two buckets, filling one another ;
The emptier ever dancing in the air,
The other down, unseen and full of water :
That bucket down and full of tears am I,
Drinking my griefs, whilst you mount up on high.
   Bolingbroke. I thought you had been willing to
      resign.
   K. Richard. My crown I am ; but still my griefs
      are mine :
You may my glories and my state depose,
But not my griefs ; still am I king of those.
   Bolingbroke. Part of your cares you give me with
      your crown.

----

[1] owns.

 K. Richard. Your cares set up do not pluck my
  cares down.
My care is loss of care, by old care done;
Your care is gain of care, by new care won:
The cares I give, I have, though given away;
They tend the crown, yet still with me they stay.
 Bolingbroke. Are you contented to resign the
  crown?
 K. Richard. Ay, no;—no, ay; for I must nothing be;
Therefore no no, for I resign to thee.
Now mark me, how I will undo myself. —
I give this heavy weight from off my head,
And this unwieldy sceptre from my hand,
The pride of kingly sway from out my heart;
With mine own tears I wash away my balm,
With mine own hands I give away my crown,
With mine own tongue deny my sacred state,
With mine own breath release all duteous oaths:
All pomp and majesty I do forswear;
My manors, rents, revènues I forego;
My acts, decrees, and statutes I deny:
God pardon all oaths that are broke to me!
God keep all vows unbroke that swear to thee!
Make me, that nothing have, with nothing griev'd,
And thou with all pleas'd, that hast all achiev'd!
Long mayst thou live in Richard's seat to sit,
And soon lie Richard in an earthy pit!
God save King Harry, unking'd Richard says,
And send him many years of sunshine days!
What more remains?

Northumberland.　　No more, but that you read
　　　　　　　　　　　(*Offering a paper.*)
These accusations, and these grievous crimes
Committed by your person and your followers
Against the state and profit of this land ;
That, by confessing them, the souls of men
May deem that you are worthily depos'd.

　K. Richard. Must I do so ? and must I ravel out
My weav'd-up follies ?　Gentle Northumberland,
If thy offences were upon record,
Would it not shame thee in so fair a troop
To read a lecture of them ?　If thou wouldst,
There shouldst thou find one heinous article,
Containing the deposing of a king,
And cracking the strong warrant of an oath,
Mark'd with a blot, damn'd in the book of heaven.
Nay, all of you that stand and look upon,
Whilst that my wretchedness doth bait myself,
Though some of you, with Pilate, wash your hands,
Showing an outward pity, yet you Pilates
Have here deliver'd me to my sour cross,
And water cannot wash away your sin.

　Northumberland.　My lord, despatch ; read o'er
　　these articles.

　K. Richard.　Mine eyes are full of tears, I cannot see ;
And yet salt water blinds them not so much
But they can see a sort [1] of traitors here.
Nay, if I turn mine eyes upon myself,
I find myself a traitor with the rest ;

---

[1] set, group.

For I have given here my soul's consent
To undeck the pompous body of a king;
Made glory base and sovereignty a slave,
Proud majesty a servant, state a peasant.

   Northumberland. My lord, —

     K. Richard. No lord of thine, thou haught[1] insult-
       ing man,

Nor no man's lord; I have no name, no title,
No, not that name was given me at the font,
But 'tis usurp'd. — Alack the heavy day,
That I have worn so many winters out,
And know not now what name to call myself!
O that I were a mockery king of snow,
Standing before the sun of Bolingbroke,
To melt myself away in water drops!
Good king, great king, and yet not greatly good,
An if my word be sterling yet in England,
Let it command a mirror hither straight,
That it may show me what a face I have,
Since it is bankrupt of his[2] majesty.

   Bolingbroke. Go some of you and fetch a looking-
     glass.   [*Exit an Attendant.*

   Northumberland. Read o'er this paper while the
     glass doth come.

   K. Richard. Fiend, thou torment'st me ere I come
     to hell!

   Bolingbroke. Urge it no more, my Lord Northum-
     berland.

   Northumberland. The commons will not then be
     satisfied.

[1] haughty.   [2] its.

K. Richard. They shall be satisfied : I'll read
   enough,
When I do see the very book indeed
Where all my sins are writ, and that's myself.
              (*Reënter Attendant with a glass.*)
Give me the glass, and therein will I read.
No deeper wrinkles yet ? hath sorrow struck
So many blows upon this face of mine,
And made no deeper wounds ?   O flattering glass,
Like to my followers in prosperity,
Thou dost beguile me !   Was this face the face
That every day under his household roof
Did keep ten thousand men ?   Was this the face
That, like the sun, did make beholders wink ?
Was this the face that faced so many follies,
And was at last out faced by Bolingbroke ?
A brittle glory shineth in this face :
As brittle as the glory is the face ;
           (*Dashes the glass against the ground.*)
For there it is, crack'd in a hundred shivers.
Mark, silent king, the moral of this sport,
How soon my sorrow hath destroy'd my face.
   Bolingbroke. The shadow of your sorrow hath de-
   stroy'd
The shadow of your face.
   K. Richard.   Say that again.
The shadow of my sorrow ?   Ha ! let's see : —
'Tis very true, my grief lies all within ;
And these external manners of lament
Are merely shadows to the unseen grief

That swells with silence in the tortur'd soul;
There lies the substance: and I thank thee, king,
For thy great bounty, that not only giv'st
Me cause to wail, but teachest me the way
How to lament the cause.   I'll beg one boon,
And then begone and trouble you no more.
Shall I obtain it?

Bolingbroke.   Name it, fair cousin.

K. Richard. "Fair cousin"? I am greater than a
    king:
For when I was a king, my flatterers
Were then but subjects; being now a subject,
I have a king here to my flatterer.
Being so great, I have no need to beg.

Bolingbroke. Yet ask.

K. Richard. And shall I have?

Bolingbroke. You shall.

K. Richard. Then give me leave to go.

Bolingbroke. Whither?

K. Richard. Whither you will, so I were from your
    sights.

Bolingbroke. Go, some of you, convey him to the
    Tower.

ACT V

SCENE IV. WINDSOR.   *A Room in the Castle.*

(*Enter Bolingbroke as King, York, Lords, and Atten-
    dants.   Enter Exton, with Attendants bearing a
    coffin.*)

Exton. Great king, within this coffin I present
Thy buried fear: herein all breathless lies

The mightiest of thy greatest enemies,
Richard of Bordeaux, by me hither brought.
 Bolingbroke. Exton, I thank thee not; for thou hast
  wrought
A deed of slander, with thy fatal hand,
Upon my head and all this famous land.
 Exton. From your own mouth, my lord, did I this
  deed.
 Bolingbroke. They love not poison that do poison
  need,
Nor do I thee: though I did wish him dead,
I hate the murtherer, love him murtherèd.
The guilt of conscience take thou for thy labour,
But neither my good word nor princely favour:
With Cain go wander thorough [1] shades of night,
And never show thy head by day nor light.
Lords, I protest, my soul is full of woe,
That blood should sprinkle me to make me grow:
Come, mourn with me for that I do lament,
And put on sullen black incontinent. [2]
I'll make a voyage to the Holy Land,
To wash this blood off from my guilty hand:
March sadly after; grace my mournings here;
In weeping after this untimely bier.   [*Exeunt.*

---

[1] through.   [2] immediately.

THE BATTLE OF OTTERBURNE

THE standing feud with Scotland gave rise to numberless raids across the Border. The following old ballad tells of a famous encounter between those two hot-headed young chieftains, James, Earl of Douglas, and the redoubtable Harry Percy. In 1388 Douglas, at the head of three thousand Scottish spears, made a raid into Northumberland and, before the walls of Newcastle, engaged Percy in single combat, capturing his lance with the attached pennon. Douglas retired in triumph, but Hotspur mustered the full force of the Border and, following hard on the Scottish rear, made a night attack upon the camp of Douglas at Otterburne, about twenty miles from the frontier. Then ensued a moonlight battle, fought on either side with unflinching bravery, and ending in the defeat of the English, Percy being taken prisoner. But the Douglas was slain in the midst of the fray.

It fell about the Lammas tide,[1]
    When muirmen[2] win their hay,
That the doughty Earl of Douglas rade
    Into England to fetch a prey.

And he has ta'en the Lindsays light,
    With them the Gordons gay;
But the Jardines wad not with him ride,
    And they rue it to this day.

Then they hae harried[3] the dales o' Tyne,
    And half o' Bambrough-shire,
And the Otter-dale they burned it haill,[4]
    And set it a' on fire.

Then he cam' up to New Castel,
    And rade it round about:

[1] August 1st.   [2] moormen.   [3] plundered.   [4] wholly.

" O who is the lord of this castel,
   Or who is the lady o't?"

But up and spake Lord Percy then,
   And O but he spake hie :
" It's I am the lord of this castel,
   My wife is the lady gay."

" If thou'rt the lord of this castel,
   Sae weel it pleases me !
For ere I cross the Border fell,[1]
   The tane[2] of us shall dee."

He took a lang spear in his hand,
   Shod with the metal free ;
And forth to meet the Douglas then,
   He rade richt furiouslie.

But O how pale his lady looked
   Frae aff the castle wa',
As doun before the Scottish spear
   She saw proud Percy fa' !

" Had we twa been upon the green,
   And never an eye to see,
I wad hae had you, flesh and fell,[3]
   But your sword shall gae wi' me."

" Now gae up to the Otterburne,
   And bide there dayis three,
And gin[4] I come not ere they end,
   A fause knight ca' ye me !"

[1] highland.   [2] the one.   [3] skin.   [4] if.

" The Otterburne is a bonnie burn,[1]
  'Tis pleasant there to be ;
But there is nought at Otterburne
  To fend my men and me.

" The deer rins wild on hill and dale,
  The birds fly wild frae tree to tree ;
But there is neither bread nor kale,[2]
  To fend[3] my men and me.

" Yet I will stay at Otterburne,
  Where you shall welcome be ;
And, if ye come not at three dayis end,
  A fause lord I'll ca' thee."

" Thither will I come," Earl Percy said,
  " By the might of our Ladye ! "
" There will I bide thee," said the Douglas,
  " My troth I plight to thee ! "

They lichted[4] high on Otterburne,
  Upon the bent[5] sae broun ;
They lichted high on Otterburne,
  And pitched their pallions[6] doun.

And he that had a bonnie boy,
  He sent his horse to grass ;
And he that had not a bonnie boy,
  His ain servant he was.

Then up and spake a little boy,
  Was near of Douglas' kin —

[1] brook.   [2] broth.   [3] sustain.   [4] alighted.
    [5] open field.   [6] tents (pavilions).

" Methinks I see an English host
　　Come branking [1] us upon !

" Nine wargangs [2] beiring braid and wide,
　　Seven banners beiring high ;
It wad do any living gude,
　　To see their colours fly ! "

" If this be true, my little boy,
　　That thou tells unto me,
The brawest bower [3] o' the Otterburne
　　Sall be thy morning fee. [4]

" But I hae dreamed a dreary dream,
　　Ayont the Isle o' Skye, —
I saw a deid man win a fight,
　　And I think that man was I."

He belted on his gude braid-sword,
　　And to the field he ran ;
But he forgot the hewmont [5] strong,
　　That should have kept his brain.

When Percy wi' the Douglas met,
　　I wot he was fu' fain : [6]
They swakkit [7] swords, and they twa swat,
　　Till the blude ran down like rain.

But Percy wi' his gude braid-sword,
　　That could sae sharply wound,
Has wounded Douglas on the brow,
　　That he fell to the ground.

[1] prancing.　　　[2] wagons.　　　[3] finest house.　　　[4] reward.
[5] helmet.　　　[6] joyful.　　　[7] smote.

And then he called his little foot-page,
   And said — " Run speedilie,
And fetch my ae [1] dear sister's son,
   Sir Hugh Montgomerie.

" My nephew gude ! " the Douglas said,
   " What recks the death of ane ?
Last night I dreamed a dreary dream,
   And ken the day's thy ain ! [1]

" My wound is deep ; I fain wad sleep !
   Tak' thou the vanguard o' the three,
And bury me by the bracken bush,
   That grows on yonder lily lea.

" O bury me by the bracken bush,
   Beneath the blumin' brier ;
Let never living mortal ken [2]
   That a kindly Scot lies here ! "

He lifted up that noble lord,
   Wi' the saut [3] tear in his e'e ;
And he hid him by the bracken bush,
   That his merry men might not see.

The moon was clear, the day drew near,
   The spears in flinders flew ;
And many a gallant Englishman
   Ere day the Scotsmen slew.

The Gordons gay, in English blude
   They wat their hose and shoon ;

[1] own.   [2] know.   [3] salt.

The Lindsays flew like fire about,
　Till a' the fray was dune.

The Percy and Montgomery met,
　That either of other was fain;
They swakkit[1] swords, and sair they swat,
　And the blude ran down between.

" Now yield thee, yield thee, Percy!" he said,
　" Or else I will lay thee low!"
" To whom maun I yield," Earl Percy said,
　" Since I see that it maun be so?"

" Thou shalt not yield to lord or loun,[2]
　Nor yet shalt thou yield to me;
But yield thee to the bracken bush
　That grows on yonder lily lea!"

This deed was done at the Otterburne
　About the breaking o' the day;
Earl Douglas was buried at the bracken bush,
　And the Percy led captive away.

KING HENRY THE FOURTH

WILLIAM SHAKESPEARE

ALL the thirteen years of his reign, Henry IV. was occupied with the struggle to maintain himself on the throne. Richard's friends refused to believe that their king was dead, and gave ready credence to an impostor who was harboured at the court of Scotland. The great barons who had taken Henry's part against Richard, the Percys of Northumberland and the Mortimers of the Marches, were dissatisfied

---

[1] smote.　　　　　　　　[2] a person of low rank.

with the king they had made, and levied war against him. The insurgents were joined by the Welsh and the Scotch, and the usurper seemed likely to be overwhelmed. The battle of Shrewsbury (1403) was a decisive victory for the House of Lancaster.

Ten years later, Henry IV., worn out by the anxieties of his reign, tormented by remorse for the murder of Richard, haunted by doubts as to his title to the crown, jealous and suspicious even of his eldest son, lay dying in the Jerusalem Chamber at Westminster Abbey. This barren fulfilment of a cherished hope seemed the crowning mockery of his troubled life.

PART I. ACT I

Scene I. London. *The Palace.*

(Enter King Henry, Prince John of Lancaster, the Earl of Westmoreland, Sir Walter Blunt, and others.)

King. So shaken as we are, so wan with care,
Find we a time for frighted peace to pant,
And breathe short-winded accents of new broils
To be commenc'd in strands afar remote.
No more the thirsty entrance of this soil
Shall daub her lips with her own children's blood ;
No more shall trenching war channel her fields,
Nor bruise her flowerets with the armèd hoofs
Of hostile paces : those opposèd eyes,
Which, like the meteors of a troubled heaven,
All of one nature, of one substance bred,
Did lately meet in the intestine shock
And furious close of civil butchery,
Shall now, in mutual well-beseeming ranks,
March all one way and be no more oppos'd
Against acquaintance, kindred, and allies :

The edge of war, like an ill-sheathèd knife,
No more shall cut his master. Therefore, friends,
As far as to the sepulchre of Christ,
Whose soldier now, under whose blessed cross
We are impressèd and engag'd to fight,
Forthwith a power of English shall we levy;
Whose arms were moulded in their mothers' womb
To chase these pagans in those holy fields
Over whose acres walk'd those blessèd feet
Which fourteen hundred years ago were nail'd
For our advantage on the bitter cross.
But this our purpose is a twelve month old,
And bootless 'tis to tell you we will go;
Therefore [1] we meet not now. Then let me hear
Of you, my gentle cousin Westmoreland,
What yesternight our council did decree
In forwarding this dear expedience.[2]

    Westmoreland. My liege, this haste was hot in
        question,[3]
And many limits of the charge [4] set down
But yesternight: when all athwart there came
A post from Wales loaden with heavy news;
Whose worst was, that the noble Mortimer,
Leading the men of Herefordshire to fight
Against the irregular and wild Glendower,
Was by the rude hands of that Welshman taken,
And a thousand of his people butcherèd;
Upon whose dead corpse there was such misuse,

---

[1] for that purpose.   [2] expedition.   [3] under earnest discussion.
[4] estimates of the cost.

Such beastly, shameless transformation,
By those Welshwomen done, as may not be
Without much shame retold or spoken of.

    King. It seems then that the tidings of this broil
Brake off our business for the Holy Land.

    Westmoreland. This match'd with other did, my
        gracious lord ;
For more uneven and unwelcome news
Came from the north, and thus it did import :
On Holy-rood day, the gallant Hotspur there,
Young Harry Percy, and brave Archibald,
That ever-valiant and approvèd Scot,
At Holmedon met,
Where they did spend a sad and bloody hour,
As by discharge of their artillery,
And shape of likelihood, the news was told ;
For he that brought them, in the very heat
And pride of their contention did take horse,
Uncertain of the issue any way.

    King. Here is a dear, a true-industrious friend,
Sir Walter Blunt, new-lighted from his horse,
Stain'd with the variation of each soil
Betwixt that Holmedon and this seat of ours ;
And he hath brought us smooth and welcome news.
The Earl of Douglas is discomfited :
Ten thousand bold Scots, two and twenty knights,
Balk'd [1] in their own blood did Sir Walter see
On Holmedon's plains. Of prisoners, Hotspur took
Mordake the Earl of Fife, and eldest son

[1] heaped.

To beaten Douglas, and the Earl of Athol,
Of Murray, Angus, and Menteith ;
And is not this an honourable spoil ?
A gallant prize ? ha ! cousin, is it not ?
   Westmoreland. In faith,
It is a conquest for a prince to boast of.
   King. Yea, there thou mak'st me sad and mak'st
     me sin
In envy that my Lord Northumberland
Should be the father to so blest a son,
A son who is the theme of honour's tongue ;
Amongst a grove, the very straightest plant,
Who is sweet Fortune's minion and her pride ;
Whilst I, by looking on the praise of him,
See riot and dishonour stain the brow
Of my young Harry. O that it could be prov'd
That some night-tripping fairy had exchang'd
In cradle-clothes our children where they lay,
And call'd mine Percy, his Plantagenet!
Then would I have his Harry, and he mine.
But let him from my thoughts. — What think you, coz,
Of this young Percy's pride ? the prisoners,
Which he in this adventure hath surpris'd,
To his own use he keeps, and sends me word,
I shall have none but Mordake Earl of Fife.
   Westmoreland. This is his uncle's teaching, this is
     Worcester,
Malevolent to you in all aspects ;
Which makes him prune himself, and bristle up
The crest of youth against your dignity.

King. But I have sent for him to answer this ;
And for this cause awhile we must neglect
Our holy purpose to Jerusalem.
Cousin, on Wednesday next our council we
Will hold at Windsor : so inform the lords ;
But come yourself with speed to us again,
For more is to be said and to be done
Than out of anger can be utterèd.
Westmoreland. I will, my liege.

ACT II

Scene   IV.   *The Boar's-Head Tavern, Eastcheap.
The Prince, Poins, and Hostess.*

(*Enter Falstaff.*)

Prince. Here comes lean Jack, here comes bare-
bone. — How now, my sweet creature of bombast ! [1]
How long is 't ago, Jack, since thou sawest thine own
knee ?

Falstaff. My own knee ! when I was about thy
years, Hal, I was not an eagle's talon in the waist ;
I could have crept into any alderman's thumb-ring :
a plague of sighing and grief ! it blows a man up like
a bladder.   There's villainous news abroad : here was
Sir John Bracy from your father ; you must to the
court in the morning.   That same mad fellow of the
north, Percy, and he of Wales, that gave Amamon
the bastinado and swore the devil his true liegeman

---

[1] cotton-stuffing.

upon the cross of a Welsh hook — what a plague call you him ?

Poins. O, Glendower.

Falstaff. Owen, Owen, the same ; and his son-in-law Mortimer, and old Northumberland, and that sprightly Scot of Scots, Douglas, that runs o' horseback up a hill perpendicular, —

Prince. He that rides at high speed and with his pistol kills a sparrow flying.

Falstaff. You have hit it.

Prince. So did he never the sparrow.

Falstaff. Well, that rascal hath good mettle in him ; he will not run.

Prince. Why, what a rascal art thou then to praise him so for running !

Falstaff. O' horseback, ye cuckoo ; but afoot he will not budge a foot.

Prince. Yes, Jack, upon instinct.

Falstaff. I grant ye, upon instinct. Well, he is there too, and one Mordake, and a thousand blue-caps more. Worcester is stolen away to-night ; thy father's beard is turned white with the news : you may buy land now as cheap as stinking mackerel.—But tell me, Hal, art not thou horrible afeard ? thou being heir-apparent, could the world pick thee out three such enemies again as that fiend Douglas, that spirit Percy, and that devil Glendower ? Art thou nôt horribly afraid ? doth not thy blood thrill at it ?

Prince. Not a whit, i' faith ; I lack some of thy instinct.

Falstaff. Well, thou wilt be horribly chid to-morrow when thou comest to thy father; if thou love me, practise an answer.

Prince. Do thou stand for my father, and examine me upon the particulars of my life.

Falstaff. Shall I? content; this chair shall be my state, this dagger my sceptre, and this cushion my crown.

Prince. Thy state is taken for a joined-stool,[1] thy golden sceptre for a leaden dagger, and thy precious rich crown for a pitiful bald crown!

Falstaff. Well, an the fire of grace be not quite out of thee, now shalt thou be moved. Give me a cup of sack to make my eyes look red, that it may be thought I have wept; for I must speak in passion, and I will do it in King Cambyses' vein.

Prince. Well, here is my leg.[2]

Falstaff. And here is my speech. — Stand aside, nobility.

Hostess. O Jesu, this is excellent sport, i' faith!

Falstaff. Weep not, sweet queen, for trickling tears are vain.

Hostess. O, the father, how he holds his countenance!

Falstaff. For God's sake, lords, convey my tristful queen;

For tears do stop the flood-gates of her eyes.

Hostess. O Jesu, he doth it as like one of these harlotry[3] players as ever I see!

Falstaff. Peace, good pint-pot; peace, good tickle-

---

[1] a folding chair.   [2] obeisance.   [3] vagabond.

brain. — Harry, I do not only marvel where thou spendest thy time, but also how thou art accompanied; for though the camomile, the more it is trodden on the faster it grows, yet youth, the more it is wasted the sooner it wears. That thou art my son, I have partly thy mother's word, partly my own opinion, but chiefly a villainous trick of thine eye and a foolish hanging of thy nether lip, that doth warrant me. If then thou be son to me, here lies the point; why, being son to me, art thou so pointed at? Shall the blessed son of heaven prove a micher[1] and eat black-berries? —a question not to be asked. Shall the son of England prove a thief and take purses? — a question to be asked. There is a thing, Harry, which thou hast often heard of, and it is known to many in our land by the name of pitch: this pitch, as ancient writers do report, doth defile; so doth the company thou keepest: for, Harry, now I do not speak to thee in drink but in tears, not in pleasure but in passion, not in words only, but in woes also: and yet there is a virtuous man whom I have often noted in thy company, but I know not his name.

Prince. What manner of man, an it like your majesty?

Falstaff. A goodly portly man, i' faith, and a corpulent; of a cheerful look, a pleasing eye, and a most noble carriage; and, as I think, his age some fifty, or, by 'r lady, inclining to three score; and now I remember me, his name is Falstaff: if that man

[1] truant.

should be lewdly given, he deceiveth me; for, Harry, I see virtue in his looks. If then the tree may be known by the fruit, as the fruit by the tree, then, peremptorily I speak it, there is virtue in that Falstaff; him keep with, the rest banish. And tell me now, thou naughty varlet, tell me, where hast thou been this month?

Prince. Dost thou speak like a king? Do thou stand for me, and I'll play my father.

Falstaff. Depose me? If thou dost it half so gravely, so majestically, both in word and manner, hang me up by the heels for a rabbit-sucker or a poulter's hare.

Prince. Well, here I am set.

Falstaff. And here I stand. — Judge, my masters.

Prince. Now, Harry, whence come you?

Falstaff. My noble lord, from Eastcheap.

Prince. The complaints I hear of thee are grievous.

Falstaff. 'Sblood, my lord, they are false; — nay, I'll tickle ye for a young prince, i' faith.

Prince. Swearest thou, ungracious boy? Henceforth ne'er look on me. Thou art violently carried away from grace: there is a devil haunts thee in the likeness of a fat old man; a tun of man is thy companion. Why dost thou converse with that trunk of humours, that bolting-hutch[1] of beastliness, that swollen parcel of dropsies, that huge bombard[2] of sack, that reverend vice, that grey iniquity, that father

---

[1] bin for sifting meal.   [2] leathern bottle.

ruffian, that vanity in years? Wherein is he good, but to taste sack and drink it? wherein neat and cleanly, but to carve a capon and eat it? wherein cunning, but in craft? wherein crafty, but in villainy? wherein villainous, but in all things? wherein worthy, but in nothing?

Falstaff. I would your grace would take me with you: whom means your grace?

Prince. That villainous, abominable misleader of youth, Falstaff, that old white-bearded Satan.

Falstaff. My lord, the man I know.

Prince. I know thou dost.

Falstaff. But to say I know more harm in him than in myself, were to say more than I know. That he is old, the more the pity, his white hairs do witness it. If sack and sugar be a fault, God help the wicked! if to be old and merry be a sin, then many an old host that I know is damned: if to be fat be to be hated, then Pharaoh's lean kine are to be loved. No, my good lord; banish Peto, banish Bardolph, banish Poins; but for sweet Jack Falstaff, kind Jack Falstaff, true Jack Falstaff, valiant Jack Falstaff, and therefore more valiant, being, as he is, old Jack Falstaff, banish not him thy Harry's company, banish not him thy Harry's company; banish plump Jack, and banish all the world.

Prince. I do, I will.

ACT IV

Scene I. *The Rebel Camp near Shrewsbury. Hot-
spur, Worcester, and Douglas.*

(*Enter Sir Richard Vernon.*)

Hotspur. My cousin Vernon! welcome, by my soul.
Vernon. Pray God my news be worth a welcome,
    lord.
The Earl of Westmoreland, seven thousand strong,
Is marching hitherwards; with him Prince John.
    Hotspur. No harm; what more?
    Vernon.   And further, I have learn'd
The king himself in person is set forth,
Or hitherwards intended speedily,
With strong and mighty preparation.
    Hotspur. He shall be welcome too.   Where is his
        son,
The nimble-footed madcap Prince of Wales,
And his comrades, that daff'd [1] the world aside,
And bid it pass?
    Vernon.   All furnish'd, all in arms;
All plum'd like estridges [2] that wing the wind;
Baited [3] like eagles having lately bath'd;
Glittering in golden coats, like images;
As full of spirit as the month of May,
And gorgeous as the sun at midsummer;
Wanton as youthful goats, wild as young bulls.
I saw young Harry, with his beaver on,

---

[1] doffed, waved off.   [2] ostriches.   [3] preening themselves.

His cuisses [1] on his thighs, gallantly arm'd,
Rise from the ground like feather'd Mercury,
And vaulted with such ease into his seat,
As if an angel dropp'd down from the clouds,
To turn and wind a fiery Pegasus
And witch the world with noble horsemanship.
 Hotspur. No more, no more : worse than the sun
  in March,
This praise doth nourish agues. Let them come ;
They come like sacrifices in their trim,
And to the fire-eyed maid of smoky war
All hot and bleeding will we offer them :
The mailèd Mars shall on his altar sit
Up to the ears in blood. I am on fire
To hear this rich reprisal is so nigh
And yet not ours. Come, let me take my horse,
Who is to bear me like a thunderbolt
Against the bosom of the Prince of Wales :
Harry to Harry shall, hot horse to horse,
Meet and ne'er part till one drop down a corse.
O that Glendower were come !
 Vernon.   There is more news :
I learn'd in Worcester, as I rode along,
He cannot draw his power this fourteen days.
 Douglas. That's the worst tidings that I hear of yet.
 Worcester. Ay, by my faith, that bears a frosty
  sound.
 Hotspur. What may the king's whole battle reach
  unto ?

      [1] thigh-armor.

Vernon. To thirty thousand.

Hotspur.   Forty let it be :
My father and Glendower being both away,
The powers of us may serve so great a day.
Come, let us take a muster speedily :
Doomsday is near ; die all, die merrily.

ACT V

SCENE IV.   *The Battle-field of Shrewsbury.   The
King and Douglas.*

Douglas. Another king ! they grow like Hydra's
      heads :
I am the Douglas, fatal to all those
That wear those colours on them : what art thou,
That counterfeit'st the person of a king ?

King. The king himself ; who, Douglas, grieves at
      heart
So many of his shadows thou hast met
And not the very king.   I have two boys
Seek Percy and thyself about the field :
But, seeing thou fall'st on me so luckily,
I will assay thee : so defend thyself.

Douglas. I fear thou art another counterfeit ;
And yet, in faith, thou bear'st thee like a king :
But mine I am sure thou art, whoe'er thou be,
And thus I win thee.

        (*They fight ; the King being in danger, reënter
            Prince of Wales.*)

Prince. Hold up thy head, vile Scot, or thou art like
Never to hold it up again ! the spirits

Of valiant Shirley, Stafford, Blunt, are in my arms:
It is the Prince of Wales that threatens thee,
Who never promiseth but he means to pay.

(*They fight; Douglas flies.*)

Cheerly, my lord! how fares your grace?
Sir Nicholas Gawsey hath for succour sent,
And so hath Clifton: I'll to Clifton straight.

King. Stay, and breathe awhile:
Thou hast redeem'd thy lost opinion,
And show'd thou mak'st some tender of [1] my life,
In this fair rescue thou hast brought to me.

Prince. O God! they did me too much injury
That ever said I hearken'd for your death.
If it were so, I might have let alone
The insulting hand of Douglas over you,
Which would have been as speedy in your end
As all the poisonous potions in the world,
And sav'd the treacherous labour of your son.

King. Make up to Clifton; I'll to Sir Nicholas
 Gawsey. [*Exit.*

(*Enter Hotspur.*)

Hotspur. If I mistake not, thou art Harry Mon-
 mouth.

Prince. Thou speak'st as if I would deny my name.

Hotspur. My name is Harry Percy.

Prince. Why, then I see
A very valiant rebel of the name.
I am the Prince of Wales; and think not, Percy,
To share with me in glory any more:

---

[1] hast some regard for.

Two stars keep not their motion in one sphere;
Nor can one England brook a double reign,
Of Harry Percy and the Prince of Wales.

   Hotspur. Nor shall it, Harry ; for the hour is come
To end the one of us ; and would to God
Thy name in arms were now as great as mine !

   Prince. I'll make it greater ere I part from thee ;
And all the budding honours on thy crest
I'll crop, to make a garland for my head.

   Hotspur. I can no longer brook thy vanities.

                                (*They fight.*)

                (*Enter Falstaff.*)

   Falstaff. Well said, Hal ! to it, Hal ! — Nay, you
     shall find no boy's play here, I can tell you.

(*Reënter Douglas; he fights with Falstaff, who falls
    down as if he were dead, and exit Douglas. Hot-
    spur is wounded, and falls.*)

   Hotspur. O, Harry, thou hast robb'd me of my
     youth !
I better brook the loss of brittle life
Than those proud titles thou hast won of me ;
They wound my thoughts worse than thy sword my
     flesh :
But thought's the slave of life, and life time's fool ;
And time, that takes survey of all the world,
Must have a stop.   O, I could prophesy,
But that the earthy and cold hand of death
Lies on my tongue ! — No, Percy, thou art dust,
And food for —   (*Dies.*)

Prince. For worms, brave Percy; fare thee well,
  great heart!
Ill-weav'd ambition, how much art thou shrunk!
When that this body did contain a spirit,
A kingdom for it was too small a bound;
But now two paces of the vilest earth
Is room enough: this earth that bears thee dead
Bears not alive so stout a gentleman.
If thou wert sensible of courtesy,
I should not make so dear a show of zeal;
But let my favours[1] hide thy mangled face;
And, even in thy behalf, I'll thank myself
For doing these fair rites of tenderness.
Adieu, and take thy praise with thee to heaven!
Thy ignominy sleep with thee in the grave,
But not remember'd in thy epitaph! —
                    (*He spieth Falstaff on the ground.*)
What, old acquaintance! could not all this flesh
Keep in a little life? Poor Jack, farewell!
I could have better spar'd a better man:
O, I should have a heavy miss of thee,
If I were much in love with vanity!
Death hath not struck so fat a deer to-day,
Though many dearer, in this bloody fray.
Embowell'd will I see thee by and by:
Till then in blood by noble Percy lie.   [*Exit.*
  Falstaff. (*Rising up.*)   Embowelled! if thou em-
bowel me to-day, I'll give you leave to powder me
and eat me too to-morrow! 'Sblood! 'twas time to
counterfeit, or that hot termagant Scot had paid me
_____
[1] Silken scarf worn over armor.

scot and lot too. Counterfeit? I lie, I am no coun-
terfeit: to die is to be a counterfeit; for he is but the
counterfeit of a man who hath not the life of a man:
but to counterfeit dying, when a man thereby liveth,
is to be no counterfeit, but the true and perfect image
of life indeed. The better part of valour is discretion;
in which better part I have saved my life. Zounds!
I am afraid of this gunpowder Percy, though he be
dead. How if he should counterfeit too and rise? by
my faith, I am afraid he would prove the better coun-
terfeit. Therefore I'll make him sure; yea, and I'll
swear I killed him. Why may not he rise as well as
I? Nothing confutes me but eyes, and nobody sees
me. Therefore, sirrah (*stabbing him*), with a new
wound in your thigh, come you along with me.

(*Takes up Hotspur on his back.*)

PART II. ACT IV

Scene V. *Chamber. The King lying on a bed. Clar-
ence, Gloucester, Warwick, and others in attendance.*

   King. Warwick! Gloucester! Clarence!
(*Reënter Warwick, Gloucester, Clarence, and the rest.*)
   Clar. Doth the king call?
   War. What would your majesty? How fares your
     grace?
   King. Why did you leave me here alone, my
     lords?
   Clar. We left the prince my brother here, my
     liege,

Who undertook to sit and watch by you.

   King. The Prince of Wales! Where is he? Let
me see him:
He is not here.

   War. This door is open; he is gone this way.

   Glou. He came not through the chamber where we
stay'd.

   King. Where is the crown? who took it from my
pillow?

   War. When we withdrew, my liege, we left it
here.

   King. The prince hath ta'en it hence: go, seek
him out.
Is he so hasty that he doth suppose
My sleep my death?
Find him, my Lord of Warwick; chide him hither.

                         [*Exit Warwick.*
This part of his conjoins with my disease,
And helps to end me. See, sons, what things you
are!
How quickly nature falls into revolt
When gold becomes her object!
For this the foolish over-careful fathers
Have broke their sleep with thoughts, their brains
with care,
Their bones with industry;
For this they have engross'd and pilèd up
The canker'd heaps of strange-achievèd gold;
For this they have been thoughtful to invest
Their sons with arts and martial exercises:

When, like the bee, culling from every flower
The virtuous sweets,
Our thighs pack'd with wax, our mouths with honey,
We bring it to the hive; and, like the bees,
Are murder'd for our pains.   This bitter taste
Yield his engrossments [1] to the ending father.

(Reënter Warwick.)

Now, where is he that will not stay so long
Till his friend sickness hath determin'd me?
    War. My lord, I found the prince in the next
      room,
Washing with kindly [2] tears his gentle cheeks,
With such a deep demeanour in great sorrow,
That tyranny, which never quaff'd but blood,
Would, by beholding him, have wash'd his knife
With gentle eye-drops.   He is coming hither.
    King. But wherefore did he take away the crown?

(Reënter Prince Henry.)

Lo, where he comes.   Come hither to me, Harry.
Depart the chamber, leave us here alone.
            [Exeunt Warwick and the rest.
    Prince. I never thought to hear you speak again.
    King. Thy wish was father, Harry, to that thought:
I stay too long by thee, I weary thee.
Dost thou so hunger for mine empty chair
That thou wilt needs invest thee with my honours
Before thy hour be ripe?   O foolish youth!
Thou seek'st the greatness that will overwhelm thee.

    [1] accumulations.   [2] natural, unfeigned.

Stay but a little; for my cloud of dignity
Is held from falling with so weak a wind
That it will quickly drop: my day is dim.
Thou hast stolen that which after some few hours
Were thine without offence; and at my death
Thou hast seal'd up my expectation:
Thy life did manifest thou lovedst me not,
And thou wilt have me die assured of it.
Thou hidest a thousand daggers in thy thoughts,
Which thou hast whetted on thy stony heart,
To stab at half an hour of my life.
What! canst thou not forbear me half an hour?
Then get thee gone and dig my grave thyself,
And bid the merry bells ring to thine ear
That thou art crownèd, not that I am dead.
Let all the tears that should bedew my hearse
Be drops of balm to sanctify thy head:
Only compound me with forgotten dust;
Give that which gave thee life unto the worms.
Pluck down my officers, break my decrees;
For now a time is come to mock at form:
Harry the fifth is crown'd: up, vanity!
Down, royal state! all you sage counsellors, hence!
And to the English court assemble now,
From every region, apes of idleness!
Now, neighbour confines, purge you of your scum:
Have you a ruffian that will swear, drink, dance,
Revel the night, rob, murder, and commit
The oldest sins the newest kind of ways?
Be happy, he will trouble you no more;

England shall double gild his treble guilt,
England shall give him office, honour, might;
For the fifth Harry from curb'd licence plucks
The muzzle of restraint, and the wild dog
Shall flesh his tooth on every innocent.
O my poor kingdom, sick with civil blows!
When that my care could not withhold thy riots,
What wilt thou do when riot is thy care?
O, thou wilt be a wilderness again,
Peopled with wolves, thy old inhabitants!

    Prince. O, pardon me, my liege! but for my tears,
The moist impediments unto my speech,
I had forestall'd this dear and deep rebuke,
Ere you with grief had spoke and I had heard
The course of it so far.   There is your crown;
And He that wears the crown immortally
Long guard it yours!   If I affect it more
Than as your honour and as your renown,
Let me no more from this obedience rise,
Which my most inward true and duteous spirit
Teacheth, this prostrate and exterior bending.
God witness with me, when I here came in,
And found no course of breath within your majesty,
How cold it struck my heart!   If I do feign,
O, let me in my present wildness die,
And never live to show the incredulous world
The noble change that I have purposèd!
Coming to look on you, thinking you dead,
And dead almost, my liege, to think you were,
I spake unto this crown as having sense,

And thus upbraided it : " The care on thee depending .
Hath fed upon the body of my father ;
Therefore, thou best of gold art worst of gold :
Other, less fine in carat, is more precious,
Preserving life in medicine potable ; [1]
But thou, most fine, most honour'd, most renown'd,
Hast eat thy bearer up." Thus, my most royal liege,
Accusing it, I put it on my head,
To try with it, as with an enemy
That had before my face murder'd my father,
The quarrel of a true inheritor.
But if it did infect my blood with joy,
Or swell my thoughts to any strain of pride ;
If any rebel or vain spirit of mine
Did with the least affection of a welcome
Give entertainment to the might of it,
Let God for ever keep it from my head,
And make me as the poorest vassal is,
That doth with awe and terror kneel to it !
   King. O my son,
God put it in thy mind to take it hence,
That thou mightst win the more thy father's love,
Pleading so wisely in excuse of it !
Come hither, Harry, sit thou by my bed ;
And hear, I think, the very latest counsel
That ever I shall breathe. God knows, my son,
By what by-paths and indirect crook'd ways
I met this crown ; and I myself know well
How troublesome it sat upon my head.

             [1] drinkable.

To thee it shall descend with better quiet,
Better opinion, better confirmation;
For all the soil of the achievement goes
With me into the earth.   It seem'd in me
But as an honour snatch'd with boisterous hand,
And I had many living to upbraid
My gain of it by their assistances;
Which daily grew to quarrel and to bloodshed,
Wounding supposèd peace.   All these bold fears
Thou see'st with peril I have answerèd;
For all my reign hath been but as a scene
Acting that argument[1]: and now my death
Changes the mode; for what in me was purchas'd,
Falls upon thee in a more fairer sort;
So thou the garland wear'st successively.
Yet, though thou stand'st more sure than I could do,
Thou art not firm enough, since griefs are green;
And all my friends, which thou must make thy friends,
Have but their stings and teeth newly ta'en out;
By whose fell working I was first advanc'd
And by whose power I well might lodge a fear
To be again displac'd: which to avoid,
I cut them off, and had a purpose now
To lead out many to the Holy Land,
Lest rest and lying still might make them look
Too near unto my state.   Therefore, my Harry,
Be it thy course to busy giddy minds
With foreign quarrels, that action, hence borne out,
May waste the memory of the former days.

[1] subject.

More would I, but my lungs are wasted so
That strength of speech is utterly denied me. —
How I came by the crown, O God forgive ;
And grant it may with thee in true peace live !
    Prince. My gracious liege,
You won it, wore it, kept it, gave it me ;
Then plain and right must my possession be :
Which I with more than with a common pain
'Gainst all the world will rightfully maintain.

       (*Enter Prince John of Lancaster.*)

    King. Look, look, here comes my John of Lan-
      caster.
    Lancaster. Health, peace, and happiness to my
      royal father !
    King. Thou bring'st me happiness and peace, son
      John ;
But health, alack, with youthful wings is flown
From this bare wither'd trunk : upon thy sight
My worldly business makes a period.
Where is my Lord of Warwick ?
    Prince.   My Lord of Warwick !

       (*Reënter Warwick, and others.*)

    King. Doth any name particular belong
Unto the lodging where I first did swoon ?
    Warwick. 'Tis call'd Jerusalem, my noble lord.
    King. Laud be to God ! even there my life must
      end.
It hath been prophesied to me many years
I should not die but in Jerusalem,

Which vainly I suppos'd the Holy Land. —
But bear me to that chamber: there I'll lie;
In that Jerusalem shall Harry die.   [*Exeunt.*

KING HENRY THE FIFTH

WILLIAM SHAKESPEARE

THE brave and self-confident young king undertook to recover the
French provinces. He even renewed Edward III.'s claim to the
French crown. The brilliant victories won by the English were due
in part to their enthusiasm and excellent discipline, but even more to
the utter incapacity of France. The French king, Charles VI., was an
imbecile, and the land was torn by the strife of rival factions. Famine
and disease had reduced the people to a state of abject despair.
Henry V. regarded his mission as a crusade against the vices of a
demoralized nation.

ACT III

SCENE I.   FRANCE.   *Before Harfleur.*

(*Alarum.   Enter King Henry, Exeter, Bedford,
Gloucester, and Soldiers with scaling-ladders.*)

King Henry. Once more unto the breach, dear
        friends, once more;
Or close the wall up with our English dead!
In peace there's nothing so becomes a man
As modest stillness and humility;
But when the blast of war blows in our ears,
Then imitate the action of the tiger:
Stiffen the sinews, summon up the blood,

Disguise fair nature with hard-favour'd rage ;
Then lend the eye a terrible aspect ;
Let it pry through the portage[1] of the head
Like the brass cannon ; let the brow o'erwhelm it
As fearfully as doth a gallèd rock
O'erhang and jutty[2] his confounded[3] base,
Swill'd[4] with the wild and wasteful ocean.
Now set the teeth and stretch the nostril wide,
Hold hard the breath, and bend up every spirit
To his full height.   On, on, you noble English,
Whose blood is fet[5] from fathers of war-proof,
Fathers that, like so many Alexanders,
Have in these parts from morn till even fought,
And sheath'd their swords for lack of argument![6]
Dishonour not your mothers ; now attest
That those whom you call'd fathers did beget you.
Be copy[7] now to men of grosser blood,
And teach them how to war ! — And you, good yeo-
    men,
Whose limbs were made in England, show us here
The mettle of your pasture ; let us swear
That you are worth your breeding ; which I doubt
    not ;
For there is none of you so mean and base,
That hath not noble lustre in your eyes.
I see you stand like greyhounds in the slips,[8]
Straining upon the start.   The game's afoot :

---

[1] port-hole.   [2] project beyond.   [3] wasted.
[4] greedily gulped down by.   [5] fetched.
[6] business : more men to kill.   [7] examples.   [8] leash.

Follow your spirit, and upon this charge
Cry " God for Harry, England, and Saint George ! "
       [*Exeunt.   Alarum, and chambers* [1] *go off.*

ACT IV

SCENE I.   *The English Camp at Agincourt.*

(*Enter King Henry, Bedford, and Gloucester.*)

   King Henry. Gloucester, 'tis true that we are in
     great danger ;
The greater therefore should our courage be. —
Good morrow, brother Bedford. — God Almighty !
There is some soul of goodness in things evil,
Would men observingly distil it out ;
For our bad neighbour makes us early stirrers,
Which is both healthful and good husbandry : [2]
Besides, they are our outward consciences,
And preachers to us all, admonishing
That we should dress [3] us fairly for our end.
Thus may we gather honey from the weed,
And make a moral of the devil himself.

(*Enter Erpingham.*)

Good morrow, old Sir Thomas Erpingham :
A good soft pillow for that good white head
Were better than a churlish turf of France.
   Erpingham. Not so, my liege : this lodging likes [4]
     me better,
Since I may say, now lie I like a king.

    [1] cannon.   [2] thrift.   [3] prepare.   [4] suits.

King Henry. 'Tis good for men to love their pres-
    ent pains
Upon example; so the spirit is eas'd:
And when the mind is quicken'd, out of doubt,
The organs, though defunct and dead before,
Break up their drowsy grave and newly move,
With casted slough and fresh legerity.[1]
Lend me thy cloak, Sir Thomas. — Brothers both,
Commend me to the princes in our camp;
Do my good morrow to them, and anon
Desire them all to my pavilion.
    Gloucester. We shall, my liege.
    Erpingham. Shall I attend your grace?
    King Henry.   No, my good knight;
Go with my brothers to my lords of England:
I and my bosom must debate awhile,
And then I would no other company.
    Erpingham. The Lord in heaven bless thee, noble
      Harry!
                    [*Exeunt all but King.*
    King Henry. God-a-mercy, old heart! thou speak'st
    cheerfully.

        *   *   *   *   *   *   *

    King Henry. O God of battles! steel my soldiers'
    hearts;
Possess them not with fear; take from them now
The sense of reckoning, if the opposèd numbers
Pluck their hearts from them. Not to-day, O Lord,
O, not to-day, think not upon the fault

               [1] alacrity.

My father made in compassing the crown!
I Richard's body have interrèd new,
And on it have bestow'd more contrite tears
Than from it issued forcèd drops of blood.
Five hundred poor I have in yearly pay,
Who twice a-day their wither'd hands hold up
Toward heaven, to pardon blood; and I have built
Two chantries, where the sad and solemn priests
Sing still for Richard's soul.   More will I do;
Though all that I can do is nothing worth,
Since that my penitence comes after all,
Imploring pardon.

THE BATTLE OF AGINCOURT

MICHAEL DRAYTON

THE campaign began badly, for although Henry took Harfleur and other places along the Seine, his troops were wasted by disease and many had to be sent home. He was pushing on to Calais with but fifteen thousand men when his march was intercepted at Agincourt (1415) by a French army four times his number. The victory, like those of Cressy and Poitiers, was won by the English archers, who proved more than a match for the heavy-armored French horsemen.

Fair stood the wind for France,
When we our sails advance,
Nor now to prove our chance
    Longer will tarry;
But putting to the main,
At Caux, the mouth of Seine,
With all his martial train,
    Landed King Harry.

And taking many a fort,
Furnished in warlike sort,
Marcheth towards Agincourt,
    In happy hour;
Skirmishing day by day
With those that stopped his way,
Where the French general lay
    With all his power.

Which in his height of pride,
King Henry to deride,
His ransom to provide
    To the king sending.
Which he neglects the while,
As from a nation vile,
Yet with an angry smile
    Their fall portending.

And turning to his men,
Quoth our brave Henry then,
"Though they be one to ten,
    Be not amazèd;
Yet have we well begun,
Battles so bravely won
Have ever to the sun
    By fame been raisèd.

"And for myself," quoth he,
"This my full rest shall be,
England ne'er mourn for me,
    Nor more esteem me.

Victor I will remain,
Or on this earth lie slain,
Never shall she sustain
        Loss to redeem me.

" Poitiers and Cressy tell,
When most their pride did swell,
Under our swords they fell.
        No less our skill is,
Than when our grandsire-great,
Claiming the regal seat,
By many a warlike feat
        Lopped the French lilies."

The Duke of York so dread
The eager va'ward led;
With the main, Henry sped,
        Amongst his henchmen.
Exeter had the rear,
A braver man not there,
O Lord, how hot they were
        On the false Frenchmen!

They now to fight are gone,
Armour on armour shone,
Drum now to drum did groan,
        To hear, was wonder;
That with the cries they make,
The very earth did shake,
Trumpet to trumpet spake,
        Thunder to thunder.

Well it thine age became,
O noble Erpingham,
Which didst the signal aim
 To our hid forces ;
When from a meadow by,
Like a storm suddenly,
The English archery
 Stuck the French horses.

With Spanish yew so strong,
Arrows a cloth-yard long,
That like to serpents stung,
 Piercing the weather ;
None from his fellow starts,
But playing manly parts,
And like true English hearts,
 Stuck close together.

When down their bows they threw,
And forth their bilbos drew,
And on the French they flew,
 Not one was tardy ;
Arms were from shoulders sent,
Scalps to the teeth were rent,
Down the French peasants went,
 Our men were hardy.

This while our noble king,
His broad sword brandishing,
Down the French host did ding,
 As to o'erwhelm it,

And many a deep wound lent,
His arms with blood besprent,[1]
And many a cruel dent
    Bruisèd his helmet.

Gloucester, that duke so good,
Next of the royal blood,
For famous England stood,
    With his brave brother;
Clarence, in steel so bright,
Though but a maiden knight,
Yet in that furious fight
    Scarce such another.

Warwick in blood did wade,
Oxford the foe invade,
And cruel slaughter made,
    Still as they ran up;
Suffolk his axe did ply,
Beaumont and Willoughby
Bare them right doughtily,
    Ferrers and Fanhope.

Upon Saint Crispin's day
Fought was this noble fray,
Which fame did not delay
    To England to carry;
Oh, when shall English men
With such acts fill a pen,
Or England breed again
    Such a King Harry?

        [1] sprinkled.

KING HENRY V. AND THE HERMIT OF DREUX

ROBERT SOUTHEY

BY the Treaty of Troyes (1420), Henry V. was recognized as heir to the throne of France and regent of the realm during the life of the mad king. He obtained the hand of the French princess Katherine in marriage, and nothing seemed lacking to complete his victory. But the French people, hating a foreign rule, rose in revolt, and the French towns had to be recaptured one by one. The resources of England were heavily taxed to support the war, and the king himself sickened and died (1422). The French chronicler relates how, while Henry V. was besieging Dreux, on the river Blaise, an ancient hermit came to his hut and, denouncing his ruthless ambition, warned him that God would punish his cruel deeds.

He pass'd unquestion'd through the camp,
    Their heads the soldiers bent
In silent reverence, or begg'd
    A blessing as he went;
And so the Hermit pass'd along
    And reached the royal tent.

King Henry sate in his tent alone,
    The map before him lay,
Fresh conquests he was planning there
    To grace the future day.

King Henry lifted up his eyes
    The intruder to behold;
With reverence he the Hermit saw,
    For the holy man was old,
His look was gentle as a Saint's,
    And yet his eye was bold.

" Repent thee, Henry, of the wrongs
   Which thou hast done this land !
O King, repent in time, for know
   The judgment is at hand.

" I have pass'd forty years of peace
   Beside the river Blaise,
But what a weight of woe hast thou
   Laid on my latter days !

" I used to see along the stream
   The white sail gliding down,
That wafted food in better times
   To yonder peaceful town.

" Henry ! I never now behold
   The white sail gliding down ;
Famine, Disease, and Death, and Thou
   Destroy that wretched town.

" I used to hear the traveller's voice
   As here he passed along,
Or maiden as she loiter'd home
   Singing her even-song.

" No traveller's voice may now be heard,
   In fear he hastens by ;
But I have heard the village maid
   In vain for succour cry.

" I used to see the youths row down
   And watch the dripping oar,

As pleasantly their viol's tones
    Came soften'd to the shore.

" King Henry, many a blacken'd corpse
    I now see floating down !
Thou man of blood ! repent in time,
    And leave this leaguer'd town."

" I shall go on," King Henry cried,
    " And conquer this good land ;
Seest thou not, Hermit, that the Lord
    Hath given it to my hand ? "

The Hermit heard King Henry speak,
    And angrily look'd down ;
His face was gentle, and for that
    More solemn was his frown.

" What if no miracle from Heaven
    The murderer's arm control,
Think you for that the weight of blood
    Lies lighter on his soul ?

" Thou conqueror King, repent in time
    Or dread the coming woe !
For, Henry, thou hast heard the threat,
    And soon shalt feel the blow ! "

King Henry forced a careless smile,
    As the Hermit went his way ;
But Henry soon remember'd him
    Upon his dying day.

THE KING'S TRAGEDY

DANTE GABRIEL ROSSETTI

IF England could boast in Henry V. a martial hero for king, Scotland could lay claim to a royal poet. James I., the ablest of Scotch rulers, spent his boyhood in captivity in England. He was carefully educated and gathered wisdom from his observation of English laws and customs. He was with Henry V. in France during part of the second campaign. Early in the reign of Henry VI. (1424), James was allowed, in his thirtieth year, to return to his kingdom, carrying with him an English bride. The jealous Scots dubbed him the Saxon king. James I. had high ideals for Scotland, and did all that one man might to reform the abuses which had crept into the government. A curb was placed on the power of the great nobles, and the poor were defended against oppression. But the king's stern enforcement of justice made him bitter enemies among the fierce Scotch lords. They plotted against his life and finally murdered him before his purposes for Scotland were accomplished.

Through all the days of his gallant youth
  The princely James was pent,
By his friends at first and then by his foes,
  In long imprisonment.

For the elder Prince, the kingdom's heir,
  By treason's murderous brood
Was slain; and the father quaked for the child
  With the royal mortal blood.

I' the Bass Rock fort, by his father's care,
  Was his childhood's life assured;
And Henry the subtle Bolingbroke,
Proud England's King, 'neath the southron yoke
  His youth for long years immured.

Yet in all things meet for a kingly man
    Himself did he approve;
And the nightingale through his prison-wall
    Taught him both lore and love.

For once, when the bird's song drew him close
    To the opened window-pane,
In her bower beneath a lady stood,
A light of life to his sorrowful mood,
    Like a lily amid the rain.

And for her sake, to the sweet bird's note,
    He framed a sweeter Song,
More sweet than ever a poet's heart
    Gave yet to the English tongue.

She was a lady of royal blood;
    And when, past sorrow and teen,
He stood where still through his crownless years
    His Scottish realm had been,
At Scone were the happy lovers crowned,
    A heart-wed King and Queen.

But the bird may fall from the bough of youth,
    And song be turned to moan,
And Love's storm-cloud be the shadow of Hate,
When the tempest-waves of a troubled State
    Are beating against a throne.

Yet well they loved; and the god of Love,
    Whom well the King had sung,
Might find on the earth no truer hearts
    His lowliest swains among.
      *   *   *   *   *   *   *

'Twas in the Charterhouse of Perth,
  In the fair-lit Death-chapelle,
That the slain King's corpse on bier was laid
  With chaunt and requiem-knell.

And all with royal wealth of balm
  Was the body purified;
And none could trace on the brow and lips
  The death that he had died.

In his robes of state he lay asleep
  With orb and sceptre in hand;
And by the crown he wore on his throne
  Was his kingly forehead spann'd.

And, girls, 'twas a sweet sad thing to see
  How the curling golden hair,
As in the day of the poet's youth,
  From the King's crown clustered there.

And if all had come to pass in the brain
  That throbbed beneath those curls,
Then Scots had said in the days to come
That this their soil was a different home
  And a different Scotland, girls!

And the Queen sat by him night and day,
  And oft she knelt in prayer,
All wan and pale in the widow's veil
  That shrouded her shining hair.

* * * * * * *

And the month of March wore nigh to its end,
    And still was the death-pall spread;
For she would not bury her slaughtered lord
    Till his slayers all were dead.

And now of their dooms dread tidings came,
    And of torments fierce and dire;
And nought she spake,— she had ceased to speak,—
    But her eyes were a soul on fire.

But when I told her the bitter end
    Of the stern and just award,
She leaned o'er the bier, and thrice three times
    She kissed the lips of her lord.

And then she said, — " My King, they are dead!"
    And she knelt on the chapel-floor,
And whispered low with a strange proud smile, —
    " James, James, they suffered more!"

Last she stood up to her queenly height,
    But she shook like an autumn leaf,
As though the fire wherein she burned
Then left her body, and all were turned
    To winter of life-long grief.

And " O James!" she said, — " My James!" she
    said, —
    " Alas for the woeful thing,
That a poet true and a friend of man,
In desperate days of bale and ban,
    Should needs be born a King!"

KING HENRY THE SIXTH

WILLIAM SHAKESPEARE

THE death of Henry V. (1422) left the kingdom with no strong man to rule it, since the heir to the throne was an infant of nine months. The boy was carefully educated, and became both good and learned, but he lacked energy and determination. He was much influenced by his relatives, the Beauforts. Their efforts to bring the French wars to a close, even on humiliating terms, rendered them and the king hateful to the people. Discontent found expression in Jack Cade's Rebellion (1451), a popular demonstration quite as formidable as the Peasants' Revolt, and as easily quelled.

When the king lapsed into imbecility (1453), the "want of governance" could no longer be endured. Even the birth of Prince Edward could not restore confidence in the House of Lancaster. London and the commons declared for Edward of York, and he was crowned king in 1461. At the battle of Towton Field, fought that same year, the Lancastrians were ruined. Henry, Queen Margaret, and the little prince found refuge in Scotland. After many vicissitudes, the unhappy Henry was murdered in the Tower.

PART I. ACT I

SCENE I. *Westminster Abbey.*

(*Dead March. Enter the Funeral of King Henry the Fifth, attended on by the Duke of Bedford, Regent of France; the Duke of Gloster, Protector; the Duke of Exeter, the Earl of Warwick, the Bishop of Winchester, Heralds, etc.*)

Bedford. Hung be the heavens with black, yield day to night!
Comets, importing change of times and states,
Brandish your crystal tresses in the sky,

And with them scourge the bad revolting stars
That have consented unto Henry's death!
King Henry the Fifth, too famous to live long!
England ne'er lost a king of so much worth.

Gloster. England ne'er had a king until his time.
Virtue he had, deserving to command :
His brandish'd sword did blind men with his [1] beams :
His arms spread wider than a dragon's wings ;
His sparkling eyes, replete with wrathful fire,
More dazzled and drove back his enemies
Than mid-day sun fierce bent against their faces.
What should I say? his deeds exceed all speech ;
He ne'er lift up his hand but conquerèd.

Exeter. We mourn in black : why mourn we not
in blood ?
Henry is dead and never shall revive :
Upon a wooden coffin we attend,
And death's dishonourable victory
We with our stately presence glorify,
Like captives bound to a triumphant car.
What! shall we curse the planets of mishap
That plotted thus our glory's overthrow ?
Or shall we think the subtle-witted French
Conjurors and sorcerers, that afraid of him
By magic verses have contriv'd his end ?

*   *   *   *   *   *   *

(*Enter a Messenger.*)

Messenger. My honourable lords, health to you all!
Sad tidings bring I to you out of France,

[1] its.

Of loss, of slaughter and discomfiture :
Guienne, Champagne, Rheims, Orleans,
Paris, Guysors, Poictiers, are all quite lost.

> *Bedford.* What say'st thou, man, before dead
> Henry's corse?

Speak softly, or the loss of those great towns
Will make him burst his lead and rise from death.

> *Gloster.* Is Paris lost? is Rouen yielded up?

If Henry were recall'd to life again,
These news would cause him once more yield the
ghost.

> *Exeter.* How were they lost? what treachery was
> us'd?

> *Messenger.* No treachery; but want of men and
> money.

Amongst the soldiers this is mutterèd, —
That here you maintain several factions,
And whilst a field should be dispatch'd and fought,
You are disputing of your generals :
One would have lingering wars with little cost;
Another would fly swift, but wanteth wings;
A third thinks, without expense at all,
By guileful fair words peace may be obtain'd.
Awake, awake, English nobility!
Let not sloth dim your honours new-begot :
Cropp'd are the flower-de-luces in your arms;
Of England's coat one-half is cut away.

> *Exeter.* Were our tears wanting to this funeral,

These tidings would call forth their flowing tides.

*   *   *   *   *   *   *

Exeter. Remember, lords, your oaths to Henry
    sworn,
Either to quell the Dauphin utterly,
Or bring him in obedience to your yoke.
    Bedford. I do remember it; and here **take** my leave,
To go about my preparation.   *[Exit.*
    Gloster. I'll to the Tower with all the haste I can,
To view the artillery and munition;
And then I will proclaim young Henry king.   *[Exit.*
    Exeter. To Eltham will I, where the young king is,
Being ordain'd his special governor,
And for his safety there I'll best devise.   *[Exit.*
    Winchester. Each hath his place and function to
    attend:
I am left out; for me nothing remains.
But long I will not be Jack out of office:
The king from Eltham I intend to steal
And sit at chiefest stern [1] of public weal.

PART II. ACT II

Scene II. London. The Duke of York's Garden.
(<i>Enter York, Salisbury, and Warwick.</i>)</center>

    York. Now, my good Lords of Salisbury and War-
    wick,
Our simple supper ended, give me leave
In this close [2] walk to satisfy myself,
In craving your opinion of my title,
Which is infallible, to England's crown.

---

  [1] highest place.   [2] retired.

Salisbury. My lord, I long to hear it at full.

Warwick. Sweet York, begin ; and if thy claim be
    good,

The Nevils are thy subjects to command.

York. Then thus :

Edward the Third, my lord, had seven sons :

The first, Edward the Black Prince, Prince of Wales ;

The second, William of Hatfield ; and the third,

Lionel Duke of Clarence ; next to whom

Was John of Gaunt, the Duke of Lancaster ;

The fifth was Edmund Langley, Duke of York ;

The sixth was Thomas of Woodstock, Duke of
    Gloucester ;

William of Windsor was the seventh and last.

Edward the Black Prince died before his father,

And left behind him Richard, his only son,

Who after Edward the Third's death reign'd as king ;

Till Henry Bolingbroke, Duke of Lancaster,

The eldest son and heir of John of Gaunt,

Crown'd by the name of Henry the Fourth,

Seiz'd on the realm, depos'd the rightful king,

Sent his poor queen to France, from whence she came,

And him to Pomfret, where, as all you know,

Harmless Richard was murther'd traitorously.

Warwick. Father, the duke hath told the truth ;

Thus got the house of Lancaster the crown.

York. Which now they hold by force and not by
    right ;

For Richard, the first son's heir, being dead,

The issue of the next son should have reign'd.

Salisbury. But William of Hatfield died without an
   heir.
York. The third son, Duke of Clarence, from whose
   line
I claim the crown, had issue, Philippe, a daughter,
Who married Edmund Mortimer, Earl of March.
Edmund had issue, Roger Earl of March ;
Roger had issue, Edmund, Anne, and Eleanor.
   Salisbury. This Edmund, in the reign of Boling-
      broke,
As I have read, laid claim unto the crown,
And, but for Owen Glendower, had been king,
Who kept him in captivity till he died.
But to the rest.
   York.   His eldest sister, Anne,
My mother, being heir unto the crown,
Married Richard Earl of Cambridge, who was son
To Edmund Langley, Edward the Third's fifth son.
By her I claim the kingdom : she was heir
To Roger Earl of March, who was the son
Of Edmund Mortimer, who married Philippe,
Sole daughter unto Lionel Duke of Clarence :
So, if the issue of the elder son
Succeed before the younger, I am king.
   Warwick. What plain proceeding is more plain
      than this ?
Henry doth claim the crown from John of Gaunt,
The fourth son ; York claims it from the third.
Till Lionel's issue fails, his should not reign :
It fails not yet, but flourishes in thee

And in thy sons, fair slips of such a stock. —
Then, father Salisbury, kneel we together;
And in this private plot be we the first
That shall salute our rightful sovereign
With honour of his birthright to the crown.

 Both. Long live our sovereign Richard, England's
  king!

 York. We thank you, lords. But I am not your
  king

Till I be crown'd, and that my sword be stain'd
With heart-blood of the house of Lancaster;
And that's not suddenly to be perform'd,
But with advice and silent secrecy.

ACT IV

Scene II. Blackheath.

(*Drum. Enter Cade, Dick the Butcher, Smith the
 Weaver, and a Sawyer, with infinite numbers.*)

 Cade. We John Cade, so termed of our supposed
father, —

 Dick (aside). Or rather, of stealing a cade[1] of
herrings.

 Cade. For our enemies shall fall before us, inspired
with the spirit of putting down kings and princes,
— Command silence.

 Dick. Silence!

 Cade. My father was a Mortimer, —

---

[1] small barrel.

Dick (aside). He was an honest man, and a good bricklayer.

Cade. My mother a Plantagenet, —

Dick (aside). I knew her well; she was a midwife.

Cade. My wife descended of the Lacies, —

Dick (aside). She was, indeed, a pedler's daughter, and sold many laces.

Smith (aside). But now of late, not able to travel with her furred pack,[1] she washes bucks [2] here at home.

Cade. Therefore am I of an honourable house.

Dick (aside). Ay, by my faith, the field is honourable; and there was he born, under a hedge, for his father had never a house but the cage.[3]

Cade. Valiant I am.

Smith (aside). A' must needs; for beggary is valiant.

Cade. I am able to endure much.

Dick (aside). No question of that; for I have seen him whipped three market-days together.

Cade. I fear neither sword nor fire.

Smith (aside). He need not fear the sword; for his coat is of proof.

Dick (aside). But methinks he should stand in fear of fire, being burnt i' the hand for stealing of sheep.

Cade. Be brave, then; for your captain is brave, and vows reformation. There shall be in England seven halfpenny loaves sold for a penny; the three-

[1] sheepskin knapsack.   [2] household linen.   [3] jail.

hooped pot shall have ten hoops ; and I will make it felony to drink small beer. All the realm shall be in common ; and in Cheapside shall my palfrey go to grass ; and when I am king, as king I will be, —

All. God save your majesty !

Cade. I thank you, good people ;—there shall be no money ; all shall eat and drink on my score ; and I will apparel them all in one livery, that they may agree like brothers and worship me their lord.

Dick. The first thing we do, let's kill all the lawyers.

Cade. Nay, that I mean to do. Is not this a lamentable thing, that of the skin of an innocent lamb should be made parchment ? that parchment, being scribbled o'er, should undo a man ? Some say the bee stings ; but I say, 'tis the bee's wax, for I did but seal once to a thing, and I was never mine own man since. — How now ! who's there ?

(*Enter some, bringing forward the Clerk of Chatham.*)

Smith. The clerk of Chatham : he can write and read and cast accompt.[1]

Cade. Oh monstrous !

Smith. We took him setting of boys' copies.

Cade. Here's a villain !

Smith. Has a book in his pocket with red letters in 't.

Cade. Nay, then, he is a conjuror.

[1] accounts.

Dick. Nay, he can make obligations,[1] and write court-hand.[2]

Cade. I am sorry for 't : the man is a proper[3] man, of mine honour ; unless I find him guilty, he shall not die. — Come hither, sirrah, I must examine thee : what is thy name?

Clerk. Emmanuel.

Dick. They use to write it on the top of letters. — 'Twill go hard with you.

Cade. Let me alone. — Dost thou use to write thy name? or hast thou a mark to thyself, like an honest, plain-dealing man?

Clerk. Sir, I thank God, I have been so well brought up that I can write my name.

All. He hath confessed; away with him! he's a villain and a traitor.

Cade. Away with him, I say! hang him with his pen and inkhorn about his neck.

[*Exit one with the Clerk.*

(*Enter Michael.*)

Michael. Where's our general?

Cade. Here I am, thou particular fellow.

Michael. Fly, fly, fly! Sir Humphrey Stafford and his brothers are hard by, with the king's forces.

Cade. Stand, villain, stand, or I'll fell thee down. He shall be encountered with a man as good as himself; he is but a knight, is a'?

Michael. No.

---

[1] contracts.   [2] law-script.   [3] good-looking.

Cade. To equal him, I will make myself a knight presently.[1] (*Kneels.*) Rise up Sir John Mortimer. — (*Rises.*) Now have at him!

(*Enter Sir Humphrey Stafford and his Brother, with drum and soldiers.*)

Stafford. Rebellious hinds, the filth and scum of Kent,

Mark'd for the gallows, lay your weapons down;
Home to your cottages, forsake this groom.
The king is merciful, if you revolt.

Brother. But angry, wrathful, and inclin'd to blood,

If you go forward ; therefore yield, or die.

Cade. As for these silken-coated slaves, I pass[2] not ;

It is to you, good people, that I speak,
Over whom, in time to come, I hope to reign,
For I am rightful heir unto the crown.

Stafford. Villain, thy father was a plasterer;
And thou thyself a shearman,[3] art thou not?

Cade. And Adam was a gardener.

Brother. And what of that?

Cade. Marry, this : Edmund Mortimer, Earl of March,

Married the Duke of Clarence's daughter, did he not?

Stafford. Ay, sir.

Cade. By her he had two children at one birth.

Brother. That's false.

---

[1] instantly.   [2] care.   [3] tailor.

Cade. Ay, there's the question ; but I say, 'tis true.
The elder of them, being put to nurse,
Was by a beggar-woman stolen away,
And, ignorant of his birth and parentage,
Became a bricklayer when he came to age.
His son am I ; deny it, if you can.

Dick. Nay, 'tis too true ; therefore he shall be king.

Smith. Sir, he made a chimney in my father's house, and the bricks are alive at this day to testify it ; therefore deny it not.

Stafford. And will you credit this base drudge's words,
That speaks he knows not what ?

All. Ay, marry, will we ; therefore get ye gone.

Brother. Jack Cade, the Duke of York hath taught you this.

Cade (aside). He lies, for I invented it myself. — Go to, sirrah, tell the king from me, that, for his father's sake, Henry the Fifth, in whose time boys went to span-counter for French crowns, I am content he shall reign ; but I'll be protector over him.

Dick. And furthermore, we'll have the Lord Say's head for selling the dukedom of Maine.

Cade. And good reason ; for thereby is England mained, and fain to go with a staff, but that my puissance holds it up. Fellow kings, I tell you that that Lord Say can speak French ; and therefore he is a traitor.

Stafford. O gross and miserable ignorance.

Cade. Nay, answer, if you can : the Frenchmen are our enemies; go to, then, I ask but this : can he that speaks with the tongue of an enemy be a good counsellor, or no?

All. No, no ; and therefore we'll have his head.

Brother. Well, seeing gentle words will not prevail, Assail them with the army of the king.

Stafford. Herald, away; and throughout every town Proclaim them traitors that are up with Cade ; That those which fly before the battle ends May, even in their wives' and children's sight, Be hang'd up for example at their doors. — And you that be the king's friends, follow me.

[Exeunt the two Staffords, and soldiers.

Cade. And you that love the commons, follow me. Now show yourselves men ; 'tis for liberty. We will not leave one lord, one gentleman : Spare none but such as go in clouted shoon,[1] For they are thrifty honest men and such As would, but that they dare not, take our parts.

Dick. They are all in order and march toward us.

Cade. But then are we in order when we are most out of order. Come, march forward.   *[Exeunt.*

PART III. ACT II

SCENE V. *A Field of Battle near Towton.*

(*Alarum. Enter King Henry.*)

King Henry. This battle fares like to the morning's war,

_____
[1] patched or hobnailed shoes.

When dying clouds contend with growing light,
What time the shepherd, blowing of his nails,
Can neither call it perfect day nor night.
Now sways it this way, like a mighty sea,
Forc'd by the tide to combat with the wind;
Now sways it that way, like the selfsame sea
Forc'd to retire by fury of the wind.
Sometime the flood prevails, and then the wind;
Now one the better, then another best;
Both tugging to be victors, breast to breast,
Yet neither conqueror nor conquerèd:
So is the equal poise of this fell war.
Here on this molehill will I sit me down.
To whom God will, there be the victory!
For Margaret my queen, and Clifford too,
Have chid me from the battle, swearing both
They prosper best of all when I am thence.
Would I were dead! if God's good will were so;
For what is in this world but grief and woe?
O God! methinks it were a happy life,
To be no better than a homely swain;[1]
To sit upon a hill, as I do now,
To carve out dials quaintly, point by point,
Thereby to see the minutes how they run,
How many make the hour full complete,
How many hours bring about the day,
How many days will finish up the year,
How many years a mortal man may live.
When this is known, then to divide the times:

[1] plain shepherd.

So many hours must I tend my flock;
So many hours must I take my rest;
So many hours must I contemplate;
So many hours must I sport myself;
So many days my ewes have been with young;
So many weeks ere the poor fools will ean;[1]
So many years ere I shall shear the fleece.
So minutes, hours, days, months, and years,
Pass'd over to the end they were created,
Would bring white hairs unto a quiet grave.
Ah, what a life were this! how sweet! how lovely!
Gives not the hawthorn bush a sweeter shade
To shepherds looking on their silly[2] sheep,
Than doth a rich embroider'd canopy
To kings that fear their subjects' treachery?
O, yes, it doth; a thousand-fold it doth.
And to conclude, the shepherd's homely curds,
His cold thin drink out of his leather bottle,
His wonted sleep under a fresh tree's shade,
All which secure and sweetly he enjoys,
Is far beyond a prince's delicates,
His viands sparkling in a golden cup,
His body couchèd in a curious[2] bed,
When care, mistrust, and treason wait on him.

*   *   *   *   *   *   *

(*Alarums.   Excursions.   Enter   Queen   Margaret,
Prince of Wales, and Exeter.*)

　Prince. Fly, father, fly! for all your friends are
　　fled

---

[1] give birth to the lambs.　　[2] innocent.　　[2] elaborate.

And Warwick rages like a chafèd bull.
Away! for death doth hold us in pursuit.
  Queen Margaret. Mount you, my lord; towards
    Berwick post amain.
Edward and Richard, like a brace of greyhounds,
Having the fearful flying hare in sight,
With fiery eyes sparkling for very wrath,
And bloody steel grasp'd in their ireful hands,
Are at our backs; and therefore hence amain.
  Exeter. Away! for vengeance comes along with
    them.
Nay, stay not to expostulate; make speed,
Or else come after: I'll away before.
  King Henry. Nay, take me with thee, good sweet
    Exeter;
Not that I fear to stay, but love to go
Whither the queen intends.   Forward! away!
                                    [*Exeunt.*

THE DREAM OF CLARENCE

WILLIAM SHAKESPEARE

(From " King Richard the Third ")

GEORGE, Duke of Clarence, the second son of Richard of York, had desired to supplant his brother, Edward IV. To this end he joined Warwick in plotting Edward's overthrow. The York king was actually driven from England, and Henry VI. was restored (1470) on the understanding that Clarence should succeed him. When Edward returned in triumph the following year, Clarence hastened to meet him, abandoning Warwick and the Lancastrians. He fought for the Red Rose at Barnet and at Tewkesbury. His loyalty was suspected, however, and he was confined in the Tower.

ACT I

Scene IV.   London.   *A Room in the Tower.*

(Enter Clarence and Keeper.)

Keeper. Why looks your grace so heavily to-day ?
Clarence. O, I have pass'd a miserable night,
So full of fearful dreams, of ugly sights,
That, as I am a Christian faithful man,
I would not spend another such a night,
Though 't were to buy a world of happy days, —
So full of dismal terror was the time.

> *Keeper.* What was your dream, my lord ?   I pray
> you tell me.
> *Clarence.* Methought that I had broken from the
> Tower,

And was embark'd to cross to Burgundy ;
And, in my company, my brother Gloster,
Who from my cabin tempted me to walk
Upon the hatches : thence we look'd toward England,
And cited up a thousand heavy times,
During the wars of York and Lancaster,
That had befall'n us.   As we pac'd along
Upon the giddy footing of the hatches,
Methought that Gloster stumbled ; and, in falling,
Struck me, that thought to stay him, overboard
Into the tumbling billows of the main.
O Lord, methought, what pain it was to drown !
What dreadful noise of water in mine ears !
What sights of ugly death within mine eyes !
Methought I saw a thousand fearful wracks ;

A thousand men that fishes gnaw'd upon ;
Wedges of gold, great anchors, heaps of pearl,
Inestimable stones, unvalued jewels,
All scatter'd in the bottom of the sea :
Some lay in dead men's skulls; and in the holes
Where eyes did once inhabit, there were crept,
As 't were in scorn of eyes, reflecting gems,
That woo'd the slimy bottom of the deep,
And mock'd the dead bones that lay scatter'd by.

Keeper. Had you such leisure in the time of death
To gaze upon these secrets of the deep ?

Clarence. Methought I had ; and often did I strive
To yield the ghost; but still the envious flood
Stopp'd in my soul, and would not let it forth
To find the empty, vast, and wand'ring air,
But smother'd it within my panting bulk,
Which almost burst to belch it in the sea.

Keeper. Awak'd you not in this sore agony ?

Clarence. No, no, my dream was lengthen'd after
  life !
O, then began the tempest in my soul !
I pass'd, methought, the melancholy flood,
With that sour ferryman which poets write of,
Unto the kingdom of perpetual night.
The first that there did greet my stranger soul
Was my great father-in-law, renownèd Warwick ;
Who spake aloud, " What scourge for perjury
Can this dark monarchy afford false Clarence ? "
And so he vanish'd.   Then came wandering by
A shadow like an angel, with bright hair

Dabbled in blood; and he shriek'd out aloud,
" Clarence is come, — false, fleeting, perjur'd Clar-
    ence, —
That stabb'd me in the field by Tewkesbury ; —
Seize oη him, Furies ! take him unto torment ! "
With that, methought, a legion of foul fiends
Environ'd me, and howlèd in mine ears
Such hideous cries that with the very noise
I trembling wak'd, and for a season after
Could not believe but that I was in hell,
Such terrible impression made my dream.
    Keeper. No marvel, lord, though it affrighted you ;
I am afraid, methinks, to hear you tell it.
    Clarence. Ah, keeper, keeper ! I have done these
        things,
That now give evidence against my soul,
For Edward's sake ; and see how he requites me ! —
O God ! if my deep prayers cannot appease thee,
But thou wilt be aveng'd on my misdeeds,
Yet execute thy wrath in me alone ;
O, spare my guiltless wife and my poor children ! —
Keeper, I prithee sit by me awhile ;
My soul is heavy, and I fain would sleep.
    Keeper. I will, my lord ; God give your grace good
        rest ! —

THE LITTLE PRINCES

WILLIAM SHAKESPEARE

(From " King Richard the Third ")

WHEN Edward IV. died (1483) he left two sons, Edward, in his thirteenth year, and Richard, who was but eleven years of age. The coronation of the little king was set for May 4th, then for June 22d, and finally for November 2d; but the ceremony was never performed. Gloucester imprisoned the boys in the Tower, claimed the succession, and was crowned Richard III. on June 25th.

ACT III

SCENE I. LONDON. *A Street.*

(*The trumpets sound. Enter the Prince of Wales, Gloster, Buckingham, Cardinal Bouchier, and others.*)

> *Buckingham.* Welcome, sweet prince, to London, to
> your chamber.[1]
> *Gloster.* Welcome, dear cousin, my thought's sover-
> eign ;
> The weary way hath made you melancholy.
> *Prince.* No, uncle ; but our crosses on the way
> Have made it tedious, wearisome, and heavy :
> I want more uncles here to welcome me.
> *Gloster.* Sweet prince, the untainted virtue of your
> years
> Hath not yet div'd into the world's deceit.
> No more can you distinguish of a man
> Than of his outward show ; which, God he knows.
> Seldom or never jumpeth [2] with the heart.

[1] capital city.   [2] accordeth.

Those uncles which you want were dangerous;
Your grace attended to their sugar'd words,
But look'd not on the poison of their hearts:
God keep you from them, and from such false friends!

> *Prince.* God keep me from false friends! but they
> were none.
>
> *Gloster.* My lord, the mayor of London comes to
> greet you.

> (*Enter the Lord Mayor and his Train.*)

> *Mayor.* God bless your grace with health and
> happy days!
>
> *Prince.* I thank you, good my lord; and thank
> you all. —

I thought my mother and my brother York
Would long ere this have met us on the way.

*   *   *   *   *   *   *

Say, uncle Gloster, if our brother come,
Where shall we sojourn till our coronation?

> *Gloster.* Where it think'st best unto your royal self.

If I may counsel you, some day or two
Your highness shall repose you at the Tower;
Then where you please, and shall be thought most fit
For your best health and recreation.

> *Prince.* I do not like the Tower, of any place. —

Did Julius Cæsar build that place, my lord?

> *Buckingham.* He did, my gracious lord, begin that
> place,

Which, since, succeeding ages have reëdified.

> *Prince.* Is it upon record, or else reported

Successively from age to age, he built it?

Buckingham. Upon record, my gracious lord.

Prince. But say, my lord, it were not register'd,
Methinks the truth should live from age to age,
As 'twere retail'd to all posterity,
Even to the general all-ending day.

Gloster (aside). So wise, so young, they say, do
never live long.

Prince. What say you, uncle?

Gloster. I say, without characters[1] fame lives long.
(*Aside*) Thus, like the formal Vice, Iniquity,
I moralize two meanings in one word.

Prince. That Julius Cæsar was a famous man;
With what his valour did enrich his wit,
His wit set down to make his valour live.
Death makes no conquest of his conqueror;
For now he lives in fame, though not in life. —
I'll tell you what, my cousin Buckingham.

Buckingham. What, my gracious lord?

Prince. An if I live until I be a man,
I'll win our ancient right in France again,
Or die a soldier, as I liv'd a king.

Gloster (aside). Short summers lightly[2] have a for-
ward spring.

(*Enter York, Hastings, and the Cardinal.*)

Buckingham. Now, in good time, here comes the
Duke of York.

Prince. Richard of York, how fares our noble
brother?

---

[1] inscriptions; written records.   [2] commonly.

York. Well, my dread lord; so must I call you now.

Prince. Ay, brother, to our grief, as it is yours.
Too late he died that might have kept that title,
Which by his death hath lost much majesty.

Gloster. How fares our cousin, noble Lord of York?

York. I thank you, gentle uncle. O, my lord,
You said that idle weeds are fast in growth;
The prince my brother hath outgrown me far.

Gloster. He hath, my lord.

York.   And therefore is he idle?

Gloster. O, my fair cousin, I must not say so.

York. Then he is more beholding [1] to you than I.

Gloster. He may command me as my sovereign,
But you have power in me as in a kinsman.

York. I pray you, uncle, give me this dagger.

Gloster. My dagger, little cousin? with all my heart.

Prince. A beggar, brother?

York. Of my kind uncle, that I know will give;
And being but a toy, which is no grief to give.

Gloster. A greater gift than that I'll give my cousin.

York. A greater gift? O, that's the sword to it.

Gloster. Ay, gentle cousin, were it light enough.

York. O, then, I see, you'll part but with light gifts;
In weightier things you'll say a beggar nay.

Gloster. It is too weighty for your grace to wear.

[1] indebted.

York. I weigh it lightly, were it heavier.

Gloster. What! would you have my weapon, little
    lord?

York. I would, that I might thank you as you call
    me.

Gloster. How?

York. Little.

Prince. My Lord of York will still be cross in
    talk. —

Uncle, your grace knows how to bear with him.

York. You mean, to bear me, not to bear with me.—

Uncle, my brother mocks both you and me;

Because that I am little, like an ape,

He thinks that you should bear me on your shoulders.

Buckingham. With what a sharp-provided wit he
    reasons!

To mitigate the scorn he gives his uncle,

He prettily and aptly taunts himself.

So cunning, and so young, is wonderful.

Gloster. My lord, will 't please you pass along?

Myself and my good cousin Buckingham

Will to your mother, to entreat of her

To meet you at the Tower and welcome you.

York. What! will you go unto the Tower, my
    lord?

Prince. My lord protector needs will have it so.

York. I shall not sleep in quiet at the Tower.

Gloster. Why, what should you fear?

York. Marry, my uncle Clarence' angry ghost;

My grandam told me he was murther'd there.

Prince. I fear no uncles dead.

Gloster. Nor none that live, I hope.

Prince. An if they live, I hope I need not fear.
But come, my lord ; and, with a heavy heart,
Thinking on them, go I unto the Tower.
(*A sennet.*[1]   *Exeunt Prince, York, Hastings, Car-
dinal, and Attendants.*)

THE PRINCES IN THE TOWER

Thomas Heywood

(From " King Edward the Fourth ")

THE little princes, however, had many friends, and King Richard
thought them dangerous.   He therefore sent an order to the constable
of the Tower that he should put them to death.   When he refused,
Sir James Tyrell was sent with a warrant giving him control of the
Tower for one night.   The boys were then smothered under their pil-
lows by Dighton and Forrest, two of their jailers.

SCENE.   *A Room in the Tower.*

(*Enter the two young Princes, Edward and Richard,
in their gowns and caps, unbuttoned, and untrust.*[2])

Rich. How does your lordship ?

Ed. Well, good brother Richard.
How does yourself ? you told me your head ached.

Rich. Indeed it does, my lord ; feel with your hands
How hot it is.

(*Edward lays his hand on his brother's head.*)
Ed. Indeed you have caught cold,

---

[1] set of notes played on a trumpet.   [2] with garments loosened.

With sitting yesternight to hear me read.
I pray thee go to bed, sweet Dick, poor little heart.

    Rich. You'll give me leave to wait upon your
      lordship.

    Ed. I had more need, brother, to wait on you.
For you are sick ; and so am not I.

    Rich. Oh, lord, methinks this going to our bed,
How like it is to going to our grave.

    Ed. I pray thee, do not speak of graves, sweet heart.
Indeed thou frightest me.

    Rich. Why, my lord brother, did not our tutor teach
      us,
That when at night we went unto our bed,
We still should think we went unto our grave.

    Ed. Yes, that's true,
That we should do as ev'ry Christian ought,
To be prepar'd to die at every hour,
But I am heavy.[1]

    Rich. Indeed, and so am I.

    Ed. Then let us say our prayers and go to bed.
    (*They kneel, and solemn music the while within. The
        music ceaseth, and they rise.*)

    Rich. What, bleeds your grace ?

    Ed. Ay, two drops and no more.

    Rich. God bless us both ; and I desire no more.

    Ed. Brother, see here what David says, and so
      say I ;
Lord ! in thee will I trust, although I die.

        (*As the young Princes go out, enter Tirill.*)

             [1] low-spirited.

Tir. Go, lay ye down, but never more to rise.
I have put my hand into the foulest murder
That ever was committed since the world.
The very senseless stones here in the walls
Break out in tears but to behold the fact.[1]
Methinks the bodies lying dead in graves,
Should rise and cry against us. O hark (*a noise
       within*), hark,
The mandrake's shrieks are music to their cries,
The very night is frighted, and the stars
Do drop like torches, to behold this deed:
The very centre of the earth doth shake,
Methinks the Tower should rent [2] down from the top,
To let the heaven look on this monstrous deed.

(*Enter at the one door, Dighton, with Edward under
    his arm, at the other door, Forrest with Richard.*)

   Digh. Stand further, damnèd rogue, and come not
     near me.
   For. Nay, stand thou further, villain, stand aside.
   Digh. Are we not both damnd for this cursèd
     deed?
   For. It is too true.   Oh, I am damnd indeed!
          (*He looks down on the boy under his arm.*)
   Tir. I am as deep as you, although my hand
Did not the deed.
   Digh. O villain, art thou there?
   For. A plague light on thee!
   Tir. Curse not;

---

[1] deed.   [2] rend itself.

A thousand plagues will light upon us all.

(*They lay them down.*)

The priest here in the Tower will bury them.
Let us away.

KING RICHARD THE THIRD

WILLIAM SHAKESPEARE

RICHARD III. was, after John, the best-hated king in English history. He was ugly and misshapen in body, and shrewd and unscrupulous in pursuit of his ends. The worst crimes of that bloody epoch were laid to Gloucester's charge. Men believed that he had slain Prince Edward after the battle of Tewkesbury and murdered King Henry as he lay a prisoner in the Tower. The death of Clarence was attributed to him, and he doubtless caused the young sons of Edward IV. to be put out of his way. Richard's usurpation of the throne was justly regarded with horror by all classes in England. Encouraged by the general discontent, Henry Tudor, Duke of Richmond, the son of Margaret Beaufort, — great-granddaughter of John of Gaunt, — and of Edmund Tudor, a Welsh nobleman, returned from exile to claim the crown. He landed at Milford Haven, where the Welsh flocked to his standard. The leading English lords, even those most trusted by Richard, declared for Henry. At the battle of Bosworth Field (1485) the king's forces were overwhelmed and he himself was slain. The crown, bloody as it fell from Richard's helmet, was placed on the head of Henry Tudor, and he was declared king.

ACT IV

SCENE IV. *Before the Palace.*

(*Enter Lord Stanley.*)

K. Rich. How now, what news with you?

Stan. None good, my lord, to please you with the
  hearing;

Nor none so bad, but it may well be told.

K. Rich. Heyday, a riddle! neither good nor bad!
Why dost thou run so many mile about,
When thou mayst tell thy tale a nearer way?
Once more, what news?

    Stan.   Richmond is on the seas.

    K. Rich. There let him sink, and be the seas on
    him!
White-liver'd runagate, what doth he there?

    Stan. I know not, mighty sovereign, but by guess.

    K. Rich. Well, sir, as you guess, as you guess?

    Stan. Stirr'd up by Dorset, Buckingham, and Ely,
He makes for England, there to claim the crown.

    K. Rich. Is the chair empty? is the sword un-
    sway'd?
Is the king dead? the empire unpossess'd?
What heir of York is there alive but we?
And who is England's king but great York's heir?
Then, tell me, what doth he upon the sea?

    Stan. Unless for that, my liege, I cannot guess.

    K. Rich. Unless for that he comes to be your liege,
You cannot guess wherefore the Welshman comes.
Thou wilt revolt and fly to him, I fear.

    Stan. No, mighty liege; therefore mistrust me not.

    K. Rich. Where is thy power then to beat him
    back?
Where are thy tenants and thy followers?
Are they not now upon the western shore,
Safe-conducting the rebels from their ships?

    Stan. No, my good lord, my friends are in the
    north.

K. Rich. Cold friends to Richard : what do they in the north,

When they should serve their sovereign in the west ?

Stan. They have not been commanded, mighty sovereign :

Please it your majesty to give me leave,

I'll muster up my friends, and meet your grace

Where and what time your majesty shall please.

K. Rich. Ay, ay, thou wouldst be gone to join with Richmond :

I will not trust you, sir.

Stan. Most mighty sovereign,

You have no cause to hold my friendship doubtful :

I never was nor never will be false.

K. Rich. Well,

Go muster men ; but, hear you, leave behind

Your son, George Stanley : look your faith be firm,

Or else his head's assurance is but frail.

Stan. So deal with him as I prove true to you.

[*Exit.*

ACT V

SCENE III. *Bosworth Field. Enter King Richard in arms with Norfolk, the Earl of Surrey, and others.*

K. Rich. Here pitch our tents, even here in Bosworth field. —

My Lord of Surrey, why look you so sad ?

Sur. My heart is ten times lighter than my looks.

K. Rich. My Lord of Norfolk, —

Nor. Here, most gracious liege.

K. Rich. Norfolk, we must have knocks; ha! must we not?

Nor. We must both give and take, my gracious lord.

K. Rich. Up with my tent there! here will I lie to-night:

But where to-morrow? Well, all's one for that.

Who hath descried the number of the foe?

Nor. Six or seven thousand is their utmost power.

K. Rich. Why, our battalion trebles that account:

Besides, the king's name is a tower of strength,

Which they upon the adverse party want.

Up with my tent there! Valiant gentlemen,

Let us survey the vantage of the field;

Call for some men of sound direction:

Let's want no discipline, make no delay;

For, lords, to-morrow is à busy day.   [*Exeunt.*

*   *   *   *   *   *   *

(*Reënter King Richard, Ratcliff, Attendants, and Forces.*)

K. Rich. What said Northumberland as touching Richmond?

Rat. That he was never trainèd up in arms.

K. Rich. He said the truth: and what said Surrey, then?

Rat. He smiled and said, "The better for our purpose."

K. Rich. He was in the right; and so indeed it is.
          (*The clock striketh.*)

Tell the clock there.   Give me a calendar.
Who saw the sun to-day?

 Rat.   Not I, my lord.

 K. Rich. Then he disdains to shine; for by the
  book

He should have brav'd[1] the east an hour ago:
A black day will it be to somebody.
Ratcliff!

 Rat. My lord?

 K. Rich.   The sun will not be seen to-day;
The sky doth frown and lour upon our army.
I would these dewy tears were from[2] the ground.
Not shine to-day! Why, what is that to me
More than to Richmond? for the selfsame heaven
That frowns on me looks sadly upon him.

(Reënter Norfolk.)

 Nor. Arm, arm, my lord; the foe vaunts in the
  field.

 K. Rich. Come, bustle, bustle.   Caparison my
  horse.

Call up Lord Stanley, bid him bring his power:
I will lead forth my soldiers to the plain,
And thus my battle shall be orderèd:
My foreward shall be drawn out all in length,
Consisting equally of horse and foot;
Our archers shall be placèd in the midst:
John Duke of Norfolk, Thomas Earl of Surrey,
Shall have the leading of this foot and horse.

[1] made glorious.   [2] away from.

They thus directed, we will follow
In the main battle, whose puissance on either side
Shall be well wingèd with our chiefest horse.
This, and Saint George to boot! What think'st thou,
      Norfolk?
   Nor. A good direction, warlike sovereign.

SCENE IV. *Another part of the field.   Alarum;
   excursions.   Enter Norfolk and forces fighting; to
   him Catesby.*

Cate. Rescue, my Lord of Norfolk, rescue, rescue!
The king enacts more wonders than a man,
Daring an opposite [1] to every danger:
His horse is slain, and all on foot he fights,
Seeking for Richmond in the throat of death.
Rescue, fair lord, or else the day is lost!

         (*Alarums.   Enter King Richard.*)

   K. Rich. A horse! a horse! my kingdom for a
      horse!
   Cate. Withdraw, my lord; I'll help you to a horse.
   K. Rich. Slave, I have set my life upon a cast,
And I will stand the hazard of the die.
I think there be six Richmonds in the field;
Five have I slain to-day instead of him.
A horse! a horse! my kingdom for a horse!
                                    [*Exeunt.*

                  [1] daring to oppose himself.

PERKIN WARBECK

JOHN FORD

HENRY VII. had much ado to keep the crown upon his head. Richard III. had left no heir, but the Yorkist party gave their support to various pretenders. The most notable of these was Perkin Warbeck, a Flemish trader of courtly face and manners, who succeeded in convincing the Irish friends of the House of York that he was Richard, the younger son of Edward IV. He landed in Cornwall (1497), and attempted to rouse the English in his behalf, but he met with little encouragement. The people had grown weary of bloodshed and were too well content with a king who was able to restore law and order to be willing to renew the dynastic controversy. Parliament had made good all defects in the hereditary title of the Tudors by vesting the crown in Henry VII. and his heirs, and men gladly accepted this settlement as final.

ACT V

SCENE II.

(Enter Lord Dawbeney, with a Guard, leading in Perkin Warbeck and his Followers, chained.)

Daw. Life to the king, and safety fix his throne!
I here present you, royal sir, a shadow
Of majesty, but in effect a substance
Of pity; a young man, in nothing grown
To ripeness but the ambition of your mercy, —
Perkin, the Christian world's strange wonder.
  K. Hen.   Dawbeney,
We observe no wonder: I behold, 'tis true,
An ornament of nature, fine and polished,
A handsome youth indeed, but not admire him.
How came he to thy hands?

Daw.   From sanctuary
At Bewley, near Southampton; registered,
With these few followers, for persons privileged.
  K. Hen. I must not thank you, sir; you were to
    blame
T' infringe the liberty of houses sacred:
Dare we be irreligious?
  Daw.   Gracious lord,
They voluntarily resigned themselves
Without compulsion.
  K. Hen.   So? 'twas very well;
'Twas very, very well. — Turn now thine eyes,
Young man, upon thyself and thy past actions;
What revels in combustion through our kingdom
A frenzy of aspiring youth hath danced,
Till, wanting breath, thy feet of pride have slipt
To break thy neck!
  War.   But not my heart; my heart
Will mount till every drop of blood be frozen
By death's perpetual winter: if the sun
Of majesty be darkened, let the sun
Of life be hid from me in an eclipse
Lasting and universal. Sir, remember
There was a shooting-in of light when Richmond,
Not aiming at a crown, retired, and gladly,
For comfort to the Duke of Bretaine's court.
Richard, who swayed the sceptre, was reputed
A tyrant then; yet then a dawning glimmered
To some few wandering remnants, promising day
When first they ventured on a frightful shore
At Milford Haven: —

Daw.   Whither speeds his boldness?
Check his rude tongue, great sir.
   K. Hen.   O, let him range:
The player's on the stage still, 'tis his part;
He does but act. — What followed?
   War.   Bosworth Field;
Where, at an instant, to the world's amazement,
A morn to Richmond, and a night to Richard,
Appeared at once: the tale is soon applied;
Fate, which crowned these attempts when least assured,
Might have befriended others like resolved.
   K. Hen. A pretty gallant!

          *   *   *   *   *   *   *

Urswick, command the dukeling and these fellows
                                    (*They rise.*)
To Digby, the lieutenant of the Tower:
With safety let them be conveyed to London.
It is our pleasure no uncivil outrage,
Taunts or abuse be suffered to their persons;
They shall meet fairer law than they deserve.
Time may restore their wits, whom vain ambition
Hath many years distracted.
   War.   Noble thoughts
Meet freedom in captivity: the Tower, —
Our childhood's dreadful nursery!
   K. Hen.   No more!
   Urs. Come, come, you shall have leisure to be-
      think ye.
      [*Exit Urswick with Perkin Warbeck and his Fol-
      lowers, guarded.*

K. Hen. Was ever so much impudence in forgery?
The custom, sure, of being styled a king
Hath fastened in his thought that he is such;
But we shall teach the lad another language:
'Tis good we have him fast.
    Daw.   The hangman's physic
Will purge this saucy humour.
    K. Hen.   Very likely.

SCENE III.   LONDON.   *The Tower-hill.*

(*Enter Constable and Officers, Perkin Warbeck, Urs-
    wick, followed by the rabble.   Enter Sheriff
    with Warbeck's Followers, halters about their
    necks.*)

Oxf. Look ye; behold your followers, appointed
To wait on ye in death!
    War.   Why, peers of England,
We'll lead 'em on courageously: I read
A triumph over tyranny upon
Their several foreheads. — Faint not in the moment
Of victory! our ends, and Warwick's head,
Innocent Warwick's head, — for we are prologue
But to his tragedy, — conclude the wonder
Of Henry's fears; and then the glorious race
Of fourteen kings, Plantagenets, determines
In this last issue male; Heaven be obeyed!
Impoverish time of its amazement, friends,
And we will prove as trusty in our payments
As prodigal to nature in our debts.
Death? pish! 'tis but a sound; a name of air;

A minute's storm, or not so much : to tumble
From bed to bed, be massacred alive
By some physicians, for a month or two,
In hope of freedom from a fever's torments,
Might stagger manhood ; here the pain is past
Ere sensibly 'tis felt.   Be men of spirit !
Spurn coward passion ! so illustrious mention
Shall blaze our names, and style us kings o'er Death.
    Daw. Away, impostor beyond precedent !
        [*Exeunt Sheriff and Officers with the Prisoners.*
No chronicle records his fellow.

THE FIRST VOYAGE OF JOHN CABOT

JOHN CABOT applied to Henry VII. in 1495 for authority to explore
the New World. The parsimonious monarch granted the letters patent,
but gave no financial aid. Only when the adventurers had returned,
reporting the discovery of Cape Breton, did the king bestow a beggarly
£10. Nevertheless, few of his contemporaries had more faith in the
future of America than Henry Tudor.

" He chases shadows," sneered the Bristol tars.
" As well fling nets to catch the golden stars
As climb the surges of earth's utmost sea."
But for the Venice pilot, meagre, wan,
His swarthy sons beside him, life began
With that slipt cable, when his dream rode free.

And Henry, on his battle-wrested throne,
The Councils done, would speak in musing tone
Of Cabot, not the cargo he might bring.

" Man's heart, though morsel scant for hungry crow,
Is greater than a world can fill, and so
Fair fall the shadow-seekers!" quoth the king.

KING HENRY THE EIGHTH

Recollection of his Portrait in Trinity Lodge, Cambridge

William Wordsworth

The second Tudor came to the throne unhampered by rivals. He was handsome, good-humored, pleasure-loving, a man born to popularity and success. His imperious temper was not resented, for the people were weary of weak government and welcomed a masterful king. In reckless pursuit of his own selfish purposes Henry reformed the church, abolished the monasteries, and gave England a leading place in the politics of Europe.

The imperial stature, the colossal stride,
Are yet before me; yet do I behold
The broad, full visage, chest of amplest mould,
The vestments 'broidered with barbaric pride;
And lo! a poniard, at the Monarch's side,
Hangs ready to be grasped in sympathy
With the keen threatenings of that fulgent eye,
Below the white-rimmed bonnet far descried.
Who trembles now at thy capricious mood?
'Mid those surrounding Worthies, haughty King,
We rather think, with grateful mind sedate,
How Providence educeth, from the spring
Of lawless will, unlooked-for streams of good,
Which neither force shall check nor time abate!

KING HENRY THE EIGHTH

JACOBEAN PLAY DOUBTFULLY ASCRIBED TO SHAKESPEARE AND FLETCHER

HENRY'S first queen was Katharine of Aragon, the widow of his elder brother Arthur. The ecclesiastical law forbade marrying with so near a relative, but for reasons of state the match was thought desirable, and a special dispensation was secured from the Pope. The legality of the arrangement was not called in question until 1527, when, after twenty years of wedded life, there being but one child living and that a daughter, the king became convinced that the marriage with Katharine had been a mistake, perhaps a sin. Henry's close friend and adviser was Thomas Wolsey, a man of great ability, on whom had been conferred the highest honors in church and state. Cardinal, Archbishop of York, and Chancellor of the Realm, he enjoyed enormous wealth and well-nigh royal powers. To him was entrusted the task of accomplishing a divorce. Wolsey's appeal to the Pope was unsuccessful, and the king in anger deposed him from the chancellorship (1529), confiscated his estates, and threw him into the Tower on a charge of high treason.

ACT II

SCENE IV. *A Hall in Black-friars.*

(*Pomp of Court and Clergy. Enter the King with his Train, followed by the Queen with hers.*)

Wolsey. Whilst our commission from Rome is read,
Let silence be commanded.
King Henry. What's the need?
It hath already publicly been read,
And on all sides th' authority allow'd;
You may, then, spare that time.

Wolsey.   Be't so. — Proceed.

Scribe. Say, Henry King of England, come into
   the court.

Crier. Henry King of England, come into the
   court.

King Henry. Here.

Scribe. Say, Katharine Queen of England, come
   into the court.

Crier. Katharine Queen of England, come into
   the court.

(*The Queen makes no answer, rises out of her chair,
   goes about the court, comes to the King, and kneels
   at his feet ; then speaks.*)

   Queen Katharine. Sir, I desire you do me right
      and justice,

And to bestow your pity on me ; for

I am a most poor woman, and a stranger,

Born out of your dominions ; having here

No judge indifferent, nor no more assurance

Of equal friendship and proceeding.   Alas, sir,

In what have I offended you ? what cause

Hath my behaviour given to your displeasure,

That thus you should proceed to put me off,

And take your good grace from me ?   Heaven witness

I have been to you a true and humble wife,

At all times to your will conformable :

Ever in fear to kindle your dislike,

Yea, subject to your countenance, glad or sorry,

As I saw it inclin'd.   When was the hour

I ever contradicted your desire,
Or made it not mine too? Or which of your
    friends
Have I not strove to love, although I knew
He were mine enemy? what friend of mine,
That had to him deriv'd your anger, did I
Continue in my liking? nay, gave notice
He was from thence discharg'd. Sir, call to mind
That I have been your wife, in this obedience,
Upward of twenty years, and have been blest
With many children by you: if in the course
And process of this time you can report,
And prove it too, against mine honour aught,
My bond to wedlock or my love and duty,
Against your sacred person, in God's name,
Turn me away; and let the foul'st contempt
Shut door upon me, and so give me up
To the sharp'st kind of justice. Please you, sir,
The king, your father, was reputed for
A prince most prudent, of an excellent
And unmatch'd wit and judgment: Ferdinand,
My father, King of Spain, was reckon'd one
The wisest prince, that there had reign'd by many
A year before: it is not to be question'd
That they had gather'd a wise council to them
Of every realm, that did debate this business,
Who deem'd our marriage lawful. Wherefore I
    humbly
Beseech you, sir, to spare me, till I may
Be by my friends in Spain advis'd, whose counsel

I will implore : if not, i' th' name of God,
Your pleasure be fulfill'd !
 Wolsey.   You have here, lady,
(And of your choice) these reverend fathers ; men
Of singular integrity and learning,
Yea, the elect o' th' land, who are assembled
To plead your cause. It shall be therefore bootless
That longer you desire the court, as well
For your own quiet as to rectify
What is unsettled in the king.
 Campeius.   His grace
Hath spoken well, and justly : therefore, madam,
It's fit this royal session do proceed,
And that without delay their arguments
Be now produc'd and heard.
 Queen Katharine.   Lord cardinal,
To you I speak.
 Wolsey. Your pleasure, madam ?
 Queen Katharine.   Sir,
I am about to weep ; but, thinking that
We are a queen (or long have dream'd so), certain
The daughter of a king, my drops of tears
I'll turn to sparks of fire.
 Wolsey.   Be patient yet.
 Queen Katharine. I will, when you are humble ;
  nay, before,
Or God will punish me. I do believe,
Induc'd by potent circumstances, that
You are mine enemy, and make my challenge
You shall not be my judge ; for it is you

Have blown this coal betwixt my lord and me, —
Which God's dew quench ! Therefore I say again,
I utterly abhor, yea, from my soul
Refuse you for my judge ; whom, yet once more,
I hold my most malicious foe, and think not
At all a friend to truth.

   Wolsey.   I do profess
You speak not like yourself ; who ever yet
Have stood to charity and display'd th' effects
Of disposition gentle, and of wisdom
O'ertopping woman's power.   Madam, you do me
     wrong :
I have no spleen against you ; nor injustice
For you, or any : how far I have proceeded,
Or how far further shall, is warranted
By a commission from the consistory,[1]
Yea, the whole consistory of Rome.   You charge me
That I have blown this coal : I do deny it.
The king is present : if it be known to him
That I gainsay my deed, how may he wound,
And worthily, my falsehood ! yea, as much
As you have done my truth.   If he know
That I am free of your report, he knows
I am not of your wrong : therefore in him
It lies to cure me ; and the cure is to
Remove these thoughts from you : the which·before
His highness shall speak in, I do beseech
You, gracious madam, to unthink your speaking,
And to say so no more.

                  [1] College of cardinals.

Queen Katharine.   My lord, my lord,
I am a simple woman, much too weak
T' oppose your cunning.   You're meek and humble-
        mouth'd ;
You sign your place and calling, in full seeming,[1]
With meekness and humility, but your heart
Is cramm'd with arrogancy, spleen, and pride.
You have, by fortune and his highness' favours,
Gone slightly [2] o'er low steps, and now are mounted
Where powers [3] are your retainers ; and your words,
Domestics to you, serve your will as 't please
Yourself pronounce their office.   I must tell you,
You tender more your person's honour than
Your high profession spiritual ; that again
I do refuse you for my judge, and here,
Before you all, appeal unto the Pope,
To bring my whole cause 'fore his Holiness,
And to be judg'd by him.

    (*She curtsies to the King, and offers to depart.*)
    Chamberlain.   The queen is obstinate,
Stubborn to justice, apt [4] to accuse it, and
Disdainful to be tried by 't : 'tis not well.
She's going away.

    King Henry.   Call her again.

    Crier. Katharine Queen of England, come into the
        court.

    Griffith. Madam, you are call'd back.

    Queen Katharine. What need you note it ? pray
        you, keep your way :

---

[1] show.   [2] smoothly, quickly.   [3] people of high authority.
                            [4] ingenious.

When you are call'd, return. — Now the Lord help!
They vex me past my patience. — Pray you, pass on:
I will not tarry; no, nor ever more
Upon this business my appearance make
In any of their courts.

        [Exeunt Queen and her Attendants.

  King Henry.   Go thy ways, Kate:
That man i' th' world who shall report he has
A better wife, let him in naught be trusted,
For speaking false in that. Thou art, alone
(If thy rare qualities, sweet gentleness,
Thy meekness saint-like, wife-like government,[1]
Obeying in commanding, and thy parts
Sovereign and pious else, could speak thee out),
The queen of earthly queens. She's noble born;
And like her true nobility she has
Carried herself towards me.

ACT III

SCENE II. *Ante-chamber to the King's apartment.*
Cardinal Wolsey alone.

  Wolsey. Farewell, a long farewell, to all my greatness!
This is the state of man: to-day he puts forth
The tender leaves of hopes; to-morrow blossoms,
And bears his blushing honours thick upon him;
The third day comes a frost, a killing frost,
And, — when he thinks, good easy man, full surely

---

[1] demeanor.

His greatness is a-ripening, — nips his root,
And then he falls as I do. I have ventur'd,
Like little wanton [1] boys that swim on bladders,
This many summers in a sea of glory,
But far beyond my depth : my high-blown pride
At length broke under me, and now has left me
Weary and old with service, to the mercy
Of a rude stream, that must for ever hide me.
Vain pomp and glory of this world, I hate ye :
I feel my heart new open'd.   O, how wretched
Is that poor man that hangs on princes' favours !
There is betwixt that smile we would aspire to,
That sweet aspect of princes, and their ruin,
More pangs and fears than wars or women have ;
And when he falls, he falls like Lucifer,
Never to hope again.—

(*Enter Cromwell, amazedly.*)

                    Why, how now, Cromwell !
  Cromwell. I have no power to speak, sir.
    Wolsey.   What ! amaz'd
At my misfortunes ? can thy spirit wonder
A great man should decline ?   Nay, an you weep,
I am fallen indeed.
    Cromwell.   How does your grace ?
    Wolsey.   Why, well :
Never so truly happy, my good Cromwell.
I know myself now ; and I feel within me
A peace above all earthly dignities,

[1] playful, reckless.

A still and quiet conscience.   The king has cur'd
    me,
I humbly thank his grace, and from these shoulders,
These ruin'd pillars, out of pity, taken
A load would sink a navy — too much honour.
O, 'tis a burthen, Cromwell, 'tis a burthen
Too heavy for a man that hopes for heaven!
    Cromwell. I am glad your grace has made that
    right use of it.
    Wolsey. I hope I have: I am able now, methinks,
Out of a fortitude of soul I feel,
To endure more miseries and greater far
Than my weak-hearted enemies dare offer.
What news abroad?
    Cromwell.   The heaviest and the worst
Is your displeasure with the king.
    Wolsey.   God bless him!
    Cromwell. The next is, that Sir Thomas More is
    chosen
Lord Chancellor in your place.
    Wolsey.   That's somewhat sudden:
But he's a learnèd man.   May he continue
Long in his highness' favour, and do justice
For truth's sake, and his conscience; that his bones,
When he has run his course and sleeps in blessings,
May have a tomb of orphans' tears wept on 'em!
What more?
    Cromwell. That Cranmer is return'd with welcome,
Install'd Lord Archbishop of Canterbury.
    Wolsey. That's news indeed!

Cromwell.   Last, that the Lady Anne,
Whom the king hath in secrecy long married,
This day was view'd in open as his queen
Going to chapel; and the voice is now
Only about her coronation.
   Wolsey. There was the weight that pull'd me
       down.   O Cromwell!
The king has gone beyond me: all my glories
In that one woman I have lost for ever.
No sun shall ever usher forth mine honours,
Or gild again the noble troops that waited
Upon my smiles.   Go, get thee from me, Cromwell;
I am a poor fallen man, unworthy now
To be thy lord and master.   Seek the king:
That sun, I pray, may never set!   I have told him
What and how true thou art: he will advance thee.
Some little memory of me will stir him
(I know his noble nature) not to let
Thy hopeful service perish too.   Good Cromwell,
Neglect him not; make use now, and provide
For thine own future safety.
   Cromwell.   O my lord!
Must I then leave you? must I needs forego
So good, so noble, and so true a master?
Bear witness, all that have not hearts of iron,
With what a sorrow Cromwell leaves his lord! —
The king shall have my service; but my prayers
For ever and for ever shall be yours.
   Wolsey. Cromwell, I did not think to shed a tear
In all my miseries; but thou hast forc'd me,

Out of thy honest truth, to play the woman.
Let's dry our eyes; and thus far hear me, Cromwell:
And, when I am forgotten, as I shall be,
And sleep in dull, cold marble, where no mention
Of me more must be heard of, say, I taught thee;
Say, Wolsey, that once trod the ways of glory,
And sounded all the depths and shoals of honour,
Found thee a way, out of his wrack, to rise in;
A sure and safe one, though thy master miss'd it.
Mark but my fall, and that that ruin'd me.
Cromwell, I charge thee, fling away ambition:
By that sin fell the angels; how can man, then,
The image of his Maker, hope to win by 't?
Love thyself last: cherish those hearts that hate
    thee:
Corruption wins not more than honesty.
Still in thy right hand carry gentle peace,
To silence envious tongues: be just, and fear not.
Let all the ends thou aim'st at be thy country's,
Thy God's, and truth's: then if thou fall'st, O
    Cromwell!
Thou fall'st a blessèd martyr.   Serve the king;
And, prithee, lead me in:
There take an inventory of all I have,
To the last penny; 'tis the king's: my robe,
And my integrity to heaven, is all
I dare now call mine own.   O Cromwell, Cromwell!
Had I but serv'd my God with half the zeal
I serv'd my king, he would not in mine age
Have left me naked to mine enemies.

FLODDEN FIELD

Sir Walter Scott

(From " Marmion," Canto VI)

HENRY VII. had hoped to secure peace with Scotland by giving his daughter Margaret to James IV. in marriage; but the ambition of Henry VIII. led him to renew the claim to overlordship, and war broke out. At the battle of Flodden Field (1513) James IV. was killed and the Scotch army was ruined.

From the sharp ridges of the hill,
All downward to the banks of Till,
   Was wreathed in sable smoke.
Volumed and fast, and rolling far,
The cloud enveloped Scotland's war,
   As down the hill they broke;
Nor martial shout, nor minstrel tone,
Announced their march; their tread alone,
At times one warning trumpet blown,
   At times a stifled hum,
Told England, from his mountain-throne
   King James did rushing come. —
Scarce could they hear, or see their foes,
   Until at weapon-point they close. —
They close, in clouds of smoke and dust,
With sword-sway, and with lance's thrust;
   And such a yell was there,
Of sudden and portentous birth,
As if men fought upon the earth,
And fiends in upper air;
O life and death were in the shout,
Recoil and rally, charge and rout,

And triumph and despair.
Long look'd the anxious squires ; their eye
Could in the darkness nought descry.

At length the freshening western blast
Aside the shroud of battle cast ;
And, first, the ridge of mingled spears
Above the brightening cloud appears ;
And in the smoke the pennons flew,
As in the storm the white sea-mew.
Then mark'd they, dashing broad and far,
The broken billows of the war,
And plumèd crests of chieftains brave,
Floating like foam upon the wave ;
　But nought distinct they see :
Wide raged the battle on the plain ;
Spears shook, and falchions flash'd amain ;
Fell England's arrow-flight like rain ;
Crests rose, and stoop'd, and rose again,
　Wild and disorderly.
Amid the scene of tumult, high
They saw Lord Marmion's falcon fly :
And stainless Tunstall's banner white,
And Edmund Howard's lion bright,
Still bear them bravely in the fight :
　Although against them come,
Of gallant Gordons many a one,
And many a stubborn highlandman,
And many a rugged Border clan,
　With Huntly, and with Home.
　　*　　*　　*　　*　　*　　*　　*

But as they left the dark'ning heath,
More desperate grew the strife of death.
The English shafts in volleys hail'd,
In headlong charge their horse assail'd;
Front, flank, and rear, the squadrons sweep
To break the Scottish circle deep,
    That fought around their King.
But yet, though thick the shafts as snow,
Though charging knights like whirlwinds go,
Though bill-men ply the ghastly blow,
Unbroken was the ring;
The stubborn spear-men still made good
Their dark impenetrable wood,
Each stepping where his comrade stood,
    The instant that he fell.
No thought was there of dastard flight;
Link'd in the serried phalanx tight,
Groom fought like noble, squire like knight,
    As fearlessly and well;
Till utter darkness closed her wing
O'er their thin host and wounded King.
Then skilful Surrey's sage commands
Led back from strife his shatter'd bands;
And from the charge they drew,
As mountain-waves, from wasted lands
    Sweep back to ocean blue.
Then did their loss his foemen know;
Their King, their Lords, their mightiest low,
They melted from the field, as snow,
When streams are swoln and south winds blow,
    Dissolves in silent dew.

Tweed's echoes heard the ceaseless plash,
  While many a broken band,
Disorder'd, through her currents dash,
  To gain the Scottish land ;
To town and tower, to down and dale,
To tell red Flodden's dismal tale,
And raise the universal wail.
Tradition, legend, tune, and song,
Shall many an age that wail prolong ;
Still from the sire the son shall hear
Of the stern strife and carnage drear,
  Of Flodden's fatal field,
Where shiver'd was fair Scotland's spear,
  And broken was her shield.

EDINBURGH AFTER FLODDEN

William Edmondstoune Aytoun

THE death of James IV. left Scotland a prey to all the dangers of
a long minority. His son, James V., was hardly a twelvemonth old.
When but thirty years of age he died, leaving an infant daughter, Mary
Stuart, sole heir to the throne.

I

News of battle ! — news of battle !
  Hark ! 'tis ringing down the street :
And the archways and the pavement
  Bear the clang of hurrying feet.
News of battle ! who hath brought it ?
  News of triumph ? Who should bring

Tidings from our noble army,
  Greetings from our gallant King?
All last night we watched the beacons
  Blazing on the hills afar,
Each one bearing, as it kindled,
  Message of the opened war.
All night long the northern streamers
  Shot across the trembling sky:
Fearful lights, that never beckon
  Save when kings or heroes die.

II

News of battle! Who hath brought it?
  All are thronging to the gate;
"Warder — warder! open quickly!
  Man — is this a time to wait?"
And the heavy gates are opened:
  Then a murmur long and loud,
And a cry of fear and wonder
  Bursts from out the bending crowd.
For they see in battered harness
  Only one hard-stricken man;
And his weary steed is wounded,
  And his cheek is pale and wan:
Spearless hangs a bloody banner
  In his weak and drooping hand —
God! can that be Randolph Murray,
  Captain of the city band?

III

Round him crush the people, crying,
  "Tell us all — oh, tell us true!

Where are they who went to battle,
  Randolph Murray, sworn to you?
Where are they, our brothers — children?
  Have they met the English foe?
Why art thou alone, unfollowed?
  Is it weal or is it woe?"
Like a corpse the grisly warrior
  Looks from out his helm of steel;
But no word he speaks in answer —
  Only with his armèd heel
Chides his weary steed, and onward
  Up the city streets they ride;
Fathers, sisters, mothers, children,
  Shrieking, praying by his side.
"By the God that made thee, Randolph!
  Tell us what mischance hath come."
Then he lifts his riven banner,
  And the asker's voice is dumb.

IV

The elders of the city
  Have met within their hall —
The men whom good King James had charged
  To watch the tower and wall.
"Your hands are weak with age," he said,
  "Your hearts are stout and true;
So bide ye in the Maiden Town,
  While others fight for you.
My trumpet from the Border-side
  Shall send a blast so clear,

That all who wait within the gate
   That stirring sound may hear.
Or, if it be the will of heaven
   That back I never come,
And if, instead of Scottish shouts,
   Ye hear the English drum, —
Then let the warning bells ring out,
   Then gird you to the fray,
Then man the walls like burghers stout,
   And fight while fight you may.
'Twere better that in fiery flame
   The roofs should thunder down,
Than that the foot of foreign foe
   Should trample in the town ! ''

V

Then in came Randolph Murray, —
   His step was slow and weak,
And, as he doffed his dinted helm,
   The tears ran down his cheek :
They fell upon his corslet
   And on his mailèd hand,
As he gazed around him wistfully,
   Leaning sorely on his brand.
And none who then beheld him
   But straight were smote with fear,
For a bolder and a sterner man
   Had never couched a spear.
They knew so sad a messenger
   Some ghastly news must bring ;

And all of them were fathers,
  And their sons were with the King.

VI

And up then rose the Provost —
  A brave old man was he,
Of ancient name, and knightly fame,
  And chivalrous degree.
He ruled our city like a Lord
  Who brooked no equal here,
And ever for the townsman's rights
  Stood up 'gainst prince and peer.
And he had seen the Scottish host
  March from the Borough-muir,
With music-storm and clamorous shout,
And all the din that thunders out
  When youth's of victory sure.
But yet a dearer thought had he, —
  For, with a father's pride,
He saw his last remaining son
  Go forth by Randolph's side,
With casque on head and spur on heel,
  All keen to do and dare ;
And proudly did that gallant boy
  Dunedin's [1] banner bear.
Oh ! woful now was the old man's look,
  And he spake right heavily —
" Now, Randolph, tell thy tidings,
  However sharp they be !

[1] Edinburgh's.

Woe is written on thy visage,
    Death is looking from thy face:
Speak! though it be of overthrow —
    It cannot be disgrace!"

VII

Right bitter was the agony
    That wrung that soldier proud:
Thrice did he strive to answer,
    And thrice he groaned aloud.
Then he gave the riven banner
    To the old man's shaking hand,
Saying — "That is all I bring ye
    From the bravest of the land!
Ay! ye may look upon it —
    It was guarded well and long,
By your brothers and your children,
    By the valiant and the strong.
One by one they fell around it,
    As the archers laid them low,
Grimly dying, still unconquered,
    With their faces to the foe.
Ay! ye may well look upon it —
    There is more than honour there,
Else, be sure, I had not brought it
    From the field of dark despair.
Never yet was royal banner
    Steeped in such a costly dye;
It hath lain upon a bosom
    Where no other shroud shall lie.

Sirs! I charge you, keep it holy,
  Keep it as a sacred thing,
For the stain ye see upon it
  Was the life-blood of your King!"

LAMENT FOR FLODDEN FIELD

JANE ELLIOTT

WHEN night fell at last on Flodden Field, ten thousand Scots lay
dead upon the hillside.

I've heard them lilting [1] at our ewe-milking,
  Lasses a' lilting before dawn o' day;
But now they are moaning on ilka [2] green loaning [3] —
  The Flowers of the Forest are a' wede away.

At bughts, [4] in the morning, nae blythe lads are
    scorning, [5]
  Lasses are lonely and dowie [6] and wae; [7]
Nae daffin', [8] nae gabbin', [9] but sighing and sabbing,
  Ilk ane lifts her leglin [10] and hies her away.

In har'st, at the shearing, nae youths now are jeering,
  Bandsters [11] are lyart, [12] and runkled, [13] and grey;
At fair or at preaching, nae wooing, nae fleeching [14] —
  The Flowers of the Forest are a' wede away.

At e'en, in the gloaming, nae younkers are roaming
  'Bout stacks wi' the lasses at bogle [15] to play;

[1] singing blithely.   [2] every.   [3] lane.
[4] cattle-pens.   [5] teasing.   [6] downcast.
[7] sorrowful.   [8] joking.   [9] chattering.
[10] milk-pail.   [11] sheaf-binders. [12] grizzled.
[13] wrinkled.   [14] coaxing.   [15] ghost.

But ilk ane sits drearie, lamenting her dearie —
The Flowers of the Forest are weded away.

Dool and wae [1] for the order, sent our lads to the
Border!
The English, for ance, by guile wan the day;
The Flowers of the Forest, that fought aye the fore-
most,
The prime of our land, are cauld in the clay.

We'll hear nae mair lilting at the ewe-milking;
Women and bairns are heartless and wae;
Sighing and moaning on ilka green loaning —
The Flowers of the Forest are a' wede away.

LADY JANE GREY

JOHN WEBSTER

(From "The Famous History of Sir Thomas Wyatt")

HENRY VIII. left three children, — Mary, the daughter of Katharine
of Aragon; Elizabeth, daughter of Anne Boleyn; and an only son,
Edward, who succeeded him. Edward VI. was a boy of nine years
when he came to the throne (1546). His short reign was troubled by
ecclesiastical controversy and by plots as to the succession. The king
was induced by his Protestant advisers to set aside both his sisters and
to declare in favor of Lady Jane Grey, the daughter of the younger
sister of Henry VIII., and a Protestant. Lady Jane was actually
crowned (July 10, 1553), but she reigned only eleven days. The
friends of Mary Tudor proclaimed Henry's daughter queen, and she
was everywhere acknowledged as the rightful successor to the throne.
Lady Jane and her husband, Guildford Dudley, were arrested and con-
fined in the Tower. They were tried for treason and condemned, but

[1] dole and woe

the order for their execution was withheld some months. The re-
bellion of Sir Thomas Wyatt soon rendered Mary morbidly jealous
of her rival, and the death warrant was sent to the Tower (February
9, 1554).

SCENE. *A Room in Sion House, London.*
(*Enter Guildford and Jane.*)

Guild. Our cousin king is dead.

Jane. Alas, how small an urn contains a king!
He, that rul'd all even with his princely breath,
Is forc'd to stoop now to the stroke of death.
Heard you not the proclamation?

Guild. I hear of it, and I give credit to it:
What great men fear to be, their fears make greater.
Our fathers grow ambitious,
And would force us sail in mighty tempests,
And are not lords of what they do possess.
Are not thy thoughts as great?

Jane. I have no thoughts so rank, so grown to head
As are our fathers' pride.
Troth, I do enjoy a kingdom, having thee;
And so[1] my pain be prosperous in that,
What care I though a sheep-cote be my palace
Or fairest roof of honour.   [*Exeunt.*

*　　*　　*　　*　　*　　*　　*

SCENE. *An Apartment in the Castle of Framlingham.*
(*Enter Queen Mary, with a prayer-book in her hand,*
like a nun.)

Mary. Thus like a nun, not like a princess born,
Descended from the royal Henry's loins,

[1] if.

Live I environ'd in a house of stone.
My brother Edward lives in pomp and state;
I in a mansion here all ruinate.
Their rich attire, delicious banquetting,
Their several pleasures, all their pride and honour,
I have forsaken for a rich prayer-book.
The golden mines of wealthy India
Are all as dross comparèd to thy sweetness:
Thou art the joy and comfort of the poor;
The everlasting bliss in thee we find.
This little volume, enclosèd in this hand,
Is richer than the empire of this land.

(*Enter Sir Henry Bedingfield.*)

Beding. Pardon me, madam, that so boldly I press
Into your chamber: I salute your highness
With the high style of queen.

Mary. Queen! may it be?
Or jest you at my lowering misery?

Beding. Your brother king is dead,
And you the Catholic queen must now succeed.

Mary. I see my God at length hath heard my prayer.
You, Sir Harry, for your glad tidings,
Shall be held in honour and due regard.

(*Enter Sir Thomas Wyatt.*)

Wyatt. Health to the Lady Mary!
Mary. And why not queen, Sir Thomas?
Wyatt. Ask that of Suffolk's duke, and great
Northumberland,
Who in your stead have crown'd another.

Mary. Another queen, Sir Thomas, we alive,
The true immediate heiress of our dread father!

Wyatt. Nothing more true than that,
Nothing more true than you are the true heir.
Come, leave this cloister, and be seen abroad :
Your very sight will stir the people's hearts,
And make them cheerly for Queen Mary cry.
One comfort I can tell you : the tenants
Of the Dukes Northumberland and Suffolk
Denied their aid in these unlawful arms ;
To all the council I denied my hand,
And for King Henry's issue still will stand.

Mary. Your counsel, good Sir Thomas, is so pithy
That I am won to like it.

Wyatt. Come, let us straight
From hence, from Framlingham. Cheer your spirits.
I'll to the dukes at Cambridge, and discharge
Them all. — Prosper me, God, in these affairs !
I lov'd the father well, I lov'd the son,
And for the daughter I through death will run.

        [Exeunt.

 * * * * * * *

SCENE. LONDON. *A Room in the Royal Palace. —
Queen Mary, Wyatt, Arundel, and Lords.*

Arun. Count Egmont, the ambassador from Spain,
Attends your highness' answer 'bout those letters
Sent from the emperor in his son's behalf.

 * * * * * * *

Wyatt. Which of you all dares justify this match,
And be not touch'd in conscience with an oath ?

Remember, O, remember, I beseech you,
King Henry's last will and his last act at court!
I mean that royal act of parliament
That does prohibit Spaniards from the land,
That will and act to which you all are sworn ;
And do not damn your souls with perjury.

    Q. Mary. But that we know thee, Wyatt, to be true
Unto the crown of England and to us,
Thy over-boldness should be paid with death :
But cease, for fear your liberal tongue offend. —
With one consent, my lords, you like this match ?

    Omnes, except Wyatt. We do, great sovereign.

    Q. Mary.   Call in Count Egmont, honourable lords.

            (*Enter Egmont.*)

We have determin'd of your embassy,
And thus I plight our love to Philip's heart.
Embark you straight ; the wind blows wondrous fair :
Till he shall land in England I'm all care.

              [*Exeunt all except `Wyatt.*

    Wyatt. And ere he land in England, I will offer
My loyal breast for him to tread upon.
O, who so forward, Wyatt, as thyself
To raise this troublesome queen in this her throne?
Philip is a Spaniard, a proud nation,
Whom naturally our countrymen abhor.
Assist me, gracious heavens, and you shall see
What hate I bear unto their slavery !
I'll into Kent, there muster up my friends,
To save this country, and this realm defend.

                  [*Exit.*

SCENE. *A Room in the Tower.   Enter Guildford,*
Jane, and Lieutenant.

Guild. Good morrow to the partner of my woe.

Jane. Good morrow to my lord, my lovely Dudley :
Why do you look so sad, my dearest lord ?

Guild. Nay, why doth Jane thus with a heavy eye,
And a defected look, salute the day ?
Sorrow doth ill become thy silver brow :
Sad grief lies dead, so long as thou liv'st fair ;
In my Jane's joy I do not care for care.

Jane. My looks, my love, are sorted with my heart :
The sun himself doth scantly show his face.
Out of this firm grate you may perceive
The Tower-hill throng'd with store of people,
As if they gap'd for some strange novelty.

Guild. Though sleep do seldom dwell in men of
care,
Yet I did this night sleep, and this night dream'd
My princely father, great Northumberland,
Was married to a stately bride ;
And then methought, just on his bridal day,
A poison'd draught did take his life away.

Jane. Let not fond visions so appal my love ;
For dreams do oftentimes contràry prove.

Guild. The nights are tedious, and the days are
sad :
And see you how the people stand in heaps,
Each man sad-looking on his oppos'd object,
As if a general passion possess'd them ?
Their eyes do seem as dropping as the moon,

As if preparèd for a tragedy;
For never swarms of people there do tread,
But to rob life and to enrich the dead,
And show they wept.

Lieut. My lord, they did so, for I was there.

Guild. I pray, resolve us, good Master Lieutenant,
Who was it yonder that tender'd up his life
To nature's death?

Lieut. Pardon me, my lord;
'Tis felony to acquaint you with the death
Of any prisoner; yet, to resolve your grace,
It was your father, great Northumberland,
That this day lost his head.

Guild. Peace rest his soul!
His sins be buried in his grave,
And not remember'd in his epitaph! —
But who comes here?

Jane. My father prisoner!

(*Enter Suffolk, guarded forth.*)

Suff. O Jane, now naught but fear! thy title and
Thy state thou now must leave for a small grave.
Had I been contented to ha' been great, I had stood;
But now my rising is pull'd down with blood.
Farewell! — Point me my house of prayers.

Jane.   Is grief
So short? 'Twas wont to be full of words, 'tis true;
But now death's lesson bids a cold adieu.
Farewell! Thus friends on desperate journeys part;
Breaking off words with tears, that swell the heart.

[*Exit Suffolk, guarded.*

Lieut. 'Tis the pleasure of the queen that you
    part lodgings
Till your arraignment, which must be to-morrow.
Jane. Good Master Lieutenant, let us pray to-
    gether.
Lieut. Pardon me, madam, I may not; they that
    owe [1] you, sway me.
Guild. Entreat not, Jane: though he our bodies
    part,
Our souls shall meet: farewell, my love!
Jane. My Dudley, my own heart!   [*Exeunt.*

A PRAISE OF PRINCESS MARY

John Heywood

"Bloody Mary" has not left an amiable memory, but she had at
least one faithful friend. John Heywood, singer, jester, playwright,
and actor, was chief entertainer to Henry VIII.'s court, and, though a
loyal Romanist, was protected by the young King Edward. His at-
tachment to Mary was genuine. When the fanatic queen lay on her
death-bed, he was called to try and cheer her with his sprightly talk
and stories. The following song he wrote for her when she was a
princess of eighteen, in deep disgrace as daughter of the divorced
Katharine and with no other voice than this poor singer's raised in
her honor.

If all the world were sought full far,
    Who could find such a wight?
Her beauty twinkleth like a star
    Within the frosty night.

----
[1] own.

Her colour comes and goes
    With such a goodly grace,
More ruddy than the rose,
    Within her lively face.

The mirth that she doth use
    Is mixt with shamefastness.
All vices she eschews
    And hateth idleness.

She doth as far exceed
    These women nowadays,
As doth the flower the weed,
    And more, a thousand ways.

This praise I shall her give, —
    When Death doth what he can,
Her honest name shall live
    Within the mouth of man.

QUEEN MARY

LORD TENNYSON

THE girlhood of Mary had been an unhappy one. Her Spanish blood and her devotion to the Roman Catholic religion drew upon her the cordial dislike of Henry VIII. She was guarded as though she were plotting treason, and her title to the throne was denied. The people loved her because she was ill-treated and were determined that justice should be done her. By blind pursuit of her own purposes Mary forfeited their confidence. She was bent on restoring the Pope's authority in England and on taking for a husband Philip II., King of Spain. The marriage was heartily disliked by the people and gave origin to numerous plots to place the Princess Elizabeth on the throne. The rigorous persecution of Protestants rendered the queen hateful to her subjects and had the effect of furthering the Reformation.

ACT III

Scene I. *A Street in London.*

(*The King and Queen pass, attended by Peers of the Realm, Officers of State, etc. Cannon shot off.*)

Crowd. Philip and Mary, Philip and Mary!
Long live the King and Queen, Philip and Mary!
    Stafford. They smile as if content with one another.
    Bagenhall. A smile abroad is oft a scowl at home.

    *   *   *   *   *   *   *

    (*Enter Gardiner turning back from the procession.*)

    Gardiner. Knave, wilt thou wear thy cap before
      the Queen?
    Man. My Lord, I stand so squeezed among the
      crowd
I cannot lift my hands unto my head.
    Gardiner. Knock off his cap there, some of you
      about him!
See there be others that can use their hands.
Thou art one of Wyatt's men?
    Man.   No, my Lord, no.
    Gardiner. Thy name, thou knave?
    Man.   I am nobody, my Lord.
    Gardiner (*shouting*). God's passion! knave, thy
      name?
    Man.   I have ears to hear.
    Gardiner. Ay, rascal, if I leave thee ears to hear.
Find out his name and bring it to me. (*To Attendant.*)
    Attendant.   Ay, my Lord.

Gardiner. Knave, thou shalt lose thine ears and
      find thy tongue,
And shalt be thankful if I leave thee that.

****

Rascal! — this land is like a hill of fire,
One crater opens when another shuts.
But so I get the laws against the heretic,
Spite of Lord Paget and Lord William Howard,
And others of our Parliament, revived,
I will show fire on my side — stake and fire —
Sharp work and short.   The knaves are easily cow'd.
Follow their Majesties.

                    [*Exit.   The crowd following.*

Bagenhall.   As proud as Becket.

Stafford. You would not have him murder'd as
      Becket was ?

Bagenhall. No — murder fathers murder : but I say
There is no man — there was one woman with us —
It was a sin to love her married, dead
I cannot choose but love her.

Stafford.   Lady Jane ?

Crowd (*going off*). God save their Graces !

Stafford.   Did you see her die ?

Bagenhall. No, no ; her innocent blood had blinded
      me.
You call me too black-blooded — true enough
Her dark dead blood is in my heart with mine.
If ever I cry out against the Pope
Her dark dead blood that ever moves with mine
Will stir the living tongue and make the cry.

Stafford. Yet doubtless you can tell me how she
died ?

Bagenhall. Seventeen — and knew eight languages
— in music

Peerless — her needle perfect, and her learning
Beyond the churchmen : yet so meek, so modest,
So wife-like humble to the trivial boy
Mismatch'd with her for policy !   I have heard
She would not take a last farewell of him,
She fear'd it might unman him for his end.
She could not be unmann'd — no, nor outwoman'd —
Seventeen — a rose of grace !
Girl never breathed to rival such a rose :
Rose never blew that equall'd such a bud.

Stafford. Pray you go on.

Bagenhall.   She came upon the scaffold
And said she was condemn'd to die for treason :
She had but follow'd the device of those
Her nearest kin : she thought they knew the laws.
But for herself, she knew but little law,
And nothing of the titles to the crown ;
She had no desire for that, and wrung her hands,
And trusted God would save her thro' the blood
Of Jesus Christ alone.

Stafford.   Pray you go on.

Bagenhall. Then knelt and said the Miserere Mei —
But all in English, mark you ; rose again,
And, when the headsman prayed to be forgiven,
Said, " You will give me my true crown at last.
But do it quickly ; " then all wept but she,

Who changed not colour when she saw the block,
But ask'd him, childlike: " Will you take it off
Before I lay me down ? "   " No, madam," he said,
Gasping ; and when her innocent eyes were bound,
She, with her poor blind hands feeling — " Where
    is it?
Where is it ? " — You must fancy that which follow'd,
If you have heart to do it.

  Crowd (in the distance). God save their Graces !
  Stafford. Their Graces, our disgraces ! God con-
    found them !

Scene V. Woodstock.

Elizabeth, Lady in Waiting.

  Lady. The colours of our Queen are green and
    white,
These fields are only green, they make me gape.
  Elizabeth. There's whitethorn, girl.
  Lady.   Ay, for an hour in May.
But Court is always May, buds out in masks,
Breaks into feather'd merriments, and flowers
In silken pageants.   Why do they keep us here ?
Why still suspect your Grace ?
  Elizabeth.   Hard upon both.

    (*Writes on the window with a diamond.*)

        Much suspected, of me
        Nothing proven can be,
           Quoth Elizabeth, prisoner.
  Lady. What hath your Highness written ?

Elizabeth.   A true rhyme.
Lady. Cut with a diamond; so to last like truth.
Elizabeth. Ay, if truth last.
Lady.   But truth, they say, will out,
So it must last.   It is not like a word,
That comes and goes in uttering.
Elizabeth.   Truth, a word!
The very Truth and very Word are one.
But truth of story, which I glanced at, girl,
Is like a word that comes from olden days,
And passes thro' the peoples: every tongue
Alters it passing, till it spells and speaks
Quite other than at first.
Lady.   I do not follow.

     *   *   *   *   *   *   *

Milkmaid (*singing without*).
  Shame upon you, Robin,
    Shame upon you now!
  Kiss me would you? with my hands
    Milking the cow?
    Daisies grow again,
    Kingcups blow again,
  And you came and kiss'd me milking the cow.

  Robin came behind me,
    Kiss'd me well I vow;
  Cuff him could I? with my hands
    Milking the cow?
    Swallows fly again,
    Cuckoos cry again,
  And you came and kiss'd me milking the cow.

> Come, Robin, Robin,
> Come and kiss me now;
> Help it can I? with my hands
> Milking the cow?
> Ringdoves coo again,
> All things woo again,
> Come behind and kiss me milking the cow!

Elizabeth. Right honest and red-cheek'd; Robin
　　was violent,
And she was crafty — a sweet violence,
And a sweet craft. I would I were a milkmaid,
To sing, love, marry, churn, brew, bake, and die,
Then have my simple headstone by the church,
And all things lived and ended honestly.
I could not if I would. I am Harry's daughter:

　　　*　　*　　*　　*　　*　　*　　*

I never lay my head upon the pillow
But that I think, "Wilt thou lie there to-morrow?"
How oft the falling axe, that never fell,
Hath shock'd me back into the daylight truth
That it may fall to-day! Those damp, black, dead
Nights in the Tower; dead — with the fear of death —
Too dead ev'n for a death-watch! Toll of a bell,
Stroke of a clock, the scurrying of a rat
Affrighted me, and then delighted me,
For there was life — And there was life in death —
The little murder'd princes, in a pale light,
Rose hand in hand, and whisper'd, "Come away,
The civil wars are gone forevermore:

Thou last of all the Tudors, come away,
With us is peace !" The last ? It was a dream :
I must not dream, not wink, but watch.

ACT IV

Scene III. *St. Mary's Church.*

(*Cole in the Pulpit, Lord Williams of Thame presiding. Lord William Howard, Lord Paget, and others. Cranmer enters between Soto and Villa Garcia, and the whole choir strike up " Nunc Dimittis." Cranmer is set upon a Scaffold before the people.*)

    *   *   *   *   *   *   *

   (*Cries on all sides.*) Pull him down ! Away with him.

   Cole. Ay, stop the heretic's mouth. Hale him away.

   Williams. Harm him not, harm him not, have him to the fire.

(*Cranmer goes out between two Friars, smiling; hands reached to him from the crowd. Lord William Howard and Lord Paget are left alone in the church.*)

   Paget. The nave and aisles all empty as a fool's jest!
No, here's Lord William Howard. What, my Lord,
You have not gone to see the burning ?
   Howard.   Fie !
To stand at ease, and stare as at a show,

And watch a good man bùrn.   Never again.
I saw the deaths of Latimer and Ridley.
Moreover tho' a Catholic, I would not,
For the pure honour of our common nature,
Hear what I might — another recantation
Of Cranmer at the stake.
   Paget.   You'd not hear that.
He pass'd out smiling, and he walk'd upright;
His eye was like a soldier's, whom the general
He looks to and he leans on as his God,
Hath rated for some backwardness and bidd'n him
Charge one against a thousand, and the man
Hurls his soiled life against the pikes and dies.

    *   *   *   *   *   *   *

Howard.   But see,

(Enter Peters.)

Peters, my gentleman, an honest Catholic,
Who follow'd with the crowd to Cranmer's fire.
One that would neither misreport nor lie,
Not to gain paradise : no, nor if the Pope
Charged him to do it — he is white as death.
Peters, how pale you look! you bring the smoke
Of Cranmer's burning with you.
   Peters.   Twice or thrice
The smoke of Cranmer's burning wrapt me round.
   Howard. Peters, you know me Catholic, but Eng-
     lish.
Did he die bravely?   Tell me that, or leave
All else untold.

Peters.　　　　My Lord, he died most bravely.
Howard. Then tell me all.
Paget.　　　　　　Ay, Master Peters, tell us.
Peters. You saw him how he past among the
　　crowd ;
And ever as he walk'd the Spanish friars
Still plied him with entreaty and reproach .
But Cranmer, as the helmsman at the helm
Steers, ever looking to the happy haven
Where he shall rest at night, moved to his death ;
And I could see that many silent hands
Came from the crowd and met his own ; and thus,
When we had come where Ridley burnt with Latimer,
He, with a cheerful smile, as one whose mind
Is all made up, in haste put off the rags
They had mock'd his misery with, and all in white,
His long white beard, which he had never shaven
Since Henry's death, down-sweeping to the chain,
Wherewith they bound him to the stake, he stood,
More like an ancient father of the Church,
Than heretic of these times ; and still the friars
Plied him, but Cranmer only shook his head,
Or answer'd them in smiling negatives ;
Whereat Lord Williams gave a sudden cry : —
" Make short ! make short ! " and so they lit the
　　wood.
Then Cranmer lifted his left hand to heaven,
And thrust his right into the bitter flame ;
And crying, in his deep voice, more than once,
" This hath offended — this unworthy hand ! "

So held it till it all was burn'd, before
The flame had reach'd his body; I stood near —
Mark'd him — he never uttered moan of pain :
He never stirr'd or writhed, but, like a statue,
Unmoving in the greatness of the flame,   ·
Gave up the ghost; and so past martyr-like —
Martyr I may not call him — past — but whither ?
   Paget. To purgatory, man, to purgatory.
   Peters. Nay, but, my lord, he denied purgatory.
   Paget. Why then to heaven, and God ha' mercy
     on him.

ACT V

SCENE I.   LONDON.   *Hall in the Palace.*

Queen.   Sir Nicholas Heath.

(*Enter Philip.*)

   Philip. Sir Nicholas tells you true,
And you must look to Calais when I go.
   Mary. Go! must you go, indeed — again — so
     soon ?
Why, nature's licensed vagabond, the swallow,
That might live always in the sun's warm heart,
Stays longer here in our poor north than you : —
Knows where he nested — ever comes again.
   Philip. And, Madam, so shall I.
   Mary.   O, will you ? will you ?
I am faint with fear that you will come no more.

Philip. Ay, ay ; but many voices call me hence.

Mary. Voices — I hear unhappy rumours — nay,
I say not, I believe. What voices call you
Dearer than mine that should be dearest to you?
Alas, my Lord! what voices and how many?

Philip. The voices of Castile and Aragon,
Granada, Naples, Sicily, and Milan, —
The voices of Franche-Comté, and the Netherlands,
The voices of Peru and Mexico,
Tunis and Oran, and the Philippines,
And all the fair spice-islands of the East.

Mary (*admiringly*). You are the mightiest mon-
arch upon earth,
I but a little Queen ; and so, indeed,
Need you the more ; and wherefore could you not
Helm the huge vessel of your state, my liege,
Here, by the side of her who loves you most?

Philip. No, Madam, no! a candle in the sun
Is all but smoke — a star beside the moon
Is all but lost; your people will not crown me —
Your people are as cheerless as your clime ;
Hate me and mine : witness the brawls, the gibbets.
Here swings a Spaniard — there an Englishman ;
The peoples are unlike as their complexion ;
Yet will I be your swallow and return —
But now I cannot bide.

Mary.   Not to help *me*?
They hate *me* also for my love to you,
My Philip ; and these judgments on the land —
Harvestless autumns, horrible agues, plague —

Philip. The blood and sweat of heretics at the
    stake
Is God's best dew upon the barren field.
Burn more!

  Mary.   I will, I will; and you will stay.

            *   *   *   *   *   *   *

Philip.   No!

  Mary. What, not one day?

  Philip.   You beat upon the rock.

  Mary. And I am broken there.

  Philip.   Is this the place
To wail in, Madam? what! a public hall.
Go in, I pray you.

  Mary.   Do not seem so changed.
Say go: but only say it lovingly.

            SCENE II.   *A Room in the Palace.*

            Mary and Lady Clarence.

  Mary. Clarence, they hate me; even while I
    speak
There lurks a silent dagger, listening
In some dark closet, some long gallery, drawn,
And panting for my blood as I go by.

  Lady Clarence. Nay, Madam, there be loyal
    papers too,
And I have often found them.

  Mary.   Find me one

Lady Clarence. Ay, Madam; but Sir Nicholas
    Heath, the Chancellor,
Would see your Highness.
    Mary.   Wherefore should I see him?
    Lady Clarence. Well, Madam, he may bring you
    news from Philip.
    Mary. So, Clarence.
    Lady Clarence. Let me first put up your hair;
It tumbles all abroad.
    Mary.   And the gray dawn
Of an old age that never will be mine
Is all the clearer seen. No, no; what matters?
Forlorn I am, and let me look forlorn.

          (*Enter Sir Nicholas Heath.*)

    Heath. I bring your Majesty such grievous news
I grieve to bring it. Madam, Calais is taken.
    Mary. What traitor spoke? Here, let my cousin
    Pole
Seize him and burn him for a Lutheran.
    Heath. Her Highness is unwell. I will retire.
    Lady Clarence. Madam, your Chancellor, Sir Nicho-
    las Heath.
    Mary. Sir Nicholas? I am stunn'd — Nicholas
    Heath?
Methought some traitor smote me on the head.
What said you, my good Lord, that our brave Eng-
    lish
Had sallied out from Calais and driven back
The Frenchmen from their trenches?
    Heath.   Alas! no.

That gateway to the mainland over which
Our flag hath floated for two hundred years
Is France again.

     *   *   *   *   *   *   *

    Mary. I hoped I had served God with all my might!
It seems I have not.   Ah, much heresy
Shelter'd in Calais.   Saints, I have rebuilt
Your shrines, set up your broken images ;
Be comfortable to me.   Suffer not
That my brief reign in England be defamed
Thro' all her angry chronicles hereafter
By loss of Calais.   Grant me Calais.   Philip,
We have made war upon the Holy Father
All for your sake : what good could come of that ?
    Lady Clarence. No, Madam, not against the Holy
      Father :
You did but help King Philip's war with France.
Your troops were never down in Italy.
    Mary. I am a byword.   Heretic and rebel
Point at me and make merry.   Philip gone !
And Calais gone !   Time that I were gone too !
    Lady Clarence. Nay, if the fetid gutter had a voice
And cried I was not clean, what should I care ?
Or you, for heretic cries ?   And I believe,
Spite of your melancholy Sir Nicholas,
Your England is as loyal as myself.
    Mary.   (*Seeing a paper on the floor.*)
There, there ! another paper !   Said you not
Many of these were loyal ?   Shall I try
If this be one of such ?

Lady Clarence.   Let it be, let it be.
God pardon me !   I have never yet found one.
                                        (*Aside.*)
   Mary (*reads*). "Your people hate you as your hus-
      band hates you."

Clarence, Clarence, what have I done ? what sin
Beyond all grace, all pardon ?   Mother of God,
Thou knowest never woman meant so well,
And fared so ill in this disastrous world.
My people hate me and desire my death.
   Lady Clarence.   No, Madam, no.
   Mary. My husband hates me, and desires my death.
   Lady Clarence. No, Madam ; these are libels.
   Mary. I hate myself, and I desire my death.
   Lady Clarence. Long live your Majesty ! Shall
      Alice sing you

One of her pleasant songs ?   Alice, my child,
Bring us your lute. (*Alice goes.*) They say the gloom
      of Saul

Was lighten'd by young David's harp.
   Mary.   Too young !
And never knew a Philip.   (*Reënter Alice.*) Give *me*
      the lute.

He hates me.   (*She sings.*)

Hapless doom of woman happy in betrothing !
Beauty passes like a breath and love is lost in loath-
      ing :
Low, my lute : speak low, my lute, but say the world
      is nothing —

                 Low, lute, low !

Love will hover round the flowers when they first
    awaken:
Love will fly the fallen leaf, and not be overtaken;
Low, my lute! oh, low, my lute! we fade and are for-
    saken —
                Low, dear lute, low!

                Take it away! not low enough for me.
  Alice. Your Grace hath a low voice.
  Mary.   How dare you say it?
Even for that he hates me. A low voice
Lost in the wilderness where none can hear!
A voice of shipwreck on a shoreless sea!
A low voice from the dust and from the grave.
                     (*Sitting on the ground.*)
There, am I low enough now?
  Alice. Good Lord! how grim and ghastly looks
    her Grace,
With both her knees drawn upward to her chin.
There was an old-world tomb beside my father's,
And this was open'd and the dead were found
Sitting, and in this fashion: she looks a corpse.

    Scene V. London. *A Room in the Palace.*

(*A Gallery on one side. The moonlight streaming
    through a range of windows on the wall opposite.
    Lady Clarence, Sir William Cecil, Alice.*)

          (*Enter Elizabeth.*)

Elizabeth. The Queen is dead.

Cecil.   Then here she stands ! my homa͜
Elizabeth. She knew me, and acknowledged n
   her heir,
Pray'd me to pay her debts, and keep the Faith ;
Then claspt the cross, and pass'd away in peace.
I left her lying still and beautiful,
More beautiful than in life. Why would you vex
   yourself,
Poor sister ? Sir, I swear I have no heart
To be your Queen. To reign is restless fence,
Tierce, quart, and trickery. Peace is with the dead.
Her life was winter, for her spring was nipt ;
And she loved much : pray God she be forgiven !
   Cecil. Peace with the dead, who never were at peace!
Yet she loved one so much — I needs must say —
That never English monarch dying left
England so little.
   Elizabeth.   But with Cecil's aid
And others, if our person be secured
From traitor stabs — we will make England great.

GLORIANA

EDMUND SPENSER

(From " The Faery Queene," Book V., Canto IX)

ELIZABETH was but twenty-five years of age when she came to the throne. From her mother she inherited beauty and grace; from her father, keen perception and an imperious will. The years during which she lived under a cloud of suspicion had taught her reticence and self-control. The religious controversy that Edward VI. and Mary had so much at heart, meant nothing to Elizabeth. She loved her people and aimed to make England strong and prosperous. Believing that peace was better assured by separation from the church of Rome, she held to the settlement arranged by Henry VIII. and carefully avoided entangling alliances with Romanist and Protestant alike. Philip II. desired to marry her, but she refused this and similar offers, vowing that she would live and die a virgin queen. Englishmen adored her as something more than human.

They, passing by, were guyded by degree
Unto the presence of that gratious Queene;
Who sate on high, that she might all men see,
And might of all men royally be seene,
Upon a throne of gold full bright and sheene,[1]
Adornèd all with gemmes of endless price,
As either might for wealth have gotten bene,
Or could be fram'd by workman's rare device
And all embost with lyons and with flourdelice.[2]

All over her a cloth of state was spred,
Not of rich tissew, nor of cloth of gold,
Nor of ought else that may be richest red,[3]
But like a cloud, as likest may be told,
That her brode spreading wings did wyde unfold;
Whose skirts were bordred with bright sunny beams,
Glistering like gold amongst the plights[4] enrold,
And here and there shooting forth silver streames,
'Mongst which crept little angels through the glittering gleames.

Seemèd those little angels did uphold
The cloth of state, and on their purpled wings

[1] shining.   [2] fleur-de-lys.   [3] described as.   [4] folds.

Did beare the pendants through their nimblesse [1]
  bold;
Besides, a thousand more of such as sings
Hymnes to High God, and carols heavenly things,
Encompassèd the throne on which she sate, —
She, angel-like, the heyre [2] of ancient kings
And mightie conquerors, in royall state;
Whylest kings and kesars [3] at her feet did them
  prostrate.

Thus she did sit in soverayne majestie,
Holding a sceptre in her royall hand,
The sacred pledge of peace and clemencie,
With which High God had blest her happie land,
Maugre [4] so many foes which did withstand:
But at her feet her sword was likewise layde,
Whose long rest rusted the bright steely brand;
Yet when as foes enforst, or friends sought ayde,
She could it sternely draw, that all the world dismayde.

LAMENT OF MARY, QUEEN OF SCOTS, ON THE APPROACH OF SPRING

ROBERT BURNS

MARY STUART, daughter of James V. and sole heir to the throne, had been from her babyhood the centre of intrigue and conspiracy. She had Tudor blood in her veins and was preferred to Elizabeth by zealous Romanists as heir to the English throne. Her marriage (1558) with the dauphin of France brought about a close alliance between Scotland and England's hereditary foe. On the death of her husband she returned to Scotland (1561); but a beautiful woman accustomed to the luxuries of the French court was ill-fitted to cope

[1] nimbleness.   [2] heir.   [3] Cæsars, emperors.   [4] despite.

with the unruly Scotch nobles. After six turbulent years, Mary fled the kingdom and took refuge in England. There she remained a prisoner till her execution (1587).

Now Nature hangs her mantle green
    On every blooming tree,
And spreads her sheets o' daisies white
    Out o'er the grassy lea:
Now Phœbus cheers the crystal streams,
    And gilds the azure skies;
But nought can glad the weary wight
    That fast in durance lies.

Now lav'rocks [1] wake the merry morn,
    Aloft on dewy wing:
The merle,[2] in his noontide bow'r,
    Makes woodland echoes ring;
The mavis [3] mild, wi' many a note,
    Sings drowsy day to rest:
In love and freedom they rejoice,
    Wi' care nor thrall [4] opprest.

Now blooms the lily by the bank,
    The primrose down the brae; [5]
The hawthorn's budding in the glen,
    And milk-white is the slae; [6]
The meanest hind in fair Scotland
    May rove the sweets amang;
But I, the Queen of a' Scotland,
    Maun lie in prison strang.

[1] larks. [2] European blackbird. [3] thrush.
[4] bondage. [5] hillside. [6] sloe, the blackthorn.

I was the Queen o' bonnie France,
  Where happy I hae been;
Fu' lightly rase I in the morn,
  As blithe lay down at e'en:
And I'm the Sov'reign of Scotland
  And monie a traitor there;
Yet here I lie in foreign bands,
  And never ending care.

But as for thee, thou false woman,
  My sister and my fae,
Grim Vengeance, yet, shall whet a sword
  That thro' thy soul shall gae;
The weeping blood in woman's breast
  Was never known to thee;
Nor th' balm that draps on wounds of wo
  Frae woman's pitying e'e.

My son! my son! may kinder stars
  Upon thy fortune shine;
And may those pleasures gild thy reign
  That ne'er wad blink on mine!
God keep thee frae thy mother's faes,
  Or turn their hearts to thee;
And where thou meet'st thy mother's friend,
  Remember him for me!

O! soon, to me, may summer suns
  Nae mair light up the morn!
Nae mair, to me, the autumn winds
  Wave o'er the yellow corn!

> And in the narrow house o' death
>   Let winter round me rave !
> And the next flowers that deck the spring,
>   Bloom on my peaceful grave !

THE ARMADA

(*A Fragment*)

LORD MACAULAY

THE death of Mary was the signal for war. Philip II., thwarted in his purpose to marry Elizabeth, fitted out a great fleet for the invasion of England, aiming to seize the throne and restore the land to the papal jurisdiction. From the Romanist point of view, the expedition was a crusade against heretics, and Spain gave blood and treasure without stint. Philip was bitterly hated in England, and people of all classes resented his attempt to displace their beloved queen. There was no standing army in those days, but every able-bodied man was trained to the use of weapons, and one hundred thousand soldiers were ready to take up arms at a day's notice. The royal navy was quite unequal to the defence of the coast, but English privateers had long been waging war on the galleons of Spain, and English sea-captains were eager for a final bout with the arch-enemy.

The Armada was never able to effect a landing in England. Driven by storms and harassed by a running fire from the English fleet, the Spanish men-of-war made their way up the Channel and around the north of Scotland, only to be dashed in pieces off the wild west coast of Ireland.

Attend, all ye who list to hear our noble England's
     praise ;
I sing of the thrice famous deeds she wrought in
     ancient days,
When that great fleet invincible against her bore in
     vain
The richest spoils of Mexico, the stoutest hearts of
     Spain.

It was about the lovely close of a warm summer day,
There came a gallant merchant-ship full sail to Plym-
    outh bay;
Her crew hath seen Castile's black fleet, beyond
    Aurigny's isle,
At earliest twilight, on the waves lie heaving many a
    mile.
At sunrise she escaped their van, by God's especial
    grace;
And the tall Pinta, till the noon, had held her close
    in chase.
Forthwith a guard at every gun was placed along the
    wall;
The beacon blazed upon the roof of Edgecumbe's
    lofty hall;
Many a light fishing-bark put out to pry along the
    coast;
And with loose rein and bloody spur rode inland
    many a post.
With his white hair unbonneted, the stout old sheriff
    comes;
Behind him march the halberdiers; before him sound
    the drums:
The yeomen round the market cross make clear an
    ample space;
For there behoves him to set up the standard of Her
    Grace:
And haughtily the trumpets peal, and gaily dance the
    bells,
As slow upon the labouring wind the royal blazon
    swells.

Look how the Lion of the sea lifts up his ancient
     crown,
And underneath his deadly paw treads the gay lilies
     down !
So stalked he when he turned to flight, on that famed
     Picard field,
Bohemia's plume, and Genoa's bow, and Cæsar's
     eagle shield.
So glared he when at Agincourt in wrath he turned
     to bay,
And crushed and torn beneath his claws the princely
     hunters lay.
Ho ! strike the flagstaff deep, Sir Knight: ho ! scatter
     flowers, fair maids :
Ho ! gunners, fire a loud salute : ho ! gallants, draw
     your blades :
Thou sun, shine on her joyously ; ye breezes, waft
     her wide ;
Our glorious *semper eadem*, the banner of our pride.

The freshening breeze of eve unfurled that banner's
     massy fold ;
The parting gleam of sunshine kissed that haughty
     scroll of gold ;
Night sank upon the dusky beach, and on the purple
     sea,
Such night in England ne'er had been, nor e'er again
     shall be.
From Eddystone to Berwick bounds, from Lynn to
     Milford Bay,

That time of slumber was as bright and busy as the
day;

For swift to east and swift to west the ghastly war-
flame spread,

High on St. Michael's Mount it shone: it shone on
Beachy Head:

Far on the deep the Spaniard saw, along each south-
ern shire,

Cape beyond cape, in endless range, those twinkling
points of fire.

The fisher left his skiff to rock on Tamar's glittering
waves:

The rugged miners poured to war from Mendip's sun-
less caves:

O'er Longleat's towers, o'er Cranbourne's oaks, the
fiery herald flew:

He roused the shepherds of Stonehenge, the rangers
of Beaulieu.

Right sharp and quick the bells all night rang out
from Bristol town,

And, ere the day, three hundred horse had met on
Clifton Down.

The sentinel on Whitehall gate looked forth into the
night,

And saw o'erhanging Richmond Hill the streak of
blood-red light.

The bugle's note and cannon's roar the deathlike
silence broke,

And with one start, and with one cry, the royal city
woke.

At once on all her stately gates arose the answering
    fires;

At once the wild alarum clashed from all her reeling
    spires;

From all the batteries of the Tower pealed loud the
    voice of fear;

And all the thousand masts of Thames sent back a
    louder cheer:

And from the furthest wards was heard the rush of
    hurrying feet,

And the broad streams of pikes and flags rushed
    down each roaring street;

And broader still became the blaze, and louder still
    the din,

As fast from every village round the horse came spur-
    ring in:

And eastward straight from wild Blackheath the war-
    like errand went,

And roused in many an ancient hall the gallant
    squires of Kent.

Southward from Surrey's pleasant hills flew those
    bright couriers forth;

High on bleak Hampstead's swarthy moor they started
    for the north;

And on, and on, without a pause, untired they bounded
    still;

All night from tower to tower they sprang; they sprang
    from hill to hill;

Till the proud peak unfurled the flag o'er Darwin's
    rocky dales,

Till like volcanoes flared to heaven the stormy hills
    of Wales,
Till twelve fair counties saw the blaze on Malvern's
    lonely height,
Till streamed in crimson on the wind the Wrekin's
    crest of light,
Till broad and fierce the star came forth on Ely's
    stately fane,
And tower and hamlet rose in arms o'er all the bound-
    less plain ;
Till Belvoir's lordly terraces the sign to Lincoln sent,
And Lincoln sped the message on o'er the wide vale
    of Trent :
Till Skiddaw saw the fire that burned on Gaunt's
    embattled pile,
And the red glare on Skiddaw roused the burghers
    of Carlisle.

DRAKE'S DRUM

HENRY NEWBOLT

SIR FRANCIS DRAKE was the most famous of the sea-captains who
won the glorious victory over the Armada and brought to naught the
designs of Philip II. against England. Eight years before, Drake had
sailed round the globe, provisioning his vessels on the way by plunder
from the Spanish colonies. His enemies denounced him on his return
as " the master-thief of the unknown world," but Queen Elizabeth went
aboard his ship, the " Golden Hind," and there dubbed him knight. In
anticipation of the war with Spain, Drake held the Spanish galleons to
be lawful prey and captured treasure-ships and men-of-war on the high
seas, in West Indian waters, in Cadiz harbor, wherever they might be
found. Death overtook this most valiant of pirates on an expedition

to the Spanish Main.   His body was placed in a leaden coffin and
buried off Nombre de Dios, the treasure port of Spanish America.

Drake, he's in his hammock an' a thousand mile away,
  (Capten, art tha sleepin' there below?)
Slung atween the round shot in Nombre Dios Bay,
  An' dreamin' arl the time o' Plymouth Hoe.
Yarnder lumes the island, yarnder lie the ships,
  Wi' sailor lads a-dancin' heel-an'-toe,
An' the shore-lights flashin', an' the night-tide dashin',
  He sees it arl so plainly as he saw et long ago.

Drake he was a Devon man, an' ruled the Devon seas,
  (Capten, art tha sleepin' there below?)
Rovin' tho' his death fell, he went wi' heart at ease,
  An' dreamin' arl the time o' Plymouth Hoe.
"Take my drum to England, hang et by the shore,
  ˙Strike et when your powder's runnin' low;
If the Dons sight Devon, I'll quit the port o' Heaven,
  An' drum them up the Channel as we drummed
    them long ago."

Drake he's in his hammock till the great Armadas
    come,
  (Capten, art tha sleepin' there below?)
Slung atween the round shot, listenin' for the drum,
  An' dreamin' arl the time o' Plymouth Hoe.
Call him on the deep sea, call him up the Sound,
  Call him when ye sail to meet the foe;
Where the old trade's plyin' an' the old flag flyin',
  They shall find him ware and wakin', as they found
    him long ago!

THE REVENGE

A Ballad of the Fleet

Lord Tennyson

In 1591, a squadron of royal men-of-war and privateers was sent out to the Azores in search of treasure-ships from the West Indies. Lord Thomas Howard was in command, and Sir Richard Grenville, vice-admiral. A Spanish fleet followed in hot pursuit. It was so far superior in numbers and equipment that Lord Howard ordered a retreat. Grenville delayed the sailing of his ship, the " Revenge," till he could get his sick men aboard. He then undertook to sail through instead of round about the Spanish galleons. A desperate fight followed — one vessel against fifteen, one hundred men against five thousand. For fifteen hours the English sailors held their own against overwhelming odds, only yielding when their guns were silenced. Sir Richard's exploit has been condemned as foolhardy by most historians, but it served to impress the Spaniards with the unquenchable valor of British seamen and so emphasized the impression wrought by the wreck of the Armada.

I

At Flores in the Azores Sir Richard Grenville lay,
And a pinnace like a flutter'd bird, came flying from
     far away :
" Spanish ships of war at sea ! we have sighted fifty-
     three ! "
Then sware Lord Thomas Howard : " 'Fore God I am
     no coward !
But I cannot meet them here, for my ships are out
     of gear,
And the half my men are sick. I must fly, but follow
     quick.
We are six ships of the line ; can we fight with fifty-
     three ? "

II

Then spake Sir Richard Grenville: " I know you are
    no coward;
You fly them for a moment to fight with them again.
But I've ninety men and more that are lying sick
    ashore.
I should count myself the coward if I left them, my
    Lord Howard,
To these Inquisition dogs and the devildoms of Spain."

III

So Lord Howard passed away with five ships of war
    that day,
Till he melted like a cloud in the silent summer
    heaven;
But Sir Richard bore in hand all his sick men from
    the land
Very carefully and slow,
Men of Biddeford in Devon,
And we laid them on the ballast down below;
For we brought them all aboard,
And they blest him in their pain, that they were not
    left to Spain,
To the thumbscrew and the stake, for the glory of the
    Lord.

IV

He had only a hundred seamen to work the ship and
    to fight,
And he sail'd away from Flores till the Spaniard came
    in sight,

With his huge sea-castles heaving upon the weather
    bow.
" Shall we fight or shall we fly ?
Good Sir Richard, let us know,
For to fight is but to die !
There'll be little of us left by the time this sun be set."
And Sir Richard said again : "We be all good English-
    men.
Let us bang these dogs of Seville, the children of the
    devil,
For I never turn'd my back upon Don or devil yet."

V

Sir Richard spoke, and he laugh'd, and we roared a
    hurrah, and so
The little " Revenge " ran on sheer into the heart of
    the foe,
With her hundred fighters on deck, and her ninety
    sick below ;
For half of their fleet to the right and half to the left
    were seen,
And the little " Revenge " ran on thro' the long sea-
    lane between.

VI

Thousands of their soldiers look'd down from their
    decks and laugh'd,
Thousands of their seamen made mock at the mad
    little craft
Running on and on, till delay'd

By their mountain-like " San Philip " that, of fifteen
    hundred tons,
And up-shadowing high above us with her yawning
    tiers of guns,
Took the breath from our sails, and we stay'd.

VII

And while now the great " San Philip " hung above
    us like a cloud
Whence the thunderbolt will fall
Long and loud,
Four galleons drew away
From the Spanish fleet that day,
And two upon the larboard and two upon the star-
    board lay,
And the battle-thunder broke from them all.

VIII

But anon the great " San Philip " she bethought her-
    self and went,
Having that within her womb that had left her ill-
    content ;
And the rest they came aboard us, and they fought
    us hand to hand,
For a dozen times they came with their pikes and
    musqueteers,
And a dozen times we shook 'em off as a dog that
    shakes his ears
When he leaps from the water to the land.

IX

And the sun went down, and the stars came out far
    over the summer sea,
But never a moment ceased the fight of the one and
    the fifty-three.
Ship after ship, the whole night long, their high-built
    galleons came,
Ship after ship, the whole night long, with her battle-
    thunder and flame;
Ship after ship, the whole night long, drew back with
    her dead and her shame.
For some were sunk and many were shatter'd, and
    so could fight us no more —
God of battles, was ever a battle like this in the world
    before?

X

For he said, " Fight on ! fight on ! "
Tho' his vessel was all but a wreck ;
And it chanced that, when half of the summer night
    was gone,
With a grisly wound to be drest he had left the deck,
But a bullet struck him that was dressing it suddenly
    dead,
And himself he was wounded again in the side and
    the head,
And he said, " Fight on ! fight on ! "

XI

And the night went down, and the sun smiled out far
    over the summer sea,

And the Spanish fleet with broken sides lay round us
    all in a ring;
But they dared not touch us again, for they fear'd
    that we still could sting,
So they watch'd what the end would be.
And we had not fought them in vain,
But in perilous plight were we,
Seeing forty of our poor hundred were slain,
And half of the rest of us maim'd for life
In the crash of the cannonades and the desperate strife;
And the sick men down in the hold were most of
    them stark and cold,
And the pikes were all broken or bent, and the
    powder was all of it spent;
And the masts and the rigging were lying over the
    side;
But Sir Richard cried in his English pride:
"We have fought such a fight for a day and a night
As may never be fought again!
We have won great glory, my men!
And a day less or more,
At sea or ashore,
We die — does it matter when?
Sink me the ship, Master Gunner — sink her, split
    her in twain!
Fall into the hands of God, not into the hands of
    Spain!"

XII

And the gunner said, "Ay, ay," but the seamen
    made reply:

"We have children, we have wives,
And the Lord hath spared our lives.
We will make the Spaniard promise, if we yield, to
    let us go ;
We shall live to fight again and to strike another
    blow."
And the lion there lay dying, and they yielded to the
    foe.

XIII

And the stately Spanish men to their flagship bore
    him then,
Where they laid him by the mast, old Sir Richard
    caught at last,
And they praised him to his face with their courtly
    foreign grace ;
But he rose upon their decks, and he cried :
"I have fought for Queen and Faith like a valiant
    man and true ;
I have only done my duty as a man is bound to do ;
With a joyful spirit I, Sir Richard Grenville, die ! "
And he fell upon their decks, and he died.

XIV

And they stared at the dead that had been so valiant
    and true,
And had holden the power and glory of Spain so cheap
That he dared her with one little ship and his English
    few ;
Was he devil or man ? He was devil for aught they
    knew,

But they sank his body with honour down into the deep,
And they mann'd the " Revenge " with a swarthier
    alien crew,
And away she sail'd with her loss and long'd for her
    own :
When a wind from the lands they had ruin'd awoke
    from sleep,
And the water began to heave and the weather to
    moan,
And or ever that evening ended a great gale blew,
And a wave like the wave that is raised by an earth-
    quake grew,
Till it smote on their hulls and their sails and their
    masts and their flags,
And the whole sea plunged and fell on the shot-
    shatter'd navy of Spain,
And the little " Revenge " herself went down by the
    island crags
To be lost evermore in the main.

QUEEN ELIZABETH

SARAH WILLIAMS

ELIZABETH was seventy years of age when she came to die (1603). Her long reign had been one of the most brilliant in English history. She found the nation weak, wretched, divided by a bitter religious controversy. She left it prosperous, united, and at peace. But the last years of the great queen were embittered by loneliness and by the apparent ingratitude of her people. Her friends and counsellors, the men who had made England strong and victorious, were already dead. Men of the new generation concerned themselves little with the wishes of the dying monarch, so eager were they to curry favor with her successor.

Dying, and loth to die, and long'd to die;
  Is there no pity, O my land, my land?
Is it as naught to you, ye passers-by?
  Will ye not, for a moment, listening stand?

Who shall come after me, is what ye pray;
  Truly ye have not spar'd me all my days.
Tudor, the grand old race, may pass away;
  Stuart, the weak and false, awaits your praise.

Essex, my murder'd darling, tender one,
  Should have been here, my people, but for you;
Now he but haunts me, — oh, my son, my son!
  Would that the queen had err'd, the friend been
    true!

Dudley, my one one love, my spirit halts;
  Would that it had thine now on which to lean;
Faulty thou wert, they said; come back, dear faults, —
  Have I not right to pardon, as a queen?

Truly, 'tis hard to rule, 'tis sore to love,
  All my life long the two have torn my heart;
Now that the end has come, all things to prove,
  I but repent me of my chosen part.

Now to my mother's God, who dwells afar,
  Come I, a broken queen, a woman old;
Smirch'd with the miry way my soul hath trod,
  Weary of life as with a tale twice told.
Thou who dost know what ingrate subjects are,
Hear me, assoil, receive me, God, my God.

TRIUMPH NOW

(For the Accession of James I.)

Thomas Campion

On the death of Elizabeth, James VI. of Scotland succeeded to the throne as James I. The union of the two kingdoms under one monarch promised to end the long quarrel between Scotch and English. Moreover, James had been bred a Protestant, he readily accepted the religious settlement ordained under Elizabeth, and men hoped for peace at last. But the enthusiasm for the Stuart king was destined to be short-lived. His much-praised learning proved to be pedantry and his religion a pharisaical devotion to the maintenance of ecclesiastical authority, while his statesmanship consisted in an unswerving determination to have his own way. James had written a book to prove that kings rule by divine right and are not bound by the law of the land. Yet he had none of the kingliness of the Tudors, for he was small and mean in body and stuttered in his speech. He never understood the English people and his blind self-will drove them into determined opposition to the royal authority.

> Triumph now with joy and mirth!
>   The God of Peace hath blessed our land:
> We enjoy the fruits of earth
>   Through favour of His bounteous hand.
>
> We through His most loving grace
>   A king and kingly seed behold,
> Like a sun with lesser stars
>   Or careful shepherd to his fold:
> Triumph then, and yield Him praise
> That gives us blest and joyful days.

RALEIGH'S CELL IN THE TOWER

DANTE GABRIEL ROSSETTI

SIR WALTER RALEIGH was one of the gifted men who enjoyed the favor
of Elizabeth, and who repaid her bounty by devoted service. He under-
took several voyages to the New World and was the first Englishman
who attempted to found a colony in America. Soon after James's
accession, Raleigh was arrested on charge of treason and condemned
to death (1603). The sentence was not, however, executed until 1618.
During the greater part of the intervening fifteen years, this man of
genius was held a prisoner in the Tower. He whiled away the weary
days in writing a history of the world, a work undertaken at the re-
quest of the king's eldest son, Prince Henry.

Here writ was the World's History by his hand
  Whose steps knew all the earth; albeit his world
  In these few piteous paces then was furl'd.
Here, daily, hourly, have his proud feet spann'd
This smaller speck than the receding land
  Had ever shown his ships; what time he hurl'd
  Abroad o'er new-found regions spiced and pearl'd
His country's high dominion and command.

Here dwelt two spheres. The vast terrestrial zone
  His spirit traversed; and that spirit was
    Itself the zone celestial, round whose birth
    The planets played within the zodiac's girth;
  Till hence, through unjust death unfeared, did pass
His spirit to the only land unknown.

EVEN SUCH IS TIME

SIR WALTER RALEIGH

THE following poem is said to have been written by Raleigh on the eve of his execution.

Even such is time, that takes in trust
    Our youth, our joys, our all we have,
And pays us but with earth and dust;
    Who, in the dark and silent grave,
When we have wandered all our ways,
Shuts up the story of our days;
But from this earth, this grave, this dust,
My God shall raise me up, I trust!

THE PILGRIM FATHERS

WILLIAM WORDSWORTH

RELIGIOUS controversy had not taught toleration to Englishmen. Dissenters from the established church, whether Romanist or Protestant, were punished and their services forbidden. The Puritans, a body of men who desired greater simplicity and freedom of worship, determined to plant a colony in the New World (Plymouth, 1620) with hope of being at liberty to serve God in their own way.

Well worthy to be magnified are they
Who, with sad hearts, of friends and country took
A last farewell, their loved abodes forsook,
And hallowed ground in which their fathers lay;
Then to the new-found World explored their way,
That so a Church, unforced, uncalled to brook
Ritual restraints, within some sheltering nook
Her Lord might worship and his word obey

In freedom.   Men they were who could not bend,
Blest Pilgrims, surely, as they took for guide
A will by sovereign Conscience sanctified ;
Blest while their Spirits from the woods ascend
Along a Galaxy that knows no end,
But in His glory who for sinners died.

TO KING CHARLES AND QUEEN
HENRIETTA

JAMES SHIRLEY

(From " The Triumph of Peace ")

A MAGNIFICENT masque given in honor of Charles I. (1633), ex-
pressed the enthusiasm felt for the handsome young king.   The hope
for a perpetual continuance of the Stuart dynasty, voiced in this
" Song of the Hours," was destined to speedy disappointment.

They that were never happy Hours
Till now, return to thank the powers
  That made them so.
  The Island doth rejoice,
And all her waves are echo to our voice,
Which, in no ages past, hath known
  Such treasures of her own.

Live, royal pair, and when your sands are spent
With Heaven's and your consent,
  Though late, from your high bowers,
  Look down on what was yours ;
For, till old Time his glass hath hurled,
And lost it in the ashes of the world,
We prophesy, you shall be read and seen,
In every branch, a king or queen.

THE PRESBYTERIANS

SAMUEL BUTLER

(From " Hudibras," Part I)

THE serious-minded clergy of Scotland had been cordially disliked by James I. from his boyhood. To his son they were still more obnoxious. Charles I. undertook to force the use of the English ritual upon the Scotch church and provoked a general rebellion (1639). Men of all classes entered into a solemn covenant to defend the Presbyterian faith against corruption. The Covenanters had many sympathizers in England. The Puritans, who protested against the king's evident leaning toward Rome, and the Parliamentarians, who steadily opposed the doctrine of divine right, were ready to join with the Scotch in the struggle against arbitrary government. The Presbyterians were, however, detested as breeders of dissension by the king's party and by the adherents of the established church. They were lampooned by Samuel Butler in the satirical poem, " Hudibras."

>   That stubborn crew
> Of errant saints whom all men grant
> To be the true Church Militant.
> Such as do build their faith upon
> The holy text of pike and gun ;
> Decide all controversies by
> Infallible artillery ;
> And prove their doctrine orthodox
> With apostolic blows and knocks ;
> Call fire and sword and desolation
> A godly, thorough Reformation,
> Which always must be going on,
> And still be doing, never done,
> As if Religion were intended
> For nothing else but to be mended :

A sect whose chief devotion lies
In odd, perverse antipathies,
In falling out with that or this.
And finding somewhat still amiss;
More peevish, cross, and splenetic
Than dog distract or monkey sick:
That with more care keep holyday
The wrong, than others the right way;
Compound for sins they are inclined to
By damning those they have no mind to.
Still so perverse and opposite
As if they worshipped God for spite,
The self-same thing they will abhor
One way and long another for;
Freewill they one way disavow,
Another, nothing else allow;
All piety consists therein
In them, in other men all sin.
Rather than fail they will defy
That which they love most tenderly;
Quarrel with mince-pies, and disparage
Their best and dearest friend plum-porridge;
Fat pig and goose itself oppose,
And blaspheme custard through the nose.

STRAFFORD

Robert Browning

Sir Thomas Wentworth was one of the English statesmen who opposed the doctrine of divine right. He believed that the life and liberty of the subject must be guarded against arbitrary power, but he was unwilling to follow the men who were aiming to render the king subordinate to Parliament. On the passing of the Petition of Right (1629), he broke with the reform party and offered his services to Charles. Wentworth was sent to Ireland as Lord Deputy, but returned to the king's side (1641) when the Covenanters were threatening an invasion of England. Finding that the Parliamentarians were carrying on negotiations with the Scotch, he offered to bring a loyal Irish army to the defence of the king. Charles rewarded his devotion by creating him Earl of Strafford and appointed him Lieutenant General of the English army with orders to suppress rebellion in any of the king's dominions. Indignant because of his treason to the popular cause, Pym and the reform party charged Strafford with attempting to "introduce an arbitrary and tyrannical government against law," and succeeded in forcing a bill of attainder through Parliament. Charles had promised Strafford upon the honor of a king "that he should not suffer in life, honor, or fortune," yet he signed the bill, hoping thus to avoid further trouble.

ACT I

Scene I. *A House near Whitehall. Hampden, Hollis, the younger Vane, Rudyard, Fiennes, and many of the Presbyterian Party; Loudon and other Scots Commissioners.*

Vane.   Now, by Heaven
They may be cool who can, silent who will —
Some have a gift that way! Wentworth is here,
Here, and the King's safe closeted with him

Ere this.   And when I think on all that's past
Since that man left us, how his single arm
Rolled the advancing good of England back
And set the woful past up in its place, —
Exalting Dagon where the Ark should be —
How that man has made firm the fickle King
(Hampden, I will speak out !) — in aught he feared
To venture on before; taught Tyranny
Her dismal trade, the use of all her tools,
To ply the scourge yet screw the gag so close
That strangled agony bleeds mute to death —
How he turns Ireland to a private stage
For training infant villainies, new ways
Of wringing treasure out of tears and blood,
Unheard oppressions nourished in the dark
To try how much man's nature can endure
— If he dies under it, what harm ? if not,
Why, one more trick is added to the rest
Worth a king's knowing, and what Ireland bears
England may learn to bear : how all this while
That man has set himself to one dear task,
The bringing Charles to relish more and more
Power, power without law, power and blood too —
Can I be still ?
  Hamp.   For that you should be still.
  Vane. O Hampden, then and now ! The year he
      left us,
The People in full Parliament could wrest
The Bill of Rights from the reluctant King;
And now, he'll find in an obscure small room

A stealthy gathering of great-hearted men
That take up England's cause: England is here!
   Hamp. And who despairs of England?
   Rud.   That do I,
If Wentworth comes to rule her. I am sick
To think her wretched masters, Hamilton,
The muckworm Cottington, the maniac Laud,
May yet be longed-for back again. I say,
I do despair.
   Vane.   And, Rudyard, I'll say this —
Which all true men say after me, not loud
But solemnly and as you'd say a prayer!
This King, who treads our England under foot,
Has just so much — it may be fear or craft —
As bids him pause at each fresh outrage; friends,
He needs some sterner hand to grasp his own,
Some voice to ask, "Why shrink? — am I not by?"
Now, one whom England loved for serving her,
Found in his heart to say, "I know where best
The iron heel shall bruise her, for she leans
Upon me when you trample." Witness, you!
So Wentworth heartened Charles, and England fell.
But inasmuch as life is hard to take
From England —
   Many Voices. Go on, Vane! 'Tis well said, Vane!
   Vane. — Who has not so forgotten Runnymead! —
   Voices. 'Tis well and bravely spoken, Vane! Go
     on!

   Vane. There are some little signs of late she knows
The ground no place for her! She glances round,

Wentworth has dropped the hand, is gone his way
On other service : what if she arise?
No! the King beckons, and beside him stands
The same bad man once more, with the same smile
And the same gesture.   Now shall England crouch,
Or catch at us and rise?

Voices.   The Renegade !
Haman!   Ahithophel !

Hamp.   Gentlemen of the North,
It was not thus the night your claims were urged,
And we pronounced the League and Covenant,
The cause of Scotland, England's cause as well !
Vane, there, sat motionless the whole night through.

Vane. Hampden !

Fien.   Stay, Vane !

Lou.   Be just and patient, Vane !

Vane. Mind how you counsel patience, Loudon ! you
Have still a Parliament, and this your League
To back it; you are free in Scotland still :
While we are brothers, hope's for England yet.
But know you wherefore Wentworth comes ? to
      quench
This last of hopes? that he brings war with him?
Know you the man's self ? what he dares?

Lou.   We know,
All know — 'tis nothing new.

Vane.   And what's new, then,
In calling for his life ? Why, Pym himself —
You must have heard — ere Wentworth dropped our
      cause

He would see Pym first; there were many more
Strong on the people's side and friends of his,
Eliot that's dead, Rudyard and Hampden here,
But for these Wentworth cared not; only, Pym
He would see — Pym and he were sworn, 'tis said,
To live and die together; so, they met
At Greenwich.   Wentworth, you are sure, was long,
Specious enough, the Devil's argument
Lost nothing on his lips; he'd have Pym own
A patriot could not play a purer part
Than follow in his track; they two combined
Might put down England.   Well, Pym heard him out;
One glance — you know Pym's eye — one word was
    all:
"You leave us, Wentworth! while your head is on,
I'll not leave you."

ACT V

SCENE. *The Tower. Pym, with Hampden and Vane,
    confronts Strafford, who is on the point of escape.*

   Pym. Have I done well? Speak, England! Whose
    sole sake
I still have laboured for, with disregard
To my own heart, — for whom my youth was made
Barren, my manhood waste, to offer up
Her sacrifice — this friend, this Wentworth here —
Who walked in youth with me, loved me, it may be,
And whom, for his forsaking England's cause,
I hunted by all means (trusting that she
Would sanctify all means) even to the block

Which waits for him.   And saying this, I feel
No bitterer pang than first I felt, the hour
I swore that Wentworth might leave us, but I
Would never leave him : I do leave him now.
I render up my charge (be witness, God !)
To England who imposed it.   I have done
Her bidding — poorly, wrongly, — it may be,
With ill effects — for I am weak, a man :
Still, I have done my best, my human best,
Not faltering for a moment.   It is done.
And this said, if I say — yes, I will say
I never loved but one man — David not
More Jonathan !   Even thus, I love him now :
And look for my chief portion in that world
Where great hearts led astray are turned again,
(Soon it may be, and, certes, will be soon :
My mission over, I shall not live long.) —
Ay, here I know I talk — I dare and must,
Of England, and her great reward, as all
I look for there ; but in my inmost heart,
Believe, I think of stealing quite away
To walk once more with Wentworth — my youth's
      friend
Purged from all error, gloriously renewed,
And Eliot shall not blame us.   Then indeed —
This is no meeting, Wentworth !   Tears increase
Too hot.   A thin mist — is it blood ? — enwraps
The face I loved once.   Then, the meeting be !
  Straf. I have loved England too ; we'll meet then,
      Pym ;

As well die now !   Youth is the only time
To think and to decide on a great course :
Manhood with action follows ; but 'tis dreary
To have to alter our whole life in age —
The time past, the strength gone !   As well die now.
When we meet, Pym, I'd be set right — not now !
Best die.   Then if there's any fault, fault too
Dies, smothered up.   Poor gray old little Laud
May dream his dream out of a perfect Church,
In some blind corner.   And there's no one left.
I trust the King now wholly to you, Pym !
And yet, I know not : I shall not be there :
Friends fail — if he have any.   And he's weak,
And loves the Queen, and — O, my fate is nothing —
Nothing !   But not that awful head — not that !

   * * * * * * *

 Pym. If England shall declare such will to me —
 Straf. No, not for England now, not for Heaven
  now, —
See, Pym, for my sake, mine who kneel to you !
There, I will thank you for the death, my friend !
This is the meeting : let me love you well !
 Pym. England, — I am thine own !   Dost thou
  exact
That service ?   I obey thee to the end.
 Straf. O God, I shall die first — I shall die first !

CAVALIER TUNES

ROBERT BROWNING

THE death of Strafford did not appease the reformers, nor yet the king's reluctant surrender of important powers and privileges. Pym and his fellows suspected, and with good reason, the sincerity of the royal promises, while Charles's friends believed that the Parliamentarians were meditating revolution. Both factions prepared for the inevitable struggle. The king's standard was set up at Nottingham Castle (August, 1642), and many lords and gentlemen gathered there to his support. The country districts of the north and west were usually loyal. Parliament was intrenched in London, and could count on aid from the towns of the east and south. For four years the land was devastated by the contending armies.

I

MARCHING ALONG

Kentish Sir Byng stood for his King,
Bidding the crop-headed Parliament swing:
And, pressing a troop unable to stoop
And see the rogues flourish and honest folk droop,
Marched them along, fifty-score strong,
Great-hearted gentlemen, singing this song.

God for King Charles! Pym and such carles
To the Devil that prompts 'em their treasonous
    parles!
Cavaliers, up! Lips from the cup,
Hands from the pasty, nor bite take nor sup
Till you're —

(*Chorus*) — *Marching along, fifty-score strong,*
        Great-hearted gentlemen, singing this song.

Hampden to hell, and his obsequies' knell.
Serve Hazelrig, Fiennes, and young Harry as well!
England, good cheer! Rupert is near!
Kentish and loyalists, keep we not here,

(*Chorus*) — *Marching along, fifty-score strong,*
    Great-hearted gentlemen, singing this song?

Then, God for King Charles! Pym and his snarls
To the Devil that pricks on such pestilent carles!
Hold by the right, you double your might;
So, onward to Nottingham, fresh for the fight,

(*Chorus*)— *March we along, fifty-score strong,*
    Great-hearted gentlemen, singing this song!

II

Give a Rouse

King Charles, and who'll do him right now?
King Charles, and who's ripe for fight now?
Give a rouse: here's, in hell's despite now,
King Charles!

Who gave me the goods that went since?
Who raised me the house that sank once?
Who helped me to gold I spent since?
Who found me in wine you drank once?

(*Chorus*)— *King Charles, and who'll do him right now?*
    King Charles, and who's ripe for fight now?
    Give a rouse: here's, in hell's despite now,
    King Charles!

III

Boot and Saddle

Boot, saddle, to horse, and away!
Rescue my castle before the hot day
Brightens to blue from its silvery gray.

(*Chorus*) — *Boot, saddle, to horse, and away!*

Ride past the suburbs, asleep as you'd say;
Many's the friend there, will listen and pray,
"God's luck to gallants that strike up the lay —

(*Chorus*) — *Boot, saddle, to horse, and away!*"

Forty miles off, like a roebuck at bay,
Flouts Castle Brancepeth the Roundheads' array:
Who laughs, "Good fellows ere this, by my fay,

(*Chorus*) — *Boot, saddle, to horse, and away!*"

Who? My wife Gertrude; that, honest and gay,
Laughs when you talk of surrendering, "Nay!
I've better counsellors; what counsel they?

(*Chorus*) —*Boot, saddle, to horse, and away!*"

TO ALTHEA FROM PRISON

Richard Lovelace

RICHARD LOVELACE was a poet and a great favorite at the court of Charles I. As the differences between the king and the Parliament grew more serious, Lovelace threw himself heart and soul into his royal master's cause. In April, 1642, he undertook to present to the House of Commons a petition in the king's behalf from the county of Kent. The document was received with contempt, burned by the common hangman, and Lovelace was thrown into the Gatehouse prison.   No sooner was he free than this ardent champion of royalty joined the Cavalier army.   He fought through the war and died(1658) in abject poverty, his whole fortune being spent in useless attempts to serve his sovereign.

When Love with unconfinèd wings
   Hovers within my gates,
And my divine Althea brings
   To whisper at the grates;
When I lie tangled in her hair
   And fetter'd to her eye,
The birds that wanton in the air
   Know no such liberty.

When flowing cups run swiftly round
   With no allaying Thames,
Our careless heads with roses crown'd,
   Our hearts with loyal flames;
When thirsty grief in wine we steep,
   When healths and draughts go free —
Fishes that tipple in the deep
   Know no such liberty.

When, (like committed linnets), I
   With shriller throat shall sing
The sweetness, mercy, majesty
   And glories of my King;
When I shall voice aloud how good
   He is, how great should be,
Enlargèd winds, that curl the flood,
   Know no such liberty.

Stone walls do not a prison make,
  Nor iron bars a cage ;
Minds innocent and quiet take
  That for an hermitage ;
If I have freedom in my love
  And in my soul am free,
Angels alone, that soar above,
  Enjoy such liberty.

THE BATTLE OF NASEBY

By Obadiah Bind-their-kings-in-chains-and-their-
nobles-with-links-of-iron, Sergeant in Ireton's
Regiment   Lord Macaulay

THE romantic and dashing Cavaliers had at first better fortune than
the plain and prosy Roundheads, because the latter lacked experience
in war. The weakness of the Parliament's troops was pointed out by
Oliver Cromwell. "Your troops," said he, speaking to his cousin
Hampden, "are most of them old decayed serving-men and tapsters
and such kind of fellows, and their troops are gentlemen's sons and
persons of quality. Do you think that the spirits of such base and
mean fellows will ever be able to encounter gentlemen that have honor,
courage and resolution in them? You must have men animated by a
spirit which will lead them as far as gentlemen would go, otherwise I
am sure you will always be beaten." Cromwell undertook to organize
an army of men that had the fear of God before their eyes, and would
put conscience into their service. His "ironsides" won the battle of
Naseby (1645), the decisive battle of the war, and were the chief
instrument in the final defeat of the king.

Oh! wherefore come ye forth, in triumph from the
    north,
  With your hands, and your feet, and your raiment
    all red ?

And wherefore doth your rout send forth a joyous
    shout?
  And whence be the grapes of the wine-press that
    ye tread?

Oh! evil was the root, and bitter was the fruit,
  And crimson was the juice of the vintage that we
    trod;
For we trampled on the throng of the haughty and
    the strong,
  Who sate in the high places and slew the saints of
    God.

It was about the noon of a glorious day of June,
  That we saw their banners dance and their cui-
    rasses shine,
And the Man of Blood was there, with his long
    essencèd hair,
  And Astley, and Sir Marmaduke, and Rupert of
    the Rhine.

Like a servant of the Lord, with his Bible and his
    sword,
  The General rode along us to form us for the
    fight,
When a murmuring sound broke out, and swelled
    into a shout,
  Among the godless horsemen upon the tyrant's
    right.

And hark! like the roar of billows on the shore,
  The cry of battle rises along their charging line!

For God! for the Cause! for the Church! for the
    Laws!
  For Charles, King of England, and Rupert of the
    Rhine!

The furious German comes, with his clarions and his
    drums,
  His bravoes of Alsatia and pages of Whitehall;
They are bursting on our flanks! Grasp your pikes!
    Close your ranks!
  For Rupert never comes, but to conquer, or to fall.

They are here — they rush on — we are broken —
    we are gone —
  Our left is borne before them like stubble on the
    blast.
O Lord, put forth thy might! O Lord, defend the
    right!
  Stand back to back, in God's name! and fight it to
    the last!

Stout Skippon hath a wound — the centre hath given
    ground:
  Hark! hark! what means the trampling of horse-
    men on our rear?
Whose banner do I see, boys? 'Tis he! thank God!
    'tis he, boys!
  Bear up another minute! brave Oliver is here!

Their heads all stooping low, their points all in a row,
  Like a whirlwind on the trees, like a deluge on the
    dykes,

Our cuirassiers have burst on the ranks of the Accurst,
  And at a shock have scatter'd the forest of his
    pikes.

Fast, fast, the gallants ride, in some safe nook to
    hide
  Their coward heads, predestin'd to rot on Temple
    Bar ;
And he — he turns ! he flies ! shame on those cruel
    eyes
  That bore to look on torture, and dare not look on
    war !

Ho, comrades ! scour the plain ; and, ere ye strip the
    slain,
  First give another stab to make your search secure ;
Then shake from sleeves and pockets their broad-
    pieces and lockets,
  The tokens of the wanton, the plunder of the poor.

Fools ! your doublets shone with gold, and your
    hearts were gay and bold,
  When you kiss'd your lily hands to your lemans
    to-day ;
And to-morrow shall the fox, from her chambers in
    the rocks,
  Lead forth her tawny cubs to howl about the prey.

Where be your tongues, that late mocked at heaven
    and hell and fate ?
  And the fingers that once were so busy with your
    blades ?

Your perfum'd satin clothes, your catches and your
 oaths ?

 Your stage-plays and your sonnets, your diamonds
 and your spades ?

Down, down, for ever down with the mitre and the
 crown,

 With the Belial of the Court and the Mammon of
 the Pope !

There is woe in Oxford halls, there is wail in Dur-
 ham's Stalls ;

 The Jesuit smites his bosom, the Bishop rends his
 cope.

And she of the seven hills shall mourn her children's
 ills,

 And tremble when she thinks on the edge of Eng-
 land's sword ;

And the kings of earth in fear shall shudder when
 they hear

 What the hand of God hath wrought for the
 Houses and the Word !

MAJESTY IN MISERY

DESPAIRING of beating the Parliamentarians in the field, Charles had
resort to diplomacy. He surrendered to the Scots, hoping that the
loyalists among them would defend him against his English foes. But
Scotland cared more for the Presbyterian church than for the king.
When he refused to abandon the episcopal establishment, the Scotch
authorities handed him over to Parliament. He was tried for treason and
condemned to die " as a tyrant, traitor, murderer, and public enemy."

The following lines are said to have been written by Charles I., during his imprisonment in Carisbroke Castle, 1648.

Great Monarch of the World! from whose arm
    springs
The potency and power of kings;
Record the royal woe, my sufferings.

Nature and law, by thy divine decree,
(The only work of righteous loyalty)
With this dim diadem invested me:

With it the sacred sceptre, purple robe,
Thy holy unction, and the royal globe;
Yet I am levell'd with the life of Job.

The fiercest furies that do daily tread
Upon my grief, my gray discrownèd head,
Are those that owe my bounty for their bread.

Tyranny bears the title of taxation,
Revenge and robbery are reformation,
Oppression gains the name of sequestration.

Great Britain's heir is forcèd into France,
Whilst on his father's head his foes advance;
Poor child! he weeps out his inheritance.

With my own power my majesty they wound,
In the king's name the king himself's uncrown'd,
So doth the dust destroy the diamond.

My life they prize at such a slender rate,
That in my absence they draw bills of hate,
To prove the king a traitor to the state.

Felons attain more privilege than I,
They are allowed to answer ere they die ;
'Tis death to me to ask the reason why.

But, sacred Saviour ! with thy words I woo
Thee *to forgive*, and not be bitter to
Such as thou know'st *do not know what they do.*

Augment my patience, nullify my hate,
Preserve my issue and inspire my mate ;
Yet, though we perish, bless this church and state !

THE DEATH OF CHARLES I

ANDREW MARVEL

(From the "Horatian Ode upon Cromwell's Return from Ireland ")

ON January 30, 1649, the king was beheaded in the public square before Whitehall. He bore himself with dignity and courage. " I go," said he, " from a corruptible to an incorruptible crown which nothing can disturb."

He nothing common did, or mean,
Upon that memorable scene,
    But with his keener eye
    The axe's edge did try ;

Nor call'd the gods, with vulgar spite,
To vindicate his helpless right ;
    But bowed his comely head
    Down, as upon a bed.

THE EXECUTION OF MONTROSE

WILLIAM EDMONDSTOUNE AYTOUN

JAMES GRAHAM, Marquis of Montrose, had at first sympathized with the Covenanters, and he even crossed the Tweed with the Scotch army sent against Charles in 1640. But the arbitrary methods of the Presbyterians led him to fear a democratic despotism more terrible than the tyranny of any one man, and he offered his services to the king. The Marquis was immediately appointed commander of the royal forces in Scotland. The loyalists rallied to his standard, and by brilliant generalship he won six pitched battles over the Covenanters. When Montrose learned of the execution of the king, he swore to avenge his death and hastened to attach himself to Prince Charles. The endeavor to raise an army for the young Stuart was regarded as treason by the Covenanters. Betrayed at last into the hands of his foes, Montrose was condemned to death and executed in the Grassmarket at Edinburgh.

Come hither, Evan Cameron!
　Come, stand beside my knee:
I hear the river roaring down
　Towards the wintry sea.
There's shouting on the mountain-side,
　There's war within the blast;
Old faces look upon me,
　Old forms go trooping past:
I hear the pibroch wailing
　Amidst the din of fight,
And my dim spirit wakes again
　Upon the verge of night.

'Twas I that led the Highland host
　Through wild Lochaber's snows,
What time the plaided clans came down
　To battle with Montrose.

I've told thee how the Southrons fell
   Beneath the broad claymore,
And how we smote the Campbell clan
   By Inverlochy's shore.
I've told thee how we swept Dundee,
   And tam'd the Lindsays' pride ;
But never have I told thee yet
   How the great Marquis died.

A traitor sold him to his foes ;
   O deed of deathless shame !
I charge thee, boy, if e'er thou meet
   With one of Assynt's name —
Be it upon the mountain's side,
   Or yet within the glen,
Stand he in martial gear alone,
   Or back'd by armèd men —
Face him, as thou wouldst face the man
   Who wrong'd thy sire's renown ;
Remember of what blood thou art,
   And strike the caitiff down !

They brought him to the Watergate,
   Hard bound with hempen span,
As though they held a lion there,
   And not a fenceless man.
They set him high upon a cart,
   The hangman rode below,
They drew his hands behind his back
   And bared his noble brow.

Then, as a hound is slipp'd from leash,
   They cheer'd the common throng,
And blew the note with yell and shout
   And bade him pass along.

It would have made a brave man's heart
   Grow sad and sick that day,
To watch the keen malignant eyes
   Bent down on that array.
There stood the Whig west-country lords,
   In balcony and bow;
There sat their gaunt and wither'd dames,
   And their daughters all a-row.
And every open window
   Was full as full might be
With black-rob'd Covenanting carles,
   That goodly sport to see!

But when he came, though pale and wan,
   He look'd so great and high,
So noble was his manly front,
   So calm his steadfast eye,
The rabble rout forebore to shout,
   And each man held his breath,
For well they knew the hero's soul
   Was face to face with death.
And then a mournful shudder
   Through all the people crept,
And some that came to scoff at him
   Now turn'd aside and wept.

But onwards — always onwards,
　In silence and in gloom,
The dreary pageant labour'd,
　Till it reach'd the house of doom.
Then first a woman's voice was heard
　In jeer and laughter loud,
And an angry cry and a hiss arose
　From the heart of the tossing crowd.
Then as the Græme look'd upwards,
　He saw the ugly smile
Of him who sold his king for gold,
　The master-fiend Argyle!

The Marquis gaz'd a moment,
　And nothing did he say,
But the cheek of Argyle grew ghastly pale
　And he turn'd his eyes away.
The painted harlot by his side,
　She shook through every limb,
For a roar like thunder swept the street,
　And hands were clench'd at him;
And a Saxon soldier cried aloud,
　" Back, coward, from thy place!
For seven long years thou hast not dar'd
　To look him in the face."

Had I been there with sword in hand,
　And fifty Camerons by,
That day through high Dunedin's streets
　Had peal'd the slogan-cry.

Not all their troops of trampling horse,
   Nor might of mailèd men,
Not all the rebels in the south
   Had borne us backwards then!
Once more his foot on Highland heath
   Had trod as free as air,
Or I, and all who bore my name,
   Been laid around him there!

It might not be.   They placed him next
   Within the solemn hall,
Where once the Scottish kings were thron'd
   Amidst their nobles all.
But there was dust of vulgar feet
   On that polluted floor,
And perjur'd traitors fill'd the place
   Where good men sate before.
With savage glee came Warristoun
   To read the murderous doom;
And then uprose the great Montrose
   In the middle of the room.

" Now, by my faith as belted knight,
   And by the name I bear,
And by the bright Saint Andrew's cross
   That waves above us there,
Yea, by a greater, mightier oath —
   And oh, that such should be ! —
By that dark stream of royal blood
   That lies 'twixt you and me,

I have not sought in battle-field
   A wreath of such renown,
Nor dar'd I hope on my dying day
   To win the martyr's crown!

"There is a chamber far away
   Where sleep the good and brave,
But a better place ye have nam'd for me
   Than by my father's grave.
For truth and right, 'gainst treason's might,
   This hand hath always striven,
And ye raise it up for a witness still
   In the eye of earth and heaven.
Then nail my head on yonder tower,
   Give every town a limb,
And God who made shall gather them :
   I go from you to Him!"

The morning dawn'd full darkly,
   The rain came flashing down,
And the jagged streak of the levin-bolt
   Lit up the gloomy town :
The thunder crash'd across the heaven,
   The fatal hour was come ;
Yet aye broke in with muffled beat
   The 'larum of the drum.
There was madness on the earth below
   And anger in the sky,
And young and old, and rich and poor,
   Came forth to see him die.

Ah, God! that ghastly gibbet!
  How dismal 'tis to see
The great tall spectral skeleton,
  The ladder and the tree!
Hark! hark! it is the clash of arms —
  The bells begin to toll —
" He is coming! he is coming!
  God's mercy on his soul! "
One last long peal of thunder:
  The clouds are clear'd away,
And the glorious sun once more looks down
  Amidst the dazzling day.

" He is coming! he is coming! "
  Like a bridegroom from his room,
Came the hero from his prison
  To the scaffold and the doom.
There was glory on his forehead,
  There was lustre in his eye,
And he never walk'd to battle
  More proudly than to die:
There was colour in his visage,
  Though the cheeks of all were wan,
And they marvell'd as they saw him pass,
  That great and goodly man!

He mounted up the scaffold,
  And he turn'd him to the crowd;
But they dar'd not trust the people,
  So he might not speak aloud.
But he look'd upon the heavens,
  And they were clear and blue,

And in the liquid ether
  The eye of God shone through;
Yet a black and murky battlement
  Lay resting on the hill,
As though the thunder slept within —
  All else was calm and still.

The grim Geneva ministers
  With anxious scowl drew near,
As you have seen the ravens flock
  Around the dying deer.
He would not deign them word nor sign,
  But alone he bent the knee,
And veil'd his face for Christ's dear grace
  Beneath the gallows-tree.
Then radiant and serene he rose,
  And cast his cloak away:
For he had ta'en his latest look
  Of earth and sun and day.

A beam of light fell o'er him,
  Like a glory round the shriven,
And he climb'd the lofty ladder
  As it were the path to heaven.
Then came a flash from out the cloud,
  And a stunning thunder-roll;
And no man dar'd to look aloft,
  For fear was on every soul.
There was another heavy sound,
  A hush and then a groan;
And darkness swept across the sky —
  The work of death was done!

TO THE LORD GENERAL CROMWELL

JOHN MILTON

THE monarchy was abolished after the execution of the king, and a republic was attempted with Oliver Cromwell at its head. His task was one of supreme difficulty. Prince Charles had been proclaimed king by the Scotch and the conquest of England attempted. The victories of Dunbar (September 3, 1850) and Worcester (September 3, 1651) put an end to this enterprise, but an even more serious danger grew out of dissensions among the republicans themselves. Parliamentarians, Presbyterians, Puritans, and Levellers were advocating their various schemes for the regulation of church and government, and each party was endeavoring to force the acceptance of its opinions upon the distracted state. Cromwell complained that Parliament did nothing but " overturn and overturn." He was obliged to resort to tyrannical measures in order to maintain his authority.

Cromwell, our chief of men, who, through a cloud
  Not of war only, but detractions rude,
  Guided by faith and matchless fortitude,
To peace and truth thy glorious way hast plough'd,
And on the neck of crownèd fortune proud
  Hast rear'd God's trophies, and his work pursued,
  While Darwin stream, with blood of Scots imbrued,
And Dunbar field, resounds thy praises loud,
And Worcester's laureate wreath. Yet much remains
  To conquer still; Peace hath her victories
  No less renown'd than War ; new foes arise,
Threatening to bind our souls with secular chains :
  Help us to save free conscience from the paw
  Of hireling wolves, whose gospel is their maw.

MELTING OF THE EARL'S PLATE

George Walter Thornbury

Not only in Scotland but in England as well, men were shocked by the execution of the king and by the arbitrary methods of the Commonwealth. The moderates came to believe that the only hope for law and order lay in the restoration of the monarchy, and they were willing to make every sacrifice for Prince Charles, the next heir to the throne.

Here's the gold cup all bossy with satyrs and saints,
And my race-bowl (now, women, no whining and
    plaints !)
From the paltriest spoon to the costliest thing,
We'll melt it all down for the use of the king.

Here's the chalice stamp'd over with sigil and cross, —
Some day we'll make up to the chapel the loss.
Now bring me my father's great emerald ring,
For I'll melt down the gold for the good of the king.

And bring me the casket my mother has got,
And the jewels that fall to my Barbara's lot ;
Then dry up your eyes and do nothing but sing,
For we're helping to coin the gold for the king.

This dross we'll transmute into weapons of steel,
Temper'd blades for the hand, sharpest spurs for the
    heel ;
And when Charles, with a shout, into London we bring,
We'll be glad to remember this deed for the king.

Bring the hawk's silver bells and the nursery spoon,
The crucible's ready — we're nothing too soon ;

For I hear the horse neigh that shall carry the thing
That'll bring up a smile in the eyes of the king.

There go my old spurs, and the old silver jug, —
'Twas just for a moment a pang and a tug;
But now I am ready to dance and to sing,
To think I've thrown gold in the chest of my king.

The earrings lose shape, and the coronet too,
I feel my eyes dim with a sort of a dew.
Hurrah for the posset dish ! — Everything
Shall run into bars for the use of the king.

That spoon is a sword, and this thimble a pike ;
It's but a week's garret in London belike —
Then a dash at Whitehall, and the city shall ring
With the shouts of the multitude bringing the king.

THE THREE TROOPERS

During the Protectorate

George Walter Thornbury

Men resented the tyranny of the Protector more than that of a king
born to the throne. The country gentry, especially, whose sympathies
were aristocratic and who had nothing to hope from the Puritans, hated
Cromwell and plotted his overthrow.

Into the Devil tavern
　　Three booted troopers strode,
From spur to feather spotted and splash'd
　　With the mud of a winter road.
In each of their cups they dropp'd a crust,
　　And star'd at the guests with a frown ;

Then drew their swords, and roar'd for a toast,
   "God send this Crum-well-down!"

A blue smoke rose from their pistol locks,
   Their sword blades were still wet,
There were long red smears on their jerkins of buff,
   As the table they overset.
Then into their cups they stirr'd the crusts,
   And curs'd old London town;
They wav'd their swords, and drank with a stamp,
   "God send this Crum-well-down!"

The 'prentice dropp'd his can of beer,
   The host turn'd pale as a clout;
The ruby nose of the toping squire
   Grew white at the wild men's shout.
Then into their cups they flung the crusts,
   And show'd their teeth with a frown;
They flash'd their swords as they gave the toast,
   "God send this Crum-well-down!"

The gambler dropp'd his dog's-ear'd cards,
   The waiting-women scream'd,
As the light of the fire, like stains of blood,
   On the wild men's sabres gleam'd.
Then into their cups they splash'd the crusts,
   And curs'd the fool of a town,
And leap'd on the table, and roar'd a toast,
   "God send this Crum-well-down!"

Till on a sudden fire-bells rang,
   And the troopers sprang to horse;

The eldest mutter'd between his teeth,
    Hot curses — deep and coarse.
In their stirrup cups they flung the crusts,
    And cried as they spurr'd through town,
With their keen swords drawn and their pistols cock'd,
    " God send this Crum-well-down ! "

Away they dash'd through Temple Bar,
    Their red cloaks flowing free,
Their scabbards clash'd, each back-piece shone —
    None lik'd to touch the three.
The silver cups that held the crusts
    They flung to the startled town,
Shouting again, with a blaze of swords,
    "God send this Crum-well-down ! "

CHARLES THE SECOND

WILLIAM WORDSWORTH

AFTER the defeat at Worcester, Prince Charles fled to the Continent, and for nine years wandered from court to court seeking help. Poor and well-nigh friendless, baffled by the failure of plot after plot, he never gave up hope of ultimate restoration. The death of Cromwell (1658) and the unpopularity of his son and successor, gave the long-sought opportunity. Scotland, England, and Ireland declared for Charles. He returned to London and was crowned king without a shadow of opposition (1660). "It must have been my own fault that I did not come before," said the king, " for I find no one but declares he is glad to see me." The third Stuart was, however, no less disappointing than the first. He was dissolute in private life and faithless to his public trust. His supreme concern was to avoid the necessity of going once more " upon his travels," and he was ready to approve any policy that should further his popularity.

Who comes, — with rapture greeted, and caress'd
With frantic love, — his kingdom to regain?
Him Virtue's Nurse, Adversity, in vain
Received, and fostered in her iron breast:
For all she taught of hardiest and of best,
Or would have taught, by discipline of pain
And long privation, now dissolves amain,
Or is remembered only to give zest
To wantonness. — Away, Circean revels!
But for what gain? if England soon must sink
Into a gulf which all distinction levels, —
That bigotry may swallow the good name,
And, with that draught, the life-blood: misery, shame,
By Poets loathed; from which Historians shrink.

THE OLD CAVALIER

SIR FRANCIS HASTINGS DOYLE

THE exclusion of the dissenters from public office bore heavily upon the Cavaliers, many of whom were devout Catholics.

" For our martyr'd Charles I pawn'd my plate,
    For his son I spent my all,
  That a churl might dine, and drink my wine,
    And preach in my father's hall:
  That father died on Marston Moor,
    My son on Worcester plain;
  But the king he turn'd his back on me
    When he got his own again.

" The other day, there came, God wot!
    A solemn, pompous ass,

Who begged to know if I did not go
　　To the sacrifice of Mass:
I told him fairly to his face,
　　That in the field of fight
I had shouted loud for Church and King,
　　When he would have run outright.

" He talked of the Man of Babylon
　　With his rosaries and copes,
As if a Roundhead wasn't worse
　　Than half a hundred Popes.
I don't know what the people mean,
　　With their horror and affright;
All Papists that I ever knew
　　Fought stoutly for the right.

" I now am poor and lonely,
　　This cloak is worn and old,
But yet it warms my loyal heart,
　　Through sleet, and rain, and cold,.
When I call to mind the Cavaliers,
　　Bold Rupert at their head,
Bursting through blood and fire, with cries
　　That might have wak'd the dead.

" Then spur and sword was the battle word,
　　And we made their helmets ring,
Howling like madmen, all the while,
　　For God and for the King.
And though they snuffled psalms, to give
　　The Rebel-dogs their due,

When the roaring shot pour'd close and hot
    They were stalwart men and true.

" On the fatal field of Naseby,
    Where Rupert lost the day
 By hanging on the flying crowd
    Like a lion on his prey,
I stood and fought it out, until,
    In spite of plate and steel,
The blood that left my veins that day
    Flow'd up above my heel.

" And certainly, it made those quail
    Who never quail'd before,
To look upon the awful front
    Which Cromwell's horsemen wore.
I felt that every hope was gone,
    When I saw their squadrons form,
And gather for the final charge
    Like the coming of the storm.

" Oh ! where was Rupert in that hour
    Of danger, toil, and strife ?
 It would have been to all brave men
    Worth a hundred years of life
 To have seen that black and gloomy force,
    As it poured down in line,
Met midway by the Royal horse
    And Rupert of the Rhine.

" All this is over now, and I
    Must travel to the tomb,

Though the king I serv'd has got his own,
    In poverty and gloom.
Well, well, I serv'd him for himself,
    So I must not now complain,
But I often wish that I had died
    With my son on Worcester plain."

EPITAPH ON CHARLES II

EARL OF ROCHESTER

OF the profligate noblemen at the court of Charles II., the Earl of Rochester was probably the meanest and the most brilliant. This epitaph, while too true of the witty, selfish king, comes with an ill grace from the favorite earl.

Here lies our Sovereign Lord the King,
    Whose word no man relies on,
Who never said a foolish thing,
    Nor ever did a wise one.

THE SONG OF THE WESTERN MEN

ROBERT STEPHEN HAWKER

THE "Merry Monarch" was succeeded by his brother James II. (1685), a man of different temper. James was an ardent Romanist and was bent on securing toleration for Roman Catholics. Most Englishmen feared that this would mean the restoration of the Pope's authority over the English church. The king's Declaration of Indulgence was therefore resented, and many of the clergy refused to read it to their congregations. Seven of the bishops who protested against the Declaration were thrown into the Tower on charge of seditious libel. Among them was Trelawney, Bishop of Bristol, a native of Cornwall, and very popular in his diocese. The excitement of the people, not only in Cornwall, but in London and throughout the kingdom, was so great that the jury appointed to try the bishops was overawed and gave verdict for acquittal.

A good sword and a trusty hand!
  A merry heart and true!
King James's men shall understand
  What Cornish lads can do.

And have they fix'd the where and when?
  And shall Trelawney die?
Here's twenty thousand Cornishmen
  Will know the reason why!

Out spake their captain brave and bold,
  A merry wight was he:
"If London Tower were Michael's hold,
  We'll set Trelawney free!

"We'll cross the Tamar, land to land,
  The Severn is no stay,
With 'one and all,' and hand in hand,
  And who shall bid us nay?

"And when we come to London Wall,
  A pleasant sight to view,
Come forth! come forth! ye cowards all!
  Here's men as good as you!

"Trelawney he's in keep and hold,
  Trelawney he may die;
But here's twenty thousand Cornish bold,
  Will know the reason why!"

KILLIECRANKIE

(The Burial-March of Dundee)

WILLIAM EDMONDSTOUNE AYTOUN

THE children of James II. were two daughters, Mary and Anne, both Protestants. Men hoped that the death of the king would bring the Romanizing policy to an end. But when (1688) a prince was born, this hope was frustrated, and the leading English statesmen determined to depose James and place his daughter Mary on the throne. They appealed to William of Orange, Mary's husband, to come to their aid. The Revolution of 1688 was accomplished without bloodshed so far as England was concerned. The Toleration Act, allowing freedom of worship to all but Roman Catholics, was a satisfactory settlement of the religious controversy. There was little enthusiasm for the obstinate old king, and James, remembering his father's fate, made revolution easy by fleeing to France. But in Scotland, the slight put upon the Stuart king was hotly resented. Under the inspiring leadership of the Viscount of Dundee, the Highlanders fought and won the battle of Killiecrankie. The death of Dundee was a fatal blow to James's cause, for there was no other man who could unite the jealous Scotch clans in his support.

> On the heights of Killiecrankie
>   Yester-morn our army lay:
> Slowly rose the mist in columns
>   From the river's broken way;
> Hoarsely roared the swollen torrent,
>   And the Pass was wrapt in gloom,
> When the clansmen rose together
>   From their lair amidst the broom.
> Then we belted on our tartans,
>   And our bonnets down we drew,
> And we felt our broadswords' edges,
>   And we proved them to be true;

And we prayed the prayer of soldiers,
 And we cried the gathering-cry,
And we clasped the hands of kinsmen,
 And we swore to do or die!
Then our leader rode before us
 On his war-horse black as night —
Well the Cameronian rebels
 Knew that charger in the fight! —
And a cry of exultation
 From the bearded warriors rose;
For we loved the house of Claver'se,
 And we thought of good Montrose.
But he raised his hand for silence —
 "Soldiers! I have sworn a vow:
Ere the evening star shall glisten
 On Schehallion's lofty brow,
Either we shall rest in triumph,
 Or another of the Græmes
Shall have died in battle-harness
 For his country and King James!
Think upon the Royal Martyr —
 Think of what his race endure —
Think of him whom butchers murdered
 On the field of Magus Muir: —
By his sacred blood I charge ye,
 By the ruined hearth and shrine —
By the blighted hopes of Scotland,
 By your injuries and mine —
Strike this day as if the anvil
 Lay beneath your blows the while,

Be they covenanting traitors,
 Or the brood of false Argyle!
Strike! and drive the trembling rebels
 Backwards o'er the stormy Forth;
Let them tell their pale Convention
 How they fared within the North.
Let them tell that Highland honour
 Is not to be bought nor sold,
That we scorn the prince's anger
 As we loathe his foreign gold.
Strike! and when the fight is over,
 If ye look in vain for me,
Where the dead are lying thickest
 Search for him that was Dundee!"

Loudly then the hills reëchoed
 With our answer to his call,
But a deeper echo sounded
 In the bosoms of us all.
For the lands of wide Breadelbane
 Not a man who heard him speak
Would that day have left the battle.
 Burning eye and flushing cheek
Told the clansmen's fierce emotion,
 And they harder drew their breath;
For their souls were strong within them,
 Stronger than the grasp of death.
Soon we heard a challenge-trumpet
 Sounding in the Pass below,
And the distant tramp of horses,
 And the voices of the foe:

Down we crouched amid the bracken,
  Till the Lowland ranks drew near,
Panting like the hounds in summer,
  When they scent the stately deer.
From the dark defile emerging,
  Next we saw the squadrons come,
Leslie's foot and Leven's troopers
  Marching to the tuck of drum ;
Through the scattered wood of birches,
  O'er the broken ground and heath,
Wound the long battalion slowly,
  Till they gained the plain beneath ;
Then we bounded from our covert —
  Judge how looked the Saxons then,
When they saw the rugged mountain
  Start to life with armèd men !
Like a tempest down the ridges
  Swept the hurricane of steel,
Rose the slogan of Macdonald, —
  Flashed the broadsword of Lochiell !
Vainly sped the withering volley
  'Mongst the foremost of our band —
On we poured until we met them,
  Foot to foot and hand to hand.
Horse and man went down like driftwood
  When the floods are black at Yule,
And their carcasses are whirling
  In the Garry's deepest pool.
Horse and man went down before us —
  Living foe there tarried none

On the field of Killiecrankie,
  When that stubborn fight was done!

And the evening star was shining
  On Schehallion's distant head,
When we wiped our bloody broadswords,
  And returned to count the dead.
There we found him gashed and gory,
  Stretched upon the cumbered plain,
As he told us where to seek him,
  In the thickest of the slain.
And a smile was on his visage,
  For within his dying ear
Pealed the joyful note of triumph,
  And the clansmen's clamorous cheer;
So, amidst the battle's thunder,
  Shot, and steel, and scorching flame,
In the glory of his manhood
  Passed the spirit of the Græme!

THE JACOBITE ON TOWER HILL

GEORGE WALTER THORNBURY

THE Revolution was hardly accomplished when the men who were friendly to James or were disappointed in William and Mary, began plotting for the restoration of the Stuart line. In 1696, a conspiracy was formed to assassinate the king. The plot was betrayed, however, and the leaders arrested and executed.

He tripp'd up the steps with a bow and a smile,
Offering snuff to the chaplain the while,

A rose at his button-hole that afternoon —
'Twas the tenth of the month, and the month it was
    June.

Then shrugging his shoulders he look'd at the man
With the mask and the axe, and a murmuring ran
Through the crowd, who, below, were all pushing to
    see
The gaoler kneel down, and receiving his fee.

He look'd at the mob, as they roar'd, with a stare,
And took snuff again with a cynical air.
"I'm happy to give but a moment's delight
To the flower of my country agog for a sight."

Then he look'd at the block, and with scented cravat
Dusted room for his neck, gaily doffing his hat,
Kiss'd his hand to a lady, bent low to the crowd,
Then smiling, turn'd round to the headsman and
    bow'd.

"God save King James!" he cried bravely and shrill,
And the cry reach'd the houses at foot of the hill,
"My friend with the axe, *à votre service*," he said;
And ran his white thumb long the edge of the blade.

When the multitude hiss'd he stood firm as a rock;
Then kneeling, laid down his gay head on the block;
He kiss'd a white rose, — in a moment 'twas red
With the life of the bravest of any that bled.

THE AGE OF QUEEN ANNE

Alexander Pope

(From "The Rape of the Lock," Canto III)

QUEEN ANNE, who succeeded to the throne on the death of Mary's husband (1702), was a woman of feeble intellect. She had so little will of her own that she never came into conflict with her subjects. The affairs of state were managed for her by certain favorites, of whom Churchill, Duke of Marlborough, was chief.

Close by those meads, for ever crown'd with flowers,
Where Thames with pride surveys his rising towers,
There stands a structure of majestic frame,
Which from the neighbouring Hampton takes its
    name.
Here Britain's statesmen oft the fall foredoom
Of foreign tyrants and of nymphs at home ;
Here thou, great ANNA ! whom three realms obey,
Dost sometimes counsel take — and sometimes tea.

  Hither the heroes and the nymphs resort,
To taste awhile the pleasures of a court ;
In various talk the instructive hours they passed,
Who gave the ball, or paid the visit last ;
One speaks the glory of the British Queen,
And one describes a charming Indian screen ;
A third interprets motions, looks, and eyes ;
At every word a reputation dies.
Snuff, or the fan, supply each pause of chat,
With singing, laughing, ogling, and all that.

AFTER BLENHEIM

Robert Southey

Louis XIV., king of France, had given refuge to James II. and, after the death of the exiled king, recognized his son Prince James as heir to the English crown. Louis was the most powerful monarch in Europe, and his championship of the Jacobite cause was a serious menace to the peace of England. Marlborough undertook to oppose the *grand monarque* in his continental ambitions and so joined the foes of France in the war of the Spanish succession (1704–1713). The allied armies won a great victory at Blenheim on the upper Danube and the prestige of France waned from that day. In the end Louis was obliged to abandon the Stuarts and to acknowledge a Protestant prince, George of Hanover, as successor to Queen Anne.

It was a summer evening,
    Old Kaspar's work was done,
And he before his cottage door
    Was sitting in the sun ;
And by him sported on the green
His little grandchild Wilhelmine.

She saw her brother Peterkin
    Roll something large and round
Which he beside the rivulet
    In playing there had found ;
He came to ask what he had found
That was so large and smooth and round.

Old Kaspar took it from the boy
    Who stood expectant by ;
And then the old man shook his head
    And with a natural sigh
" 'Tis some poor fellow's skull," said he,
" Who fell in the great victory.

" I find them in the garden,
 For there's many here about ;
And often when I go to plough
 The ploughshare turns them out.
For many thousand men," said he,
" Were slain in that great victory."

" Now tell us what 'twas all about,"
 Young Peterkin he cries ;
And little Wilhelmine looks up
 With wonder-waiting eyes ;
" Now tell us all about the war,
And what they fought each other for."

" It was the English," Kaspar cried,
 " Who put the French to rout ;
But what they fought each other for
 I could not well make out.
But everybody said," quoth he,
" That 'twas a famous victory.

" My father lived at Blenheim then,
 Yon little stream hard by ;
They burnt his dwelling to the ground,
 And he was forced to fly :
So with his wife and child he fled,
Nor had he where to rest his head.

" With fire and sword the country round
 Was wasted far and wide,
And many a childing mother then
 And new-born baby died :

But things like that, you know, must be
At every famous victory.

"They say it was a shocking sight
    After the field was won;
For many thousand bodies here
    Lay rotting in the sun:
But things like that, you know, must be
After a famous victory.

"Great praise the Duke of Marlbro' won
    And our good Prince Eugene;"
"Why 'twas a very wicked thing!"
    Said little Wilhelmine;
"Nay — nay — my little girl," quoth he,
"It was a famous victory.

"And everybody praised the Duke
    Who this great fight did win."
"But what good came of it at last?"
    Quoth little Peterkin: —
"Why that I cannot tell," said he,
"But 'twas a famous victory."

THREE PORTRAITS OF PRINCE CHARLES

ANDREW LANG

THE first two kings of the Hanoverian line were more German than English. They knew next to nothing about affairs of state and aroused little enthusiasm among their subjects. Disappointed office-seekers and persecuted Romanists joined the ranks of the Jacobites. James III. was not the man to push his claims, but his son, Charles Edward, was a promising lad and determined to recover the throne. Opportunity came in the outbreak of war with France (1743). Encouraged by promises of aid from Louis XV., Prince Charles landed in Scotland, and raised the royal standard at Glenfinnan (1745). The Highland clans gathered about him and he marched against Edinburgh with a considerable army. The battle of Prestonpans gave him control of Scotland. He then crossed into England and advanced as far as Derby. But France sent no aid, and the English Jacobites did not rise in his behalf. The older heads among his officers counselled retreat. On the way back to the Border, the Jacobite army was overtaken and cut to pieces at Culloden Moor (1646). Charles fled to France and spent the rest of his life wandering about from one refuge to another, growing more drunken and dissolute as hope waned. With him died the Jacobite cause.

1731

Beautiful face of a child,
   Lighted with laughter and glee,
Mirthful, and tender, and wild,
   My heart is heavy for thee!

1744

Beautiful face of a youth,
   As an eagle poised to fly forth
To the old land loyal of truth,
   To the hills and the sounds of the North:
Fair face, daring and proud,
   Lo! the shadow of doom, even now,
The fate of thy line, like a cloud,
   Rests on the grace of thy brow!

1773

Cruel and angry face,
   Hateful and heavy with wine,
Where are the gladness, the grace,
   The beauty, the mirth that were thine?

Ah, my Prince, it were well, —
   Hadst thou to the gods been dear, —
To have fallen where Keppoch fell,
   With the war-pipe loud in thine ear !
To have died with never a stain
   On the fair White Rose of Renown,
To have fallen, fighting in vain,
   For thy father, thy faith, and thy crown !
More than thy marble pile,
   With its women weeping for thee,
Were to dream in thine ancient isle,
   To the endless dirge of the sea !
But the Fates deemed otherwise ;
   Far thou sleepest from home,
From the tears of the Northern skies,
   In the secular [1] dust of Rome.
A city of death and the dead,
   But thither a pilgrim came,
Wearing on weary head
   The crowns of years and fame :
Little the Lucrine lake
   Or Tivoli said to him,
Scarce did the memories wake
   Of the far-off years and dim,
For he stood by Avernus' shore,
   But he dreamed of a Northern glen,
And he murmured, over and o'er,
   " *For Charlie and his men :* "

[1] centuried.

And his feet, to death that went,
　Crept forth to St. Peter's shrine,
And the latest Minstrel bent
　O'er the last of the Stuart line.

WHA'LL BE KING BUT CHARLIE?

LADY NAIRN

PRINCE CHARLES had landed at Moidart, a bay on the west coast of Invernesshire, where he hoped to find support among the Highland clans. When counselled to abandon the desperate enterprise, he replied, " I am come home and I will not return to France, for I am persuaded that my faithful Highlanders will stand by me." The song speaks the genuine devotion of the Celts, who made up the bulk of the army with which the Prince invaded England.

The news frae Moidart cam' yestreen,
　Will soon gar mony ferlie; [1]
For ships o' war hae just come in
　And landit Royal Charlie.

Come thro' the heather, around him gather,
　Ye're a' the welcomer early;
Around him cling wi' a' your kin;
　For wha'll be King but Charlie?
Come thro' the heather, around him gather,
Come Ronald, come Donald, come a' thegither,
And crown your rightfu', lawfu' King!
　For wha'll be King but Charlie?

The Hieland clans, wi' sword in hand,
　Frae John o' Groats to Airlie,
Hae to a man declared to stand
　Or fa' wi' Royal Charlie.

[1] make many wonder.

Come thro' the heather, around him gather,
    Ye're a' the welcomer early;
Around him cling wi' a' your kin;
    For wha'll be King but Charlie?
Come thro' the heather, around him gather,
Come Ronald, come Donald, come a' thegither,
And crown your rightfu', lawfu' King!
    For wha'll be King but Charlie?

The Lowlands a', baith great and sma',
    Wi' mony a lord and laird, hae
Declar'd for Scotia's King an' law,
    An' speir [1] ye wha but Charlie?

Come thro' the heather, around him gather,
    Ye're a' the welcomer early;
Around him cling wi' a' your kin;
    For wha'll be King but Charlie?
Come thro' the heather, around him gather,
Come Ronald, come Donald, come a' thegither,
And crown your rightfu', lawfu' King!
    For wha'll be King but Charlie?

There's ne'er a lass in a' the lan',
    But vows baith late an' early,
She'll ne'er to man gie heart nor han',
    Wha wadna fecht for Charlie.

Come thro' the heather, around him gather,
    Ye're a' the welcomer early;
Around him cling wi' a' your kin;
    For wha'll be King but Charlie?

[1] ask.

Come thro' the heather, around him gather,
Come Ronald, come Donald, come a' thegither,
And crown your rightfu', lawfu' King!
  For wha'll be King but Charlie?

Then here's a health to Charlie's cause,
  And be't complete an' early;
His very name our heart's blood warms;
  To arms for Royal Charlie!

Come thro' the heather, around him gather,
  Ye're a' the welcomer early;
Around him cling wi' a' your kin;
  For wha'll be King but Charlie?
Come thro' the heather, around him gather,
Come Ronald, come Donald, come a' thegither,
And crown your rightfu', lawfu' King!
  For wha'll be King but Charlie?

LAMENT FOR CULLODEN

ROBERT BURNS

THERE was terrible slaughter at Culloden. After the battle, the Highlanders lay in heaps upon the ground. Prince Charles was horror-struck by the sight of the carnage wrought in his behalf. He had not realized that war was so terrible.

The lovely lass o' Inverness,
Nae joy nor pleasure can she see;
For e'en and morn she cries, Alas!
And aye the saut tear blins her ee:

Drumossie moor — Drumossie day —
A waefu' day it was to me!
For there I lost my father dear,
My father dear, and brethren three.

Their winding-sheet the bluidy clay,
Their graves are growing green to see:
And by them lies the dearest lad
That ever blest a woman's ee!
Now wae to thee, thou cruel lord,
A bluidy man I trow thou be;
For mony a heart thou hast made sair
That ne'er did wrang to thine or thee.

ENGLAND, WITH ALL THY FAULTS, I LOVE THEE STILL

WILLIAM COWPER

(From "The Task," Bk. II)

THE third George was proud of being English born and English bred. He determined to make himself master of the political situation, and to be king in fact as well as in name. To this end, old and tried counsellors, such as Chatham, were set aside, and new men were called to the ministry, men who would bow to the royal will. The king's arbitrary policy soon involved England in a war with the American colonies and drove the ablest of her statesmen into opposition.

England, with all thy faults, I love thee still,
My country! and, while yet a nook is left
Where English minds and manners may be found,
Shall be constrained to love thee. Though thy clime
Be fickle, and thy year, most part, deformed

With dripping rains, or withered by a frost,
I would not yet exchange thy sullen skies
And fields without a flower, for warmer France
With all her vines ; nor for Ausonia's groves
Of golden fruitage, and her myrtle bowers.
To shake thy senate, and from heights sublime
Of patriot eloquence to flash down fire
Upon thy foes, was never meant my task ;
But I can feel thy fortunes, and partake
Thy joys and sorrows with as true a heart
As any thunderer there.   And I can feel
Thy follies too, and with a just disdain
Frown at effeminates, whose very looks
Reflect dishonour on the land I love.
How, in the name of soldiership and sense,
Should England prosper, when such things, as smooth
And tender as a girl, all essenced o'er
With odours, and as profligate as sweet,
Who sell their laurel for a myrtle wreath,
And love when they should fight — when such as
    these
Presume to lay their hand upon the ark
Of her magnificent and awful cause ?
Time was when it was praise and boast enough
In every clime, and travel where we might,
That we were born her children ; praise enough
To fill the ambition of a private man,
That Chatham's language was his mother tongue,
And Wolfe's great name compatriot with his own.
Farewell those honours, and farewell with them

The hope of such hereafter ! They have fallen
Each in his field of glory ; one in arms,
And one in council — Wolfe upon the lap
Of smiling Victory that moment won,
And Chatham, heart-sick of his country's shame !
They made us many soldiers. Chatham still
Consulting England's happiness at home,
Secured it by an unforgiving frown
If any wronged her. Wolfe, where'er he fought,
Put so much of his heart into his act,
That his example had a magnet's force,
And all were swift to follow whom all loved.
Those suns are set. Oh, rise some other such !
Or all that we have left is empty talk
Of old achievements, and despair of new.

PITT AND FOX

Sir Walter Scott

(From the Introduction to " Marmion ")

THE arbitrary methods of George III. were possible because Parliament had ceased to represent the nation. Seats in the House of Commons were bought and sold, and the king could carry any measure he chose by the judicious use of money and influence. William Pitt, the son of the " Great Commoner," and Charles Fox led the opposing parties in the House of Commons. Both thought that power should be restored to the people by abolishing the rotten boroughs and giving the right of sending members to the House of Commons to the more populous districts. Working together, the two statesmen might have accomplished this important reform, but their rivalry destroyed all chance of success.

With more than mortal powers endowed,
How high they soared above the crowd!
Theirs was no common party race,
Jostling by dark intrigue for place;
Like fabled gods, their mighty war
Shook realms and nations in its jar;
Beneath each banner proud to stand,
Looked up the noblest of the land,
Till through the British world were known
The names of Pitt and Fox alone.
Spells of such force no wizard grave
E'er framed in dark Thessalian cave,
Though his could drain the ocean dry,
And force the planets from the sky.
These spells are spent, and, spent with these,
The wine of life is on the lees.
Genius, and taste, and talent gone,
For ever tombed beneath the stone,
Where, — taming thought to human pride! —
The mighty chiefs sleep side by side.
Drop upon Fox's grave the tear,
'Twill trickle to his rival's bier;
O'er Pitt's the mournful requiem sound,
And Fox's shall the notes rebound.
The solemn echo seems to cry, —
" Here let their discord with them die;
Speak not for those a separate doom,
Whom Fate made brothers in the tomb,
But search the land of living men,
Where wilt thou find their like again?"

EDMUND BURKE

OLIVER GOLDSMITH

(From " Retaliation ")

THE most eloquent orator of the day was Fox's friend, Edmund Burke. He had eagerly advocated various projects of reform, but he was frightened by the excesses of the French Revolution, and thereafter wrote and spoke in the interest of the old order. Many Englishmen sympathized with him and preferred to put up with present abuses rather than risk such radical reforms as France was attempting.

Here lies our good Edmund, whose genius was such
We scarcely can praise it, or blame it too much ;
Who, born for the universe, narrow'd his mind,
And to party gave up what was meant for mankind ;
Though fraught with all learning, yet straining his
  throat
To persuade Tommy Townshend to lend him a
  vote ;
Who, too deep for his hearers, still went on refining,
And thought of convincing, while they thought of
  dining ;
Though equal to all things, for all things unfit ;
Too nice for a statesman, too proud for a wit,
For a patriot too cool, for a drudge disobedient,
And too fond of the *right* to pursue the expedient.
In short 'twas his fate, unemploy'd, or in place, sir,
To eat mutton cold, and cut blocks with a razor.

THE BATTLE OF THE BALTIC

Thomas Campbell

The execution of Louis XVI. and the ambitious projects of Napoleon led the English government to declare war against France. Britain had no foothold on the Continent, but her navy was the finest afloat. Her best policy was to blockade the French ports and starve out her great antagonist by preventing neutral nations from supplying France with the provisions of war. It was a policy greatly resented by commercial countries, and the states along the Baltic formed an alliance in self-defence. To break the power of this alliance, the British government sent a squadron under Parker and Nelson with instructions to destroy the Danish fleet. On the morning of April 2, 1801, the British men-of-war sailed into the harbor at Copenhagen and opened fire on the Danes. The return fire was unexpectedly strong, for every able-bodied man in the city had offered his services for the defence. Both fleets suffered severely and Parker gave the signal for retreat. But Nelson clapped a telescope to his blind eye and declared he could not see the Admiral's flag. He fought on until victory was assured and then sent ashore a flag of truce, proposing to prevent further bloodshed by an armistice. The Danes gladly consented and the Northern Maritime League came to an end.

Of Nelson and the North
Sing the glorious day's renown,
When to battle fierce came forth
All the might of Denmark's crown,
And her arms along the deep proudly shone;
By each gun the lighted brand
In a bold determined hand,
And the Prince of all the land
Led them on.

Like leviathans afloat
Lay their bulwarks on the brine;

While the sign of battle flew
On the lofty British line:
It was ten of April morn by the chime:
As they drifted on their path
There was silence deep as death;
And the boldest held his breath
For a time.

But the might of England flush'd
To anticipate the scene;
And her van the fleeter rush'd
O'er the deadly space between.
"Hearts of oak!" our captains cried, when each gun
From its adamantine lips
Spread a death-shade round the ships,
Like the hurricane eclipse
Of the sun.

Again! again! again!
And the havoc did not slack,
Till a feeble cheer the Dane
To our cheering sent us back; —
Their shots along the deep slowly boom: —
Then ceased — and all is wail,
As they strike the shatter'd sail;
Or in conflagration pale
Light the gloom.

Out spoke the victor then
As he hail'd them o'er the wave,
"Ye are brothers; ye are men!
And we conquer but to save: —

So peace instead of death let us bring :
But yield, proud foe, thy fleet
With the crews, at England's feet,
And make submission meet
To our King."

Then Denmark bless'd our chief
That he gave her wounds repose ;
And the sounds of joy and grief
From her people wildly rose,
As death withdrew his shades from the day :
While the sun look'd smiling bright
O'er a wide and woful sight,
Where the fires of funeral light
Died away.

Now joy, old England, raise !
For the tidings of thy might,
By the festal cities' blaze,
Whilst the wine cup shines in light ;
And yet amidst that joy and uproar,
Let us think of them that sleep
Full many a fathom deep
By thy wild and stormy steep,
Elsinore !

Brave hearts ! to Britain's pride
Once so faithful and so true,
On the deck of fame that died,
With the gallant good Riou :
Soft sigh the winds of Heaven o'er their grave !

While the billow mournful rolls
And the mermaid's song condoles
Singing glory to the souls
Of the brave!

NELSON

AN OLD MAN-O'-WAR'S-MAN'S YARN

GERALD MASSEY

NAPOLEON was bent on the invasion of England, but while Nelson's fleet guarded the coasts, the French army could not be carried across the Channel. The Emperor determined to rid himself of this obstacle, and he therefore ordered the combined French and Spanish fleets to give battle to the English. The great sea-fight took place off Trafalgar (1805). Napoleon's naval force was destroyed, and he was obliged thereafter to confine his ambitious projects to the Continent.

Our best beloved of all the brave
  That ever for freedom fought;
And all his wonders of the wave
  For fatherland were wrought!
He was the manner of man to show
  How victories may be won;
So swift, you scarcely saw the blow;
  You lookt — the deed was done.

You should have seen him as he trod
  The deck, our joy, and pride!
You should have seen him, like a god
  Of storm, his war-horse ride!

You should have seen him as he stood
   Fighting for his good land,
With all the iron of soul and blood
   Turned to a sword in hand.

The Nelson touch his men he taught,
   And his great stride to keep ;
His faithful fellows round him fought
   Ten thousand heroes deep.
With a red pride of life, and hot
   For him, their blood ran free ;
They "minded not the showers of shot,
   No more than peas," said he.

Napoleon saw our sea-king thwart
   His landing on our isle ;
He gnashed his teeth, he gnawed his heart,
   At Nelson of the Nile,
Who set his fleet in flames, to light
   The lion to his prey,
And lead Destruction through the night
   Upon his dreadful way.

Oh, he could do the deeds that set
   Old fighters' hearts a-fire ;
The edge of every spirit whet,
   And every arm inspire.
Yet I have seen upon his face
   The tears that, as they roll,
Show what a light of saintly grace
   May clothe a sailor's soul.

And when our darling went to meet
   Trafalgar's Judgment Day,
The people knelt down in the street
   To bless him on his way.
He felt the country of his love
   Watching him from afar ;
It saw him through the battle move :
   His heaven was in that star.

Magnificently glorious sight
   It was in that great dawn !
Like one vast sapphire flashing light,
   The sea, just breathing, shone.
Their ships, fresh painted, stood up tall
   And stately : ours were grim
And weatherworn, but one and all
   In rare good fighting trim.

Our spirits all were flying light,
   And into battle sped,
Straining for it on wings of might,
   With feet of springy tread ;
The battle light on every face ;
   Its fire in every eye ;
Our sailor blood at swiftest pace
   To catch the victory nigh.

His proudly wasted face, wave-worn,
   Was loftily serene ;
I felt the brave, bright spirit burn
   There, all too plainly seen ;

As though the sword this time was drawn
   For ever from the sheath ;
And when its work to-day was done,
   All would be dark in death.

Mast-high the famous signal ran ;
   Breathless we caught each word :
" England expects that every man
   Will do his duty." Lord,
You should have seen our faces ! heard
   Us cheering, row on row ;
Like men before some furnace stirred
   To a fiery fearful glow !

We grimly kept our vanward path ;
   Over us hummed their shot ;
But, silently, we reined our wrath,
   Held on, and answered not,
Till we could grip them face to face,
   And pound them for our own,
Or hug them in a war embrace,
   Till they or we went down.

How calm he was ! when first he felt
   The sharp edge of that fight,
Cabined with God alone he knelt ;
   The prayer still lay in light
Upon his face, that used to shine
   In battle — flash with life,
As though the glorious blood ran wine,
   Dancing with that wild strife.

And four hours after, he had done
　With winds and troubled foam.
The Reaper was borne dead upon
　Our load of harvest home.
Not till he knew the old flag flew
　Alone on all the deep;
Then said he, "Hardy, is that you?
　Kiss me." And fell asleep.

Well, 'twas his chosen death, below
　The deck in triumph trod;
'Tis well. A sailor's soul should go
　From his good ship to God.
He would have chosen death aboard,
　From all the crowns of rest;
And burial with the patriot's sword
　Upon the victor's breast.

YE MARINERS OF ENGLAND

THOMAS CAMPBELL

THE victory of Trafalgar destroyed the French and Spanish fleets and secured to Britain the mastery of the seas. There was no further fear of invasion for the island kingdom. Her only rival, the United States, was three thousand miles distant.

I

Ye Mariners of England
That guard our native seas.
Whose flag has braved, a thousand years,
The battle and the breeze!

Your glorious standard launch again
To match another foe :
And sweep through the deep,
While the stormy winds do blow ;
While the battle rages loud and long
And the stormy winds do blow.

II

The spirits of your fathers
Shall start from every wave —
For the deck it was their field of fame,
And Ocean was their grave :
Where Blake and mighty Nelson fell,
Your manly hearts shall glow,
As ye sweep through the deep,
While the stormy winds do blow ;
While the battle rages loud and long,
And the stormy winds do blow.

III

Britannia needs no bulwarks,
No towers along the steep ;
Her march is o'er the mountain-waves,
Her home is on the deep.
With thunders from her native oak
She quells the floods below —
As they roar on the shore,
When the stormy winds do blow ;
When the battle rages loud and long,
And the stormy winds do blow.

IV

The meteor flag of England
Shall yet terrific burn ;
Till danger's troubled night depart
And the star of peace return.
Then, then, ye ocean-warriors !
Our song and feast shall flow
To the fame of your name,
When the storm has ceased to blow ;
When the fiery fight is heard no more,
And the storm has ceased to blow.

AT CORUÑA

Robert Southey

THE nations of Europe had one by one yielded to Napoleon until his conquest of the Continent seemed as complete as England's control of the sea. The first opportunity to meet the great antagonist on land came when (1808) the Spanish people rose in revolt against his tyranny. An English army, under Sir Arthur Wellesley, later Duke of Wellington, was immediately sent to their aid. The French were driven from Portugal, but the attempt to shake their hold on Spain was at first unsuccessful. Sir John Moore, with an army of twenty thousand men, advanced to Salamanca, but learning that Napoleon was marching to meet him with a force twice his own, the English commander beat a hasty retreat to Coruña. Here he expected to find transports to convey his shattered troops back to England. The vessels were late, however, and Moore found himself obliged to fight (January 6, 1809). The French were beaten off at every point, but in the moment of victory, Sir John fell, mortally wounded. The English were embarked the same night.

When from these shores the British army first
Boldly advanced into the heart of Spain,

The admiring people who beheld its march
Call'd it " the Beautiful."	And surely well
Its proud array, its perfect discipline,
Its ample furniture of war complete,
Its powerful horse, its men of British mould,
All high in heart and hope, all of themselves
Assured, and in their leaders confident,
Deserved the title.	Few short weeks elapsed
Ere hither that disastrous host return'd,
A fourth of all its gallant force consumed
In hasty and precipitate retreat,
Stores, treasure and artillery, in the wreck
Left to the fierce pursuer, horse and man
Founder'd, and stiffening on the mountain snows.
But when the exulting enemy approach'd
Boasting that he would drive into the sea
The remnant of the wretched fugitives,
Here ere they reach'd their ships, they turn'd at bay.
Then was the proof of British courage seen ;
Against a foe far overnumbering them,
An insolent foe, rejoicing in pursuit,
Sure of the fruit of victory, whatsoe'er
Might be the fate of battle, here they stood
And their safe embarkation — all they sought,
Won manfully.	That mournful day avenged
Their sufferings, and redeem'd their country's name ;
And thus Coruña, which in this retreat
Had seen the else indelible reproach
Of England, saw the stain effaced in blood.

THE BURIAL OF SIR JOHN MOORE

CHARLES WOLFE

MOORE was buried at Coruña in the garden of San Carlos. A monument was erected on the spot in 1814.

Not a drum was heard, not a funeral note,
    As his corpse to the ramparts we hurried ;
Not a soldier discharged his farewell shot
    O'er the grave where our hero we buried.

We buried him darkly at dead of night,
    The sods with our bayonets turning ;
By the struggling moonbeam's misty light,
    And the lantern dimly burning.

No useless coffin enclosed his breast,
    Not in sheet nor in shroud we wound him ;
But he lay like a warrior taking his rest,
    With his martial cloak around him.

Few and short were the prayers we said,
    And we spoke not a word of sorrow ;
But we steadfastly gazed on the face that was dead,
    And we bitterly thought of the morrow.

We thought as we hollowed his narrow bed
    And smoothed down his lonely pillow,
That the foe and the stranger would tread o'er his
        head,
    And we far away on the billow !

Lightly they'll talk of the spirit that's gone,
   And o'er his cold ashes upbraid him, —
But little he'll reck, if they let him sleep on
   In the grave where a Briton has laid him.

But half of our heavy task was done
   When the clock struck the hour for retiring :
And we heard the distant and random gun
   That the foe was sullenly firing.

Slowly and sadly we laid him down,
   From the field of his fame fresh and gory ;
We carved not a line, and we raised not a stone,
   But we left him alone with his glory.

GEORGE III

(November, 1813)

WILLIAM WORDSWORTH

THE long reign of George III. came to an end in 1820. Years before his death the king was afflicted with fits of madness. By 1811, his mind was so far gone that he was unfit to attend to affairs of state, and the Prince of Wales was appointed Regent. The year 1813 was one of splendid victories. Wellington inflicted overwhelming defeat on Joseph Bonaparte at Vittoria and on Marshal Soult at the battle of the Pyrenees. The frontier towns of San Sebastian and Pamplona fell into his hands, and the French were finally driven out of Spain. The English armies were now free to combat Napoleon on French soil.

Now that all hearts are glad, all faces bright,
Our aged Sovereign sits to the ebb and flow
Of states and kingdoms, to their joy or woe,
Insensible ; he sits deprived of sight,

And lamentably wrapped in twofold night,
Whom no weak hopes deceived ; whose mind ensued,
Through perilous war, with regal fortitude,
Peace that should claim respect from lawless might.
Dread King of kings, vouchsafe a ray divine
To his forlorn condition ! let thy grace
Upon his inner soul in mercy shine ;
Permit his heart to kindle, and to embrace
(Though were it only for a moment's space)
The triumphs of this hour ; for they are THINE !

THE EVE OF WATERLOO

LORD BYRON

(Selected Stanzas from " Childe Harold's Pilgrimage," Canto III)

THE final contest with Napoleon was fought out at Waterloo. There
the allied nations of Europe brought their forces against the emperor.
Wellington and the English army lay at Brussels, expecting the ap-
proach of the French, but unaware that Napoleon had come within
fighting distance. Early in the morning of June 15, 1814, the attack
on the Prussian encampment at Charleroi opened the great battle of
four days' duration that crushed for all time the power of Napoleon.

There was a sound of revelry by night,
And Belgium's capital had gather'd then
Her Beauty and her Chivalry, and bright
The lamps shone o'er fair women and brave men ;
A thousand hearts beat happily ; and when
Music arose with its voluptuous swell,
Soft eyes look'd love to eyes which spake again,
And all went merry as a marriage bell ;
But hush ! hark ! a deep sound strikes like a rising
    knell !

Did ye not hear it? — No; 'twas but the wind,
Or the car rattling o'er the stony street;
On with the dance! let joy be unconfined;
No sleep till morn, when Youth and Pleasure meet
To chase the glowing Hours with flying feet —
But, hark! — that heavy sound breaks in once
        more,
As if the clouds its echo would repeat;
And nearer, clearer, deadlier than before!
Arm! Arm! it is — it is — the cannon's opening roar!

Ah! then and there was hurrying to and fro,
And gathering tears, and tremblings of distress,
And cheeks all pale, which but an hour ago
Blush'd at the praise of their own loveliness;
And there were sudden partings, such as press
The life from out young hearts, and choking sighs
Which ne'er might be repeated; who could guess
If ever more should meet those mutual eyes,
Since upon night so sweet such awful morn could rise?

And there was mounting in hot haste; the steed,
The mustering squadron, and the clattering car,
Went pouring forward with impetuous speed,
And swiftly forming in the ranks of war;
And the deep thunder peal on peal afar;
And near, the beat of the alarming drum
Roused up the soldier ere the morning star;
While throng'd the citizens with terror dumb,
Or whispering, with white lips — "The foe! They
        come! they come!"

THE FIELD OF WATERLOO

SIR WALTER SCOTT

(Stanzas IX–XII, XXII)

WELLINGTON'S troops encountered the French at Waterloo, a village in the neighborhood of Brussels. In the crisis of the battle, the steadiness of the English infantry won the day. The musketeers stood their ground unmoved until the French cavalry had advanced to within forty yards of their line, and then they opened a withering fire.

IX

Pale Brussels! then what thoughts were thine,
When ceaseless from the distant line
    Continued thunders came!
Each burgher held his breath, to hear
These forerunners of havoc near,
    Of rapine and of flame.
What ghastly sights were thine to meet,
When rolling through thy stately street,
The wounded showed their mangled plight
In token of the unfinished fight,
And from each anguish-laden wain
The blood-drops laid thy dust like rain!
How often in the distant drum
Heardst thou the fell Invader come,
While Ruin, shouting to his band,
Shook high her torch and gory brand! —
Cheer thee, fair City! From yon stand,
Impatient, still his outstretched hand
    Points to his prey in vain.

While maddening in his eager mood,
And all unwont to be withstood,
    He fires the fight again.

X

" On! on ! " was still his stern exclaim;
" Confront the battery's jaws of flame !
    Rush on the levelled gun !
My steel-clad cuirassiers, advance !
Each Hulan forward with his lance,
My Guard — my Chosen — charge for France,
    France and Napoleon ! "
Loud answered their acclaiming shout,
Greeting the mandate which sent out
Their bravest and their best to dare
The fate their leader shunned to share.
But He, his country's sword and shield,
Still in the battle front revealed,
Where danger fiercest swept the field,
    Came like a beam of light.
In action prompt, in sentence brief —
" Soldiers, stand firm," exclaimed the Chief,
    " England shall tell the fight ! "

XI

On came the whirlwind — like the last
But fiercest sweep of tempest-blast —
On came the whirlwind — steel-gleams broke
Like lightning through the rolling smoke ;
    The war was waked anew,

Three hundred cannon mouths roared loud,
And from their throats, with flash and cloud,
    Their showers of iron threw.
Beneath their fire, in full career,
Rushed on the ponderous cuirassier,
The lancer couched his ruthless spear,
And hurrying as to havoc near,
    The cohorts' eagles flew.
In one dark torrent, broad and strong,
The advancing onset rolled along,
Forth harbingered by fierce acclaim,
That, from the shroud of smoke and flame,
Pealed wildly the imperial name.

XII

But on the British heart were lost
The terrors of the charging host;
For not an eye the storm that viewed
Changed its proud glance of fortitude,
Nor was one forward footstep staid,
As dropped the dying and the dead.
Fast as their ranks the thunders tear,
Fast they renewed each serried square;
And on the wounded and the slain
Closed their diminished files again.
Till from their line scarce spears' lengths three,
Emerging from the smoke they see,
Helmet, and plume, and panoply, —
    Then waked their fire at once!
Each musketeer's revolving knell,

As fast, as regularly fell,
As when they practise to display
Their discipline on festal day.
 Then down went helm and lance,
Down were the eagle banners sent,
Down reeling steeds and riders went,
Corselets were pierced, and pennons rent;
 And, to augment the fray,
Wheeled full against their staggering flanks,
The English horsemen's foaming ranks
 Forced their resistless way.
Then to the musket-knell succeeds
The clash of swords — the neigh of steeds —
As plies the smith his clanging trade,
Against the cuirass rang the blade;
And while amid their scattered band
Raged the fierce rider's bloody brand,
Recoiled in common rout and fear,
Lancer and guard and cuirassier,
Horsemen and foot — a mingled host,
Their leaders fallen, their standards lost.

  * * * * * * *

XXII

Forgive, brave Dead, the imperfect lay!
Who may your names, your numbers, say?
What high-strung harp, what lofty line,
To each the dear-earned praise assign,
From high-born chiefs of martial fame
To the poor soldier's lowlier name?

Lightly ye rose that dawning day,
From your cold couch of swamp and clay,
To fill, before the sun was low,
The bed that morning cannot know. —
Oft may the tear the green sod steep,
And sacred be the heroes' sleep,
 Till time shall cease to run;
And ne'er beside their noble grave,
May Briton pass and fail to crave
A blessing on the fallen brave
 Who fought with Wellington!

ODE ON THE DEATH OF THE DUKE OF WELLINGTON

LORD TENNYSON

(Stanza VI)

NELSON died in the hour of victory. Wellington lived to serve his country in council and on the field for thirty-seven years after the battle of Waterloo. In 1852 the great general was laid to rest beside the great admiral in the cathedral of St. Paul's.

Who is he that cometh, like an honour'd guest,
With banner and with music, with soldier and with
 priest,
With a nation weeping, and breaking on my rest?
Mighty Seaman, this is he
Was great by land as thou by sea.
Thine island loves thee well, thou famous man,
The greatest sailor since the world began.
Now, to the roll of muffled drums,

To thee the greatest soldier comes;
For this is he
Was great by land as thou by sea;
His foes were thine; he kept us free;
O give him welcome, this is he
Worthy of our gorgeous rites,
And worthy to be laid by thee;
For this is England's greatest son,
He that gain'd a hundred fights,
Nor ever lost an English gun;
This is he that far away
Against the myriads of Assaye
Clash'd with his fiery few and won;
And underneath another sun,
Warring on a later day,
Round affrighted Lisbon drew
The treble works, the vast designs
Of his labour'd rampart lines,
Where he greatly stood at bay,
Whence he issued forth anew,
And ever great and greater grew,
Beating from the wasted vines
Back to France her banded swarms,
Back to France with countless blows,
Till o'er the hills her eagles flew
Beyond the Pyrenean pines,
Follow'd up in valley and in glen
With blare of bugle and clamour of men,
Roll of cannon and clash of arms,
And England pouring on her foes.

Such a war had such a close.
Again their ravening eagle rose
In anger, wheel'd on Europe-shadowing wings,
And barking for the thrones of kings;
Till one that sought but Duty's iron crown
On that loud sabbath shook the spoiler down,
A day of onsets of despair!
Dashed on every rocky square
Their surging charges foam'd themselves away;
Last, the Prussian trumpet blew;
Thro' the long-tormented air
Heaven flash'd a sudden jubilant ray,
And down we swept and charged and overthrew.
So great a soldier taught us there,
What long-enduring hearts could do
In that world-earthquake, Waterloo!
Mighty Seaman, tender and true,
And pure as he from taint of craven guile,
O saviour of the silver-coasted isle,
O shaker of the Baltic and the Nile,
If aught of things that here befall
Touch a spirit among things divine,
If love of country move thee there at all,
Be glad, because his bones are laid by thine!
And thro' the centuries let a people's voice
In full acclaim,
A people's voice,
The proof and echo of all human fame,
A people's voice, when they rejoice
At civic revel and pomp and game,

Attest their great commander's claim
With honour, honour, honour, honour to him,
Eternal honour to his name.

CROWNED AND WEDDED

ELIZABETH BARRETT BROWNING

Two of the sons of George III., George IV. and William IV., lived
to succeed him on the throne, but they left no children. The next heir
was Victoria, daughter of Edward, Duke of Kent, the fourth son of
George III. She was proclaimed queen in 1837, when but eighteen
years of age. Victoria had been carefully educated for this high posi-
tion and she keenly felt her heavy responsibility. In 1840 she was
married to her cousin, Prince Albert of Coburg and Gotha.

When last before her people's face her own fair face
    she bent,
Within the meek projection of that shade she was
    content
To erase the child-smile from her lips, which seemed
    as if it might
Be still kept holy from the world to childhood still in
    sight —
To erase it with a solemn vow, — a princely vow — to
    rule ;
A priestly vow — to rule by grace of God the pitiful;
A very godlike vow — to rule in right and righteous-
    ness,
And with the law and for the land ! — so God the
    vower bless !

The minster was alight that day, but not with fire, I
    ween,
And long-drawn glitterings swept adown that mighty
    aislèd scene.
The priests stood stolèd in their pomp, the sworded
    chiefs in theirs,
And so, the collared knights, and so, the civil minis-
    ters,
And so, the waiting lords and dames — and little
    pages best
At holding trains — and legates so, from countries
    east and west.
So, alien princes, native peers, and high-born ladies
    bright,
Along whose brows the Queen's, new crowned, flashed
    coronets to light.
And so, the people at the gates, with priestly hand on
    high,
Which bring the first anointing to all legal majesty.
And so the *Dead* — who lie in rows beneath the
    minster floor,
There, verily, an awful state maintaining evermore;
The statesman whose clean palm will kiss no bribe
    whate'er it be,
The courtier who, for no fair queen, will rise up to
    his knee,
The court-dame who, for no court-tire, will leave her
    shroud behind,
The laureate who no courtlier rhyme than "dust to
    dust" can find,

The kings and queens who having made that vow and
    worn that crown,

Descended unto lower thrones and darker, deep
    adown!

Dieu et mon droit — what is't to them? — what mean-
    ing can it have? —

The King of kings, the right of death — God's judg-
    ment and the grave.

And when betwixt the quick and dead, the young fair
    queen had vowed,

The living shouted " May she live! Victoria, live!"
    aloud.

And as the loyal shouts went up, true spirits prayed
    between,

"The blessings happy monarchs have, be thine, O
    crownèd queen!"

But now before her people's face she bendeth hers
    anew,

And calls them, while she vows, to be her witness
    thereunto.

She vowed to rule, and, in that oath, her childhood
    put away.

She doth maintain her womanhood, in vowing love
    to-day.

O, lovely lady! — let her vow! — such lips become
    such vows,

And fairer goeth bridal wreath than crown with ver-
    nal brows.

O, lovely lady! — let her vow! yea, let her vow to
    love! —

And though she be no less a queen — with purples
    hung above,
The pageant of a court behind, the royal kin around,
And woven gold to catch her looks turned maidenly
    to ground,
Yet may the bride-veil hide from her a little of that
    state,
While loving hopes, for retinues, about her sweetness
    wait.
She vows to love who vowed to rule — (the chosen
    at her side)
Let none say, God preserve the queen ! — but, rather,
    Bless the bride !
None blow the trump, none bend the knee, none vio-
    late the dream
Wherein no monarch but a wife, she to herself may
    seem.
Or if ye say, Preserve the queen ! — oh, breathe it
    inward low —
She is a *woman*, and *beloved !* — and 'tis enough but so.
Count it enough, thou noble prince, who tak'st her
    by the hand,
And claimest for thy lady-love, our lady of the
    land !
And since, Prince Albert, men have called thy spirit
    high and rare,
And true to truth and brave for truth, as some at
    Augsburg were, —
We charge thee by thy lofty thoughts, and by thy
    poet-mind

Which not by glory and degree takes measure of man-
   kind,
Esteem that wedded hand less dear for sceptre than
   for ring,
And hold her uncrowned womanhood to be the royal
   thing.

And now, upon our queen's last vow, what blessings
   shall we pray?
None, straitened to a shallow crown, will suit our lips
   to-day.
Behold, they must be free as love — they must be
   broad as free,
Even to the borders of heaven's light and earth's
   humanity.
Long live she! — send up loyal shouts — and true
   hearts pray between —
" The blessings happy *peasants* have, be thine, O
   crownèd queen! "

TO THE MEMORY OF PRINCE ALBERT

LORD TENNYSON

(From " Idylls of the King." Dedication)

PRINCE ALBERT died in 1861. He had been an ideal Prince Con-
sort, greatly aiding the queen by advice and sympathy. His voice was
always for peace and for such legislation as would better the lot of the
poor.

These to His Memory — since he held them dear,
Perchance as finding there unconsciously
Some image of himself — I dedicate,

I dedicate, I consecrate with tears —
These Idylls.
                      And indeed He seems to me
Scarce other than my own ideal knight,
"Who reverenced his conscience as his king ;
Whose glory was, redressing human wrong ;
Who spake no slander, no, nor listen'd to it ;
Who loved one only and who clave to her — "
Her — over all whose realms to their last isle,
Commingled with the gloom of imminent war,
The shadow of His loss moved like eclipse,
Darkening the world. We have lost him : he is gone :
We know him now : all narrow jealousies
Are silent ; and we see him as he moved,
How modest, kindly, all-accomplish'd, wise,
With what sublime suppression of himself,
And in what limits, and how tenderly ;
Not swaying to this faction or to that ;
Not making his high place the lawless perch
Of wing'd ambitions, nor a vantage-ground
For pleasure ; but thro' all this tract of years
Wearing the white flower of a blameless life,
Before a thousand peering littlenesses,
In that fierce light which beats upon a throne,
And blackens every blot : for where is he,
Who dares foreshadow for an only son
A lovelier life, a more unstain'd, than his ?
Or how should England dreaming of *his* sons
Hope more for these than some inheritance
Of such a life, a heart, a mind as thine,

Thou noble Father of her Kings to be,
Laborious for her people and her poor —
Voice in the rich dawn of an ampler day —
Far-sighted summoner of War and Waste
To fruitful strifes and rivalries of peace —
Sweet nature gilded by the gracious gleam
Of letters, dear to Science, dear to Art,
Dear to thy land and ours, a Prince indeed,
Beyond all titles, and a household name,
Hereafter, thro' all times, Albert the Good.

Break not, O woman's heart, but still endure ;
Break not, for thou art Royal, but endure,
Remembering all the beauty of that star
Which shone so close beside Thee, that ye made
One light together, but has past and left
The Crown of lonely splendour.
                                        May all love,
His love, unseen but felt, o'ershadow Thee,
The love of all Thy sons encompass Thee,
The love of all Thy daughters cherish Thee,
The love of all Thy people comfort Thee,
Till God's love set Thee at his side again !

TO THE QUEEN

LORD TENNYSON

(Dedication of Her Laureate's Poems)

QUEEN VICTORIA'S reign of sixty-four years is the longest in English history. It was rendered glorious by the maintenance of peace with European powers, by the development of vast colonial possessions, by wise laws intended to promote the people's rights, and by the further-ance of education and popular welfare. The Queen's ministers were men who had the confidence of the nation and they were guided by the nation's will as expressed in the House of Commons. In all their beneficent work, they had the sympathetic coöperation of Victoria.

> Revered, beloved — O you that hold
>   A nobler office upon earth
>   Than arms, or power of brain or birth
> Could give the warrior kings of old,
>
> Victoria, — since your royal grace
>   To one of less desert allows
>   This laurel greener from the brows
> Of him that utter'd nothing base ;
>
> And should your greatness, and the care
>   That yokes with empire, yield you time
>   To make demand of modern rhyme
> If aught of ancient worth be there ;
>
> Then — while a sweeter music wakes,
>   And thro' wild March the throstle calls,
>   Where all about your palace-walls
> The sun-lit almond-blossom shakes —

Take, Madam, this poor book of song;
  For tho' the faults were thick as dust
  In vacant chambers, I could trust
Your kindness.   May you rule us long,

And leave us rulers of your blood
  As noble till the latest day !
  May children of our children say,
" She wrought her people lasting good ;

" Her court was pure; her life serene ;
  God gave her peace ; her land reposed ;
  A thousand claims to reverence closed
In her as Mother, Wife, and Queen ;

" And statesmen at her council met
  Who knew the seasons, when to take
  Occasion by the hand, and make
The bounds of freedom wider yet

" By shaping some august decree,
  Which kept her throne unshaken still,
  Broad-based upon her people's will,
And compass'd by the inviolate sea."

CHARTIST SONG

Thomas Cooper

No sooner were the Napoleonic wars at an end than the English people began to demand for themselves such privileges as the French had won. First of all, they asked for power to send representatives to the House of Commons in order that they might have some share in the making of the laws. The substance of their demands was formulated in the People's Charter and the reformers were therefore called Chartists. By 1832, popular agitation had become so vigorous and so persistent that Parliament dared no longer resist. The first Reform Act was passed in that year. The right of electing representatives to the House of Commons was taken away from the rotten boroughs and given to a number of towns that had never been allowed this privilege. Moreover, the right of voting at town elections was extended to all householders. The people's representatives succeeded in carrying through some much needed reforms.

The time shall come when wrong shall end,
When peasant to peer no more shall bend;
When the lordly Few shall lose their sway,
And the Many no more their frown obey.
    Toil, brothers, toil, till the work is done,
    Till the struggle is o'er, and the Charter won!

The time shall come when the artisan
Shall homage no more the titled man;
When the moiling men who delve in the mine
By Mammon's decree no more shall pine.
    Toil, brothers, toil, till the work is done,
    Till the struggle is o'er, and the Charter won.

The time shall come when the weavers' band
Shall hunger no more in their fatherland;
When the factory-child can sleep till day,
And smile while it dreams of sport and play.
    Toil, brothers, toil, till the work is done,
    Till the struggle is o'er, and the Charter won.

The time shall come when man shall hold
His brother more dear than sordid gold;
When the negro's stain his freeborn mind

Shall sever no more from human-kind.
  Toil, brothers, toil, till the world is free,
  Till Justice and Love hold jubilee.

The time has come when kingly crown
And mitre for toys of the past are shown;
When the fierce and false alike shall fall,
And mercy and·truth encircle all.
  Toil, brothers, toil, till the world is free,
  Till Mercy and Truth hold jubilee!

The time shall come when earth shall be
A garden of joy, from sea to sea,
When the slaughterous sword is drawn no more,
And goodness exults from shore to shore.
  Toil, brothers, toil, till the world is free,
  Till Goodness shall hold high jubilee!

THE BARONS BOLD

WILLIAM JOHNSON FOX

THE Chartists were not satisfied with the measure of representation accorded the people by the Reform Act of 1832 and demanded manhood suffrage. On April 6, 1848, twenty-five thousand men assembled on Kennington Common, south of the Thames, determined to carry to the House of Commons a monster petition that the Charter should immediately be granted. The magistrates were greatly alarmed and made elaborate preparations for the defence of the city. The Chartists were unarmed and dared not meet the troops, so the great demonstration came to nothing. But suffrage has since been given to every householder in town and country alike, and the people have to-day sufficient influence in the House of Commons to carry any measure for which they make a united demand.

The Barons bold on Runnymede
  By union won their charter;
True men were they, prepar'd to bleed,
  But not their rights to barter:
And they swore that England's laws
  Were above a tyrant's word;
And they prov'd that freedom's cause
  Was above a tyrant's sword:
      Then honour we
      The memory
Of those Barons brave united;
      And like their band,
      Join hand to hand:
Our wrongs shall soon be righted.

The Commons brave, in Charles's time,
  By union made the Crown fall,
And show'd the world how royal crime
  Should lead to royal downfall:
And they swore that rights and laws
  Were above a monarch's word;
And they raised the nation's cause
  Above the monarch's sword:
      Then honour we
      The memory
Of those Commons brave, united;
      And like their band,
      Join hand to hand:
Our wrongs shall soon be righted.

The People firm, from Court and Peers,
  By union won Reform, sirs,

And, union safe, the nation steers
    Through sunshine and through storm, sirs :
And we swear that equal laws
    Shall prevail o'er lordlings' words,
And can prove that freedom's cause
    Is too strong for hireling swords :
            Then honour we
            The victory
Of the people brave, united ;
            Let all our bands
            Join hearts and hands :
Our wrongs shall all be righted.

THE CRY OF THE CHILDREN

ELIZABETH BARRETT BROWNING

THE invention of machinery and the building of great factories made the employment of children profitable, and many a father sent his boys and girls to work before they were old enough to endure the strain. There was at first no limit set to the number of hours the children might be kept at work or to the tasks that might be required of them. The suffering of the factory operatives was finally brought to the attention of Parliament, and laws for the protection of women and children were passed. Mrs. Browning's poem did much to rouse public feeling in behalf of the little toilers.

Do ye hear the children weeping, O my brothers,
        Ere the sorrow comes with years ?
They are leaning their young heads against their
        mothers,
        And *that* cannot stop their tears.
The young lambs are bleating in the meadows,
    The young birds are chirping in the nest,

The young fawns are playing with the shadows,
 The young flowers are blowing toward the west —
But the young, young children, O my brothers,
  They are weeping bitterly !
They are weeping in the playtime of the others,
  In the country of the free.

Do you question the young children in the sorrow,
  Why their tears are falling so ?
The old man may weep for his to-morrow
  Which is lost in Long Ago.
The old tree is leafless in the forest,
 The old year is ending in the frost,
The old wound, if stricken, is the sorest,
 The old hope is hardest to be lost.
But the young, young children, O my brothers,
  Do you ask them why they stand
Weeping sore before the bosoms of their mothers,
  In our happy Fatherland ?

They look up with their pale and sunken faces,
  And their looks are sad to see,
For the man's hoary anguish draws and presses
  Down the cheeks of infancy.
" Your old earth," they say, " is very dreary ;
 Our young feet," they say, " are very weak !
Few paces have we taken, yet are weary —
 Our grave-rest is very far to seek.
Ask the aged why they weep, and not the children ;
  For the outside earth is cold ;

And we young ones stand without, in our bewildering,
    And the graves are for the old.

"True," say the children, "it may happen
    That we die before our time.
Little Alice died last year — her grave is shapen
    Like a snowball, in the rime.
We looked into the pit prepared to take her.
    Was no room for any work in the close clay!
From the sleep wherein she lieth none will wake her,
    Crying, 'Get up, little Alice! it is day.'
If you listen by that grave, in sun and shower,
    With your ear down, little Alice never cries.
Could we see her face, be sure we should not know
    her,
    For the smile has time for growing in her eyes.
And merry go her moments, lulled and stilled in
    The shroud by the kirk-chime!
It is good when it happens," say the children,
    "That we die before our time."

Alas, alas, the children! they are seeking
    Death in life, as best to have.
They are binding up their hearts away from breaking,
    With a cerement from the grave.
Go out, children, from the mine and from the city,
    Sing out, children, as the little thrushes do.
Pluck your handfuls of the meadow-cowslips pretty,
    Laugh aloud, to feel your fingers let them through!
But they answer, "Are your cowslips of the meadows
    Like our weeds anear the mine?

Leave us quiet in the dark of the coal-shadows,
     From your pleasures fair and fine!

" For oh," say the children, "we are weary
     And we cannot run or leap.
If we cared for any meadows, it were merely
     To drop down in them and sleep.
Our knees tremble sorely in the stooping,
  We fall upon our faces, trying to go;
And, underneath our heavy eyelids drooping,
  The reddest flower would look as pale as snow.
For, all day, we drag our burden tiring
     Through the coal-dark, underground —
Or, all day, we drive the wheels of iron
     In the factories, round and round.

" For, all day, the wheels are droning, turning, —
     Their wind comes in our faces, —
Till our hearts turn, — our heads, with pulses burning,
     And the walls turn in their places.
Turns the sky in the high window blank and reeling,
  Turns the long light that drops adown the wall,
Turn the black flies that crawl along the ceiling,
  All are turning, all the day, and we with all.
And all the day, the iron wheels are droning,
     And sometimes we could pray,
'O ye wheels,' (breaking out in a mad moaning)
     'Stop! be silent for to-day!'"

Ay! be silent! Let them hear each other breathing
     For a moment, mouth to mouth!

Let them touch each other's hands in a fresh wreath-
    ing
      Of their tender human youth!
Let them feel that this cold metallic motion
  Is not all the life God fashions or reveals.
Let them prove their living souls against the notion
  That they live in you, or under you, O wheels! —
Still, all day, the iron wheels go onward,
      Grinding life down from its mark;
And the children's souls, which God is calling sunward,
      Spin on blindly in the dark.

Now tell the poor young children, O my brothers,
      To look up to Him and pray;
So the blessèd One who blesseth all the others,
      Will bless them another day.
They answer, "Who is God that He should hear us,
  While the rushing of the iron wheel is stirred?
When we sob aloud, the human creatures near us,
  Pass by, hearing not, or answer not a word.
And *we* hear not (for the wheels in their resounding)
      Strangers speaking at the door.
Is it likely God, with angels singing round Him,
      Hears our weeping any more?

"Two words, indeed, of praying we remember,
      And at midnight's hour of harm,
'Our Father,' looking upward in the chamber,
      We say softly for a charm.
We know no other words, except 'Our Father,'
  And we think that, in some pause of angel's song,

God may pluck them with the silence sweet to gather,
  And hold both within His right hand which is
    strong.
Our Father ! If He heard us, He would surely
    (For they call Him good and mild)
Answer, smiling down the steep world very purely,
    ' Come and rest with me, my child.'

" But no ! " say the children, weeping faster,
    " He is speechless as a stone.
And they tell us, of His image is the master
    Who commands us to work on.
Go to ! " say the children, — " up in Heaven,
  Dark, wheel-like, turning clouds are all we find.
Do not mock us ; grief has made us unbelieving —
  We look up for God, but tears have made us blind."
Do you hear the children weeping and disproving,
    O my brothers, what ye preach ?
For God's possible is taught by his world's loving,
    And the children doubt of each.

And well may the children weep before you !
    They are weary ere they run.
They have never seen the sunshine, nor the glory,
    Which is brighter than the sun.
They know the grief of man, without his wisdom.
  They sink in man's despair, without its calm ;
Are slaves, without the liberty in Christdom,
  Are martyrs, by the pang without the palm, —
Are worn, as if with age, yet unretrievingly
    The harvest of its memories cannot reap, —

Are orphans of the earthly love and heavenly.
    Let them weep! let them weep!

They look up, with their pale and sunken faces,
    And their look is dread to see,
For they mind you of their angels in high places,
    With eyes turned on Deity! —
" How long," they say, " how long, O cruel nation,
  Will you stand, to move the world, on a child's
    heart, —
Stifle down with a mailed heel its palpitation,
  And tread onward to your throne amid the mart?
Our blood splashes upward, O gold-heaper,
    And your purple shows your path!
But the child's sob in the silence curses deeper
    Than the strong man in his wrath."

THE PEOPLE'S PETITION

W. M. W. CALL

THE landlords, who were naturally interested to secure high prices
for their crops, had induced Parliament to pass a corn law (1815) im-
posing heavy taxes on all grains imported into the country. This pre-
vented foreigners from sending their grain to England, and bread,
since it must be made of English wheat, was very dear. Working-
men found it difficult to buy sufficient food for themselves and their
families. It was a grievance most keenly felt by the people of the
towns who had no garden-land. Much was said and written against
the corn law, but no argument could induce the government to aban-
don this wicked tax until 1846. Then the potato crop failed, and the
Irish peasants, deprived of their staple food, began to die of starvation.
The corn law was speedily repealed, and it has since been the policy
of Great Britain to lay import duties only upon luxuries.

O lords! O rulers of the nation!
O softly cloth'd!   O richly fed!
O men of wealth and noble station!
Give us our daily bread.

For you we are content to toil,
For you our blood like rain is shed;
Then, lords and rulers of the soil,
Give us our daily bread.

Your silken robes, with endless care,
Still weave we; still uncloth'd, unfed,
We make the raiment that ye wear:
Give us our daily bread.

In the red forge-light do we stand,
We early leave — late seek our bed,
Tempering the steel for your right hand:
Give us our daily bread.

We sow your fields, ye reap the fruit;
We live in misery and in dread;
Hear but our prayer, and we are mute:
Give us our daily bread.

Throughout old England's pleasant fields
There is no spot where we may tread,
No house to us sweet shelter yields:
Give us our daily bread.

Fathers are we; we see our sons,
We see our fair young daughters, dead;

Then hear us, O ye mighty ones!
Give us our daily bread.

'Tis vain — with cold, unfeeling eye
Ye gaze on us, uncloth'd, unfed;
'Tis vain — ye will not hear our cry,
Nor give us daily bread.

We turn from you, our lords by birth,
To him who is our Lord above;
We all are made of the same earth,
Are children of one love.

Then, Father of this world of wonders,
Judge of the living and the dead,
Lord of the lightnings and the thunders,
Give us our daily bread.

THE DAY IS COMING

WILLIAM MORRIS

MUCH has been done for the welfare of the people in England, but much yet remains to do. William Morris hoped that all distinction between rich and poor would be done away and that every man would labor for the common good. The poet's dream may yet become reality.

Come hither lads and hearken,
    for a tale there is to tell,
Of the wonderful days a-coming, when all
    shall be better than well.

And the tale shall be told of a country,
    a land in the midst of the sea,

And folk shall call it England
  in the days that are going to be.

There more than one in a thousand
  in the days that are yet to come,
Shall have some hope of the morrow,
  some joy of the ancient home.

For then, laugh not, but listen,
  to this strange tale of mine,
All folk that are in England
  shall be better lodged than swine.

Then a man shall work and bethink him,
  and rejoice in the deeds of his hand,
Nor yet come home in the even
  too faint and weary to stand.

Men in that time a-coming
  shall work and have no fear
For to-morrow's lack of earning
  and the hunger-wolf anear.

I tell you this for a wonder,
  that no man then shall be glad
Of his fellow's fall and mishap
  to snatch at the work he had.

For that which the worker winneth
  shall then be his indeed,
Nor shall half be reaped for nothing
  by him that sowed no seed.

O strange new wonderful justice!
  But for whom shall we gather the gain?
For ourselves and for each of our fellows,
  and no hand shall labour in vain.

Then all Mine and all Thine shall be Ours,
  and no more shall any man crave
For riches that serve for nothing
  but to fetter a friend for a slave.

And what wealth then shall be left us
  when none shall gather gold
To buy his friend in the market,
  and pinch and pine the sold?

Nay, what save the lovely city,
  and the little house on the hill,
And the wastes and the woodland beauty,
  and the happy fields we till;

And the homes of ancient stories,
  the tombs of the mighty dead;
And the wise men seeking out marvels,
  and the poet's teeming head;

And the painter's hand of wonder;
  and the marvellous fiddle-bow,
And the banded choirs of music:
  all those that do and know.

For all these shall be ours and all men's,
  nor shall any lack a share
Of the toil and the gain of living
  in the days when the world grows fair.

ENGLAND

JAMES LINCOLN

Who would trust England, let him lift his eyes
  To Nelson, columned o'er Trafalgar Square,
  Her hieroglyph of Duty, written where
The roar of traffic hushes to the skies;
Or mark, while Paul's vast shadow softly lies
  On Gordon's statued sleep, how praise and prayer
  Flush through the frank young faces clustering
      there
To con that kindred rune of Sacrifice.

O England, no bland cloud-ship in the blue,
  But rough oak, plunging on o'er perilous jars
Of reef and ice, our faith will follow you
  The more for tempest roar that strains your spars
And splits your canvas, be your helm but true,
  Your courses shapen by the eternal stars.

NOTES

PAGE

1 **Cassibelan**: Cassivelaunus, who was probably not the uncle but the grandfather of Cunobelaunus. The tribute had not been rendered in the ninety-five years since Cæsar's second invasion.

2 **Cloten.** Though son of the queen and stepson of the king, this Cloten is a clownish fellow, who blurts out his opinions so rudely that the Roman disdains to reply.

2 **That opportunity.** The queen says, to put it a little more simply: "As it was then their opportunity to take tribute from us, so now it is our opportunity to resume our independence."

3 **Lud's town**: London. Lud was the god of commerce. London was the principal port for trade with the Continent.

3 **Mulmutius**: a legendary character, the traditional founder of kingship in Britain.

4 **Augustus Cæsar**: the title given to all Roman emperors after Augustus. In this instance Claudius is meant.

4 **Boadicea.** Tennyson's poem under this same title, and Fletcher's tragedy "Bonduca," though too difficult for young students, will be enjoyed by more advanced readers.

5 **Rome shall perish.** The wild prophecy of the Druid was fulfilled five centuries later when the Roman Empire was invaded by barbarian tribes and the imperial city suffered sack. The troops were summoned from Britain to aid in the defence of Rome.

5 **Sounds, not arms**: an allusion to the effeminate pleasures of the later Romans.

5 **Regions Cæsar never knew.** The reference is doubtless to the British Empire.

7 **the heathen**: the pagan Saxons.

7 **One lying in the dust at Almesbury**: Guinevere, Arthur's queen, whom he had left in the nunnery of Almesbury to repent the wrongs she had done him and the kingdom.

413

10 **Excalibur**: Arthur's sword, which, the old story says, shone in his enemies' eyes as bright as thirty torches.

11 **The goodliest fellowship of famous knights** : the knights of the Round Table.

11 **Merlin** : a hoary magician and prophet, much revered at Arthur's court.

14 **Three Queens.** The chief of these queens was Arthur's sister, Morgan the Fay. With her were the Queen of Northgallis and the Queen of the Westerlands.

16 **Avilion** : Avalon, the Land of Eternal Youth, beyond the waves — the mythical paradise of the Britons. This was the home of Morgan the Fay.

18 **Monkish gown.** Monasteries were the only schools in those troubled times.

18 **Lord of the harp.** The story of Alfred's finding his way into the Danish camp disguised as a harper may not be true, but that he was both poet and musician we have good reason to believe.

18 **this noble miser of his time.** Alfred caused a lantern to be made of wood and white oxhorn, in which candles might burn steadily shut in from the wind. Each candle lasted four hours, and so the day was divided into six parts that the king might accurately plan his time.

18 **pain narrows not his cares.** Alfred suffered all his life from a distressing malady, yet he led his army on rapid and exhausting marches, gave personal attention to the execution of justice throughout his realm, and overlooked the work of artisans and architects, translators, and law-makers.

18 **remote Jerusalem.** The patriarch of Jerusalem sent letters and gifts to King Alfred.

18 **Christian India**. Asser states that embassies were sent to Alfred from the Tyrrhenean Sea. It may be that Wordsworth had Armenia in mind.

20 **Merrily sang the monks of Ely.** The lines are very old, and may have been written by Canute himself. The king was a lover of minstrelsy and a patron of poets.

20 **My queen**: the Norman princess Emma, the wife of Etheldred. After the death of the Saxon king she was married to Canute.

21 **silversticks and goldsticks great**: officers so named from the gilt

or silvered wands they bore. The colonel of a regiment of Life Guards is still called Gold Stick in England, and the field officer of the Life Guards, when on duty at the palace, is known as Silver Stick.

23 **Those fair sons:** Harold and Harthacanute, who fell to quarrelling over the succession immediately after their father's death.

23 **Look, the land is crowned with minsters.** To atone for the bloodshed by which the kingdom was won, Canute had given generously to monasteries both in England and on the Continent.

24 **communis omnibus:** common to all men.

24 **Loathsome lepers.** The monarchs of England from Edward the Confessor to Queen Anne were believed to have power to cure scrofula by a touch of the hand. Thackeray attributes this royal gift to Canute.

24 **Jewish captain:** Joshua x. 12–14.

25 **And he sternly bade them.** The words of the king, as reported by Huntingdon, were: " Let all men know how empty and worthless is the power of kings, for there is none worthy of the name but He whom heaven, earth, and sea obey by eternal laws."

26 **his golden crown of empire.** The same chronicler states that Canute "thenceforth never wore his crown of gold, but placed it as a lasting memorial on the image of our Lord."

26 **In heaven signs.** A comet appeared in the sky this year (1065), and was thought to portend disaster.

27 **the great church of Holy Peter:** Westminster Abbey.

27 **The seven sleepers.** The legend runs that seven young men of Ephesus, Christians, hid in a mountain cave to escape the persecution of the Emperor Decius. By his orders the mouth of the cavern was blocked up with stone, and here the seven youths miraculously slept 360 years, awaking then " with their faces fresh and blooming as roses," to testify to the resurrection from the dead.

27 **Tostig:** Harold's brother, Earl of Northumbria.

27 **Aldwyth:** Tostig's wife, later married to Harold.

28 **William Malet:** a Norman nobleman, one of William's retinue, but friendly to Harold.

29 **My ransom'd prisoner.** Harold's ship, bound to Flanders, was driven out of its course by contrary winds and wrecked on the coast of Ponthieu. According to the cruel custom of the times, Harold was

held for ransom by his captor. The price was paid by William that he might get possession of this formidable rival.

30 **William Rufus**: the second son of William, and his successor on the English throne.

30 **the great assembly choose their king.** The Witan was accustomed to elect the ablest of the descendants of the dead king, but its choice was not limited to the royal line.

31 **Wolfnoth**: Harold's youngest brother, a hostage at the court of Normandy. He was kept a prisoner, first in Normandy and then in England, till his death.

33 **"Work for the tanner."** William's grandfather on his mother's side had been a tanner at Falaise.

34 **Then for thine Edith.** Edith was Harold's betrothed.

34 **The Atheling.** Edgar, "the child," great-grandson of Ethelbert, was a boy of eight years. He was elected king after Harold's death, but was obliged to acknowledge William's conquest of the realm. He spent the greater part of his life in exile at the court of Scotland.

35 **my wife descends from Alfred.** Matilda of Flanders, whose ancestors were descended from Alfrith, the daughter of King Alfred, was William's wife.

39 **Stigand**: Archbishop of Canterbury, an Englishman who dreaded Norman rule.

40 **Ha Rou,** or Haro: an old French war-cry, perhaps of Gothic origin and allied to our hooray and hurrah.

40 **the gonfanon of Holy Peter.** The pope favored William's claim, and sent a consecrated banner as sign of his approval of the invasion of England.

40 **he bares his face.** In the crisis of the battle the cry arose that William had fallen. He lifted the visor of his helmet and cried, "Here is Duke William," thus encouraging his followers to fresh effort.

41 **War-woodman of old Woden.** The northern peoples, in their pagan days, had for chief god Odin or Woden, and one of their terms for a mighty warrior whose blade hewed down his enemies like trees was "Odin's Woodman." In his excitement, Stigand the Saxon, though a Christian priest, utters the old phrase.

42 **Gurth** and **Leofwin**: Harold's brothers, who fell at Senlac Hill.

43 **The day of St. Calixtus**: October 14. Calixtus was pope early in the third century.

44 **a church to God.** Battle Abbey was built to commemorate this victory.

44 **the false Northumbrian**: Morkere, who had been appointed earl of Northumbria in Tostig's place. When Tostig undertook to regain his earldom, Harold led an army to Morkere's aid and won for him the battle of Stamford Bridge (September 25, 1066). When Harold hurried south to meet William at Senlac Hill (October 14), Morkere refused to follow with his troops.

45 **Of one self-stock at first.** The Normans came originally from the same Scandinavian lands that had given birth to Angles, Jutes, Saxons, and Danes. The distinction between Norman and English, conqueror and conquered, did not disappear till the fourteenth century.

46 **mitre and pall thou hast y-sold.** William Rufus sold ecclesiastical appointments to the highest bidder without regard to the fitness of the candidate.

46 **Steading and hamlet and churches tall.** The Conqueror had devastated a good part of Hampshire to make room for the New Forest, that he might be able to hunt the wild deer in the neighborhood of Winchester.

46 **Tyrrel**, Walter: a French knight much trusted by William Rufus. Some of the chroniclers state that he intended to kill his sovereign. He himself denied on oath that he had been near the king that day. Nevertheless, he fled to France.

47 **A hart of ten**: a hart of ten antlers. The more branches a stag's horn has the more of a prize he is for the hunter.

48 **fell to sanctuarie.** The churches served as places of refuge in those wild times to all men fleeing from vengeance, no matter what their crime may have been.

49 **"Clerkly Harry."** He was called Henry Beauclerc (fine scholar) because of his devotion to letters.

49 **his elder brother's eyes were gone.** Duke Robert was thrown into prison and held there till his death, but there is no good evidence that he was blinded.

49 **The poor flung ploughshares on his road**: presumably to show that they would not till the fields for so hard a taskmaster. This is a

misrepresentation. Henry was cruel to the barons, who withstood his will, but his stern enforcement of the law in behalf of the English people won for him the title "Lion of Justice."

50 **his tribute's right**: a token of feudal allegiance.

50 **your father's foot did slip**: an allusion to the story that William the Norman stumbled when first he set foot on English ground and fell prostrate. With great presence of mind he caught up a handful of earth as a sign of ownership, and so converted the bad omen into an augury of success.

53 **The Prince's sister**: his half-sister, the Countess of Perche.

55 **When the Body of Christ goes down the street**: when the sacramental bread, or wafer, is borne in priestly procession.

57 **And he wept and mourned**. Prince William was the son of Matilda, the niece of Edgar Atheling, and therefore descended from King Alfred. Born in England, he was loved by the people as an English prince.

61 **Glocester**: Robert, Earl of Glocester, Matilda's half-brother.

62 **yon towers**: the castle of Lincoln which had recently been in Stephen's hands.

62 **The Empress**. Matilda was the widow of the Emperor Henry V.

63 **secular splendours**. Becket was a plain merchant's son, but he lived in great state. Once he went to Paris on an embassy and the people were much impressed by the magnificence of his retinue. They said, "If this be the chancellor of England, what must the king be ?"

64 **the man shall seal**. The council of Northampton was held in 1164. All the clergy present save Becket had signed the Constitutions of Clarendon, defining the relations of church and state. The signature of the Archbishop of Canterbury, primate of England, was essential to their validity. Thomas was finally induced to sign the document, but he would not affix the official seal. In fear of his life he fled to France, and spent the next six years in the attempt to induce King Henry to withdraw from his decision.

64 **My burgher's son**. Thomas was the son of Gilbert Becket, a citizen of London.

65 **the nineteen winters of King Stephen**. Henry's account of the horrors of the civil war is not exaggerated. The chronicler relates: "When the castles were made, they (the barons) filled them with devils and evil men. Then took they those men that they imagined had any property, both by night and by day, peasant men and women, and put them in prison for their gold and silver and tortured them with most terrible torture."

65 **went abroad thro' all my counties.** Henry II. spent much time journeying from place to place and visiting the courts in order to make sure that his laws were enforced without fear or favor.

66 **your courts.** The ecclesiastical courts could not award the death penalty. The king wished that, after a priest had been unfrocked, he should be made over to the civil courts for punishment. To this the church would not consent.

66 **certain wholesome usages.** The king had caused the customs observed by Henry I. to be ascertained and reduced to writing. They formed the basis of the Constitutions of Clarendon.

66 **" The meeting of the kings."** Henry was holding conference with Louis VII. of France at Montmirail when the archbishop came before the two kings and, throwing himself at his sovereign's feet, offered to submit all disputed questions to his discretion " saving God's honour and my order."

66 **The friends we were.** People said of the two men in the year before the quarrel that they had " but one heart and one mind."

68 **When he, my lord**: Philip Augustus, King of France and suzerain of the kings of England. He had joined Richard in a crusade for the deliverance of Jerusalem. The two kings swore to defend each the other's realm as he would his own. Yet Philip took advantage of Richard's captivity and invaded Normandy. Moreover, he intrigued with John, Richard's ambitious younger brother, to prevent the royal prisoner's release.

69 **Of Pensavin and Chail.** The land of the troubadours, lyric poets of mediæval France.

72 **Our vice-king John.** John was the most vicious and the best hated of all the kings of England.

74 **Sheriff of Nottingham**: the king's representative in the county court. He had been false to his trust.

77 **palmer**: a pilgrim who passed his life in journeying from shrine to shrine, living on charity. Palmers were so called from the palm-branch, carried in token that they had visited the Holy Land.

PAGE

79 **"It's good habit that makes a man."** The Earl of Huntingdon was accustomed to fine raiment, and he pulls wry faces as he disguises himself in the old tramp's patched clothes, with the numerous bags attached. The earl had not realized before how much handsome clothing does for a man's sense of personal dignity.

81 **Elinor**: Henry II.'s queen and a woman of remarkable strength of character. She had maintained order in England during the absence of Richard, and on his return effected a reconciliation between the brothers. She now takes the part of John against Geoffrey's son.

81 **Faulconbridge**: a merry nobleman connected with the royal family. In the play he embodies the spirit of English patriotism.

82 **hoarding abbots.** John plundered monasteries to secure funds with which to carry on his many wars.

82 **Imprison'd angels.** John makes a common Elizabethan pun. The angel was a gold coin, worth about two dollars and a half, having on one side a figure of the archangel Michael piercing the prostrate dragon.

82 **Bell, book, and candle**: used by the priest in performing the ceremony of excommunication. John was actually excommunicated by the pope six years later.

82 **Hubert.** Shakespeare follows old chronicles in making Hubert de Burgh the king's instrument in the plot to murder Arthur.

83 **too full of gawds.** In the clear daylight, filled with all bright and beautiful sights, John cannot speak his hideous secret. This black-souled king, who cannot understand what laughter is, instils the suggestion of murder like creeping poison into Hubert's mind.

83 **brooded**: brooding; as vigilant as a bird on brood over her young.

84 **Within the arras.** The heavy tapestries that draped mediæval walls afforded excellent hiding-places.

89 **want pleading.** Two tongues would not be enough to plead for a pair of eyes.

89 **undeserved extremes**: torture of the innocent. The fire, made to give comfortable warmth, grieves that it should be asked to cause burning agony.

90 **Prince Henry.** Afterward Henry III. In reality the prince was only nine years old at the time of his father's death.

92 **There is so hot a summer in my bosom.** One tradition has it that

John's fever was brought on by a surfeit of peaches and beer. He fell ill in the Cistercian Abbey at Swineshead, but died at Newark. Shakespeare follows here another tradition to the effect that John, the plunderer of abbeys, was poisoned by a monk.

93 **in the Washes all unwarily.** The forces John relied upon to withstand the Dauphin were overwhelmed by the tide while fording the Welland, a river flowing into the Wash.

94 **the King's own sister:** Eleanor, who was married to Earl Simon (1238), much to the indignation of the English nobles.

95 **England's prince.** When Prince Edward, the heir apparent, was christened (1239), Earl Simon stood as godfather.

95 **the King, at pinch.** In 1244, Henry summoned Simon to aid him in France, and Leicester stood by the king to the great damage of his own interests. In 1248, the king besought de Montfort to undertake the government of Gascony, and Simon, "not wishing that the king should suffer for aught that I could do for him," assumed the difficult task.

95 **Kenilworth.** This famous castle, dating from about 1120, passed after the day of the de Montforts to John of Gaunt. It afterward became a royal possession, and was given by Elizabeth to the Earl of Leicester. (See Scott's "Kenilworth.") The stately pile was demolished by the Roundheads, but its ruins still attract multitudes of visitors.

96 **The lightning in the skies.** One day when Henry III. was being rowed along the Thames, he was forced by a sudden thunderstorm to take refuge in Durham Palace, where, to his surprise, he was received by the Earl of Leicester. Said the king, "I fear thunder and lightning not a little, Lord Simon, but I fear you more than all the thunder and lightning in the world." "Fear your enemies, my Lord King," replied the earl, "those who flatter you to your ruin, not me, your constant and faithful friend."

96 **I will die under ban.** Before the battle of Lewes, de Montfort said, "Though all should forsake me, I will stand firm with my four sons, in the just cause to which my faith is pledged, nor will I fear to risk the fortunes of war."

96 **The people loved the proud French lord.** The Londoners held with Earl Simon against the king, and sent fifteen thousand men to the force, with which the earl won the battle of Lewes. Representa-

tives of the Commons were summoned for the first time to the Parliament he held at Westminster (1265).

96 **He had taught to war.** When Earl Simon saw Prince Edward's troops moving to meet him at Evesham, he said, " By the arm of St. James, they come on in fine fashion, but it was from me that they learned it."

96 **Evesham's battle-gloom.** Although the battle took place early in the morning, the skies were so clouded with storm that the combatants fought in semi-darkness.

97 **the traitor.** This charge was brought against Wallace at his trial; but he was no traitor, since he fought for his country against a would-be conqueror.

97 **laurel wreath** : placed on the head of the captive in mockery of his supposed ambition to be king. The English believed that Wallace had said he would yet wear a crown in Westminster Hall.

98 **Wallace.** In the address to his men quoted by the contemporary chronicler, Bruce made no allusion to Wallace. As a matter of fact, he fought against Wallace at Falkirk.

100 **Plantagenet** : the nickname of Geoffrey of Anjou, father of Henry II., and the name borne by all the English sovereigns of that race. As John was the worst, so Edward II. was weakest of the line.

101 **De Argentine** : Sir Giles. He fought on after the retreat of the English and fell upon the field.

102 **Edward Bruce** : the brother of Robert and later king of Ireland.

103 **No spears were there the shock to let.** The Scotch foot-soldiers, massed in solid battalions with spears pointing outward, were as awkward to handle as a porcupine.

103 **No stakes to turn the charge were set.** By Bruce's order, stakes were driven into the ground over which the English cavalry must pass.

104 **Ailsa Rock** : a beautiful crag, rising abruptly from the sea off the coast of Ayrshire. The peasants believed that the multitudes of sea-fowl nesting on this mighty crag were transformed fairies who, at the coming of Christianity, had fled the islands.

104 **Carrick spearmen.** Carrick was the ancestral estate of the Bruce family.

107 **Might have enforc'd me to have swum** : a grammatical error still too common.

PAGE

107 **Tanti**: so much for them. Gaveston makes a gesture of contempt, equivalent to snapping the fingers.

108 **Lancaster**: the proudest and most powerful of the English nobles. He was finally beheaded by Edward II. for his part in the plots against Gaveston.

108 **these two Mortimers**: uncle and nephew. They represented the chief family of the Welsh Marches. The elder Mortimer died in the Tower (1326); the younger escaped to France and joined forces with Edward's queen, Isabella, for the invasion of England. His term of triumph was brief. Edward III. had him executed (1330) for his supposed complicity in the king's murder.

109 **Kent**: Edmund, the king's half-brother, a vacillating character unable to remain long loyal either to Edward or the barons.

109 **Preach upon poles.** Political offenders were beheaded in those cruel days and their heads were fixed on poles in a public place, as London Bridge.

109 **Warwick**: this earl is represented in the play as a grizzled warrior. He is a type of the mighty feudal baron, with a force of retainers able to match the royal army. He was beheaded with Lancaster.

109 **O, our heads!** Warwick speaks in sarcastic derision.

110 **All Warwickshire will love him for my sake.**
And northward Gaveston hath many friends. Warwick and Lancaster speak ironically.

111 **receive my seal**: the great seal, emblem of sovereignty. It was usually intrusted to the chancellor and gave to him vice-regal powers.

112 **Killingworth.** Edward was forced to resign the crown at Kenilworth, the "Killingworth" of the play. He was afterward placed in charge of two ruffians, Gournay and Maltravers, who transferred him to Corfe Castle, thence to Bristol, and finally to Berkeley. Accounts differ as to details, but there is little doubt that he was cruelly treated and finally put to death by his brutal guardians.

112 **Tisiphon**: one of the Greek Furies, with writhing snakes for hair.

113 **Trussel**: the proctor of the Parliament, who renounces the homage of the realm in the name of that august body.

115 **Isabella.** The queen was the daughter of Philip the Fair, king of France. Alienated by the king's neglect, she had sought refuge and aid at Paris.

PAGE

119 Let him be king. The prince indicates Kent, not Mortimer.

119 his highness' pleasure. The reference is to Edward II., to whom his son's heart remained loyal.

123 we have more sons. Edward III. had seven sons, of whom five lived to manhood. The fourth son, John of Gaunt, Duke of Lancaster, and the fifth son, the Duke of York, figure in Shakespeare's " Richard II."

125 Prince Edward: the Black Prince, so called because he wore black armor. He was but sixteen years of age at this time. He lived to win other brilliant victories, but at ruinous cost in both money and men. Worn out at last with campaigning, he returned to England and died (1376) the year before Edward III. passed away.

125 King of Boheme: an ally of France. He was old and blind, but, eager to play a man's part, he begged the knights of his bodyguard to lead him into the thick of the fray. In order that they might keep by his side, they fastened their horses' bridles to his and so rode forward in line. The king fought gallantly, but against overwhelming odds. He was found next morning lying dead among his knights, the bridles of their horses still tied together.

126 Arise, Prince Edward, trusty knight at arms. Prince Edward had been knighted before the battle of Cressy.

127 Wat Tyler. There were several *tilers* among the insurgents. John Tyler of Dartford, who killed the tax-collector for insulting his daughter, should be distinguished from Wat Tyler of Maidstone, who commanded the insurgents at Blackheath.

128 or a Charles: Charles V. of France, the son and successor of that King John who was taken prisoner by the Black Prince at Poictiers.

128 six groats. The groat amounted to fourpence (eight cents), not a large sum, but its purchasing power was as much as that of one dollar to-day. The poll tax of 1381 was exacted from every man and woman in the kingdom above fifteen years of age, in proportion to wealth. The poorest paid at least one groat.

129 Blackheath: a moor five miles south of London, where Wat Tyler's troops gathered on the eve of the entry into London, June 12, 1381.

130 The Tower. Tyler desired to treat with the king, and Richard would have gone to meet him, but the ministers of state induced the lad to take refuge in the Tower.

PAGE

130 **Archbishop of Canterbury**: bitterly hated by the people because he had advised the poll tax. He was murdered in the Tower after the departure of the king.

130 **Walworth,** Thomas: Lord Mayor of London. He had thrown wide the gates of the city because he dared not openly resist the people, but at Smithfield he picked a quarrel with Wat Tyler and slew him in the presence of the king.

130 **Absolves you of your promise**. The good offices of the archbishop were not needed. Parliament revoked the freedom charters granted by the king.

131 **Westminster Hall**: the place devoted to sessions of the superior law courts. The trial of John Ball actually took place at St. Albans, July 14, 1381, before Sir Robert (not John) Tresilian.

132 **his strange, wild notions**. Froissart gives an interesting sample of Ball's preaching. See also William Morris's " Dream of John Ball."

137 **York**: the king's youngest uncle, as unstable in his action as was Kent in the play of " Edward II."

140 **Flint Castle**. Richard was captured at Conway Castle, where he promised to resign the crown. He was then taken to Flint Castle, where Henry met him. He consented to go to London, and there, "with cheerful mien, he read the act of renunciation."

140 **Yet looks he like a king**. The "rose-red" Richard had all the aspect of royalty, but not the substance.

141 **Northumberland**: the passionate Earl Percy of the north, already zealous in the service of the usurper.

141 **pestilence**. The Black Death that swept away half the population of England in 1349 and 1350 returned again and again in the latter half of the fourteenth century, and was dreaded as the scourge of God.

141 **The purple testament**. To open a will is to begin to execute its provisions. So Bolingbroke has come to turn his secret plan of war into bloody action.

143 **tender-hearted cousin**. The Duke of Aumerle was York's eldest son. He lost his ducal title by Henry's first Parliament, but became Duke of York on his father's death. He fell at Agincourt, leading the vanguard.

150 **Whither you will, so I were from your sights**. Richard was for some time confined in the Tower, but the conspiracies of his friends

426 *NOTES*

PAGE

made his life dangerous to the usurper. He was hurried from castle to castle, and finally hidden away in a dungeon at Pontefract, where he perished. His body was conveyed to London and exhibited to the people.

151 **a voyage to the Holy Land.** Henry IV. purposed a pilgrimage to Jerusalem in expiation of his responsibility for the death of Richard.

152 **the Otter-dale:** the valley of the Otter River, which runs south across the Border to meet the Tyne.

152 **New Castel:** Newcastle, one of the fortified places belonging to the Percy family. The Scotch army had wasted the country as far as Durham, and was returning by way of Newcastle.

154 **But there is nought at Otterburne**
   To fend my men and me.

A Scotch force was well-nigh independent of supplies. Froissart gives a graphic account of their campaign methods. Every man carried on the back of his stout mountain pony a sack of oatmeal. This, mixed with water and baked before the fire, made a nourishing oat-cake that served for bread. For meat they depended on the herds of the enemy. The horses were turned loose at night to feed over the moors.

159 **the noble Mortimer.** Edmund Mortimer, younger son of the second Earl of March and Philippa, granddaughter of Edward III. He had been sent against the Welsh by Henry IV. After his capture, he married the daughter of Glendower and joined forces with the insurgents.

160 **Holmedon.** At the battle of Holmedon Hill, fought a few months after Otterburne, the disgrace of that defeat was avenged. Five Scotch earls were there taken prisoners, among them Archibald Douglas, the descendant of the Douglas who was "buried under the bracken bush." Hotspur's refusal to surrender his prizes to the king gave rise to a fierce quarrel between the Houses of Lancaster and Northumberland.

161 **my young Harry.** This depreciation of Prince Hal is doubtless exaggerated. The boy had rendered effective service in the field before the battle of Shrewsbury.

161 **Worcester.** Thomas of Worcester, Hotspur's uncle, later proved false to the king.

162 **Boar's Head:** a famous tavern in Eastcheap, London.

162 **that gave Amamon the bastinado.** Owen Glendower, the leader of the Welsh insurgents, was reputed to be a master of the Black Art, and so Falstaff laughingly alludes to him as whipping demons and swearing the devil into his service.

163 **upon instinct.** This is a joke on Falstaff, who has just excused his own running away on a certain occasion by that plea.

163 **blue-caps:** Scots, so called because of their blue bonnets.

164 **King Cambyses:** the ranting tyrant of an old-fashioned Elizabethan tragedy.

164 **convey my tristful queen:** lead aside my sorrowful queen. Falstaff affects the lofty language of the stage.

166 **a rabbit-sucker or a poulter's hare.** A sucking rabbit is small; a hare hanging up by the hind legs in the poulterer's window looks long and slender. The joke comes in comparing Falstaff to these.

168 **Shrewsbury** (1403). Here all the enemies of the House of Lancaster gathered for a final test of arms. Glendower and Mortimer brought the Welsh tribesmen. Harry Percy, whose wife was Mortimer's sister, led his vassals from Northumberland. James III. of Scotland, who had harbored the false Richard II. at his court, now sent an army to fight for Philippa's grandson. The event might have been disastrous to the Lancastrian dynasty but for the tardiness of the Welsh who did not arrive upon the scene till after the defeat of the Scotch and English forces.

169 **Douglas.** Hotspur's captive fought valiantly at the battle of Shrewsbury. He was taken prisoner and secured release only after the payment of a heavy ransom.

170 **Another king! they grow like hydra's heads.** The hydra had nine heads, and as fast as one was cut away three more would spring in its place. So Douglas, determined to kill the king, had already met " many marching in his coats."

172 **Hotspur** was killed at Shrewsbury. There is no historic evidence, however, that Prince Hal slew him.

180 **to busy giddy minds with foreign quarrels.** Henry V.'s renewing of the French war was probably suggested by his desire to furnish occupation to the restless barons.

181 **Jerusalem.** Henry IV. fell ill while at his devotions in Westminster

Abbey, and was carried to the abbot's lodging, where he died in a room called after the sacred city of Jerusalem.

182 **Harfleur**. Henry's first exploit in France was the siege and capture of the fortified port at the mouth of the Seine.

182 **King Henry**. This representation of Henry V. is in accordance with history. A fifteenth-century chronicler says of him: " In his youth he had been wild and reckless and spared nothing of his lusts or desires, but as soon as he was crowned he was changed into a new man, and all his intent was to live virtuously."

184 **a churlish turf of France**. The English bivouacked in the open air the night before the battle of Agincourt, and spent in prayer and preparation the hours that the French were giving to carousal.

186 **I Richard's body have interrèd new**. When Henry Bolingbroke was sent into exile and the Lancastrian estates confiscated, Richard made generous provision for the support and education of young Prince Hal. Henry V.'s first concern on coming to the throne was to have Richard's body honorably interred at Westminster.

187 **Which in his height of pride**. The French sent the English king the sum of money that would be necessary to ransom him when he should be captured. King Henry took no open notice of the insult, but bided his time.

188 **Loss to redeem me**. In the address to his troops before the battle, Henry declared that England should never pay ransom for him. He was perhaps thinking of the French king John, captured at Poictiers, and long held a prisoner in England.

188 **our grandsire-great**. Edward III., great-grandfather of Henry V.

188 **Lopped the French lilies**. Since the fleur-de-lis is the French emblem, to lop the French lilies is to cut down the pride and power of France.

189 **Erpingham**: the aged knight who gave the signal for advance.

189 **bilbos**: swords so called from Bilbao in Spain where they were manufactured.

190 **Bruisèd his helmet**. The king, who fought on foot, was attacked by a French knight, and forced to his knees. The dented helmet was taken back to London as a trophy, but the king refused to let it be displayed to the people.

190 **Saint Crispin's day**: October 25th. Crispin and his brother Cris-

pian were Roman missionaries of the fourth century, who supported themselves on their preaching tours by shoemaking. After their martyrdom they became the tutelar saints of shoemakers.

194 **The princely James.** James I. was the third king of the Stuart line, and the great-great-great-grandson of Robert Bruce.

194 **the elder Prince:** David, Duke of Rothesay, who was murdered (1402) by his uncle, Duke of Albany. (See Scott's "Fair Maid of Perth.")

194 **the father quaked for the child.** James's father, Robert III., was a man of weak intellect and feeble will. He was quite unequal to the protection or suitable education of his son. The boy, when but eight years of age, was given in charge to the bishop of St. Andrews. In 1205 James was sent to France for greater safety, but the ship was captured by an English vessel and the prince fell into the hands of Henry IV.

194 **Bass Rock:** a fortress at the mouth of the Frith of Forth.

195 **a sweeter Song:** the "Kingis Quair," a poem long believed to have been written by James at about nineteen years of age. Modern scholarship, however, does not find the evidence of his authorship convincing, and even questions whether he was a poet at all.

195 **a lady of royal blood:** Jane, the daughter of the Earl of Somerset and granddaughter of John of Gaunt. The match was approved by English statesmen, and it was hoped a better understanding between the two British kingdoms might thus be brought about. The mutual devotion of the royal pair excited the wonder and admiration of the profligate Scotch court.

195 **Scone:** the abbey where the kings of Scotland were regularly crowned.

195 **the tempest-waves of a troubled state.** James's ideals for Scotland were in advance of the age. The turbulent Scottish nobles, embittered by the king's uncompromising curtailment of their privileges, conspired against him.

196 **the Charterhouse of Perth.** The King was done to death in the cloister of the Black Friars at Perth where he had gone to keep the Christmas festival. The mutilated body was buried in the convent of the Carthusians near by.

196 **girls.** The poet has put the story into the mouth of one of the

queen's maids of honor, Kate Barlass, so called because she was the lass who, at the time of the king's murder, barred the door with her own arm against the assassins. She is pictured as telling the tale over, in her old age, to a group of girls. The entire ballad should be read, for it is no less true as history than beautiful as poetry.

197   March. James was murdered on February 20th. Within forty days all the men who had share in his slaying were hunted down, tortured, and executed with vindictive barbarity.

198   King Henry the Sixth. It is not probable that Shakespeare was the original author of these three plays. Part I. is especially unworthy of him. Perhaps two or three dramatists wrote the plays together, and Shakespeare revised their work.

198   John, Duke of Bedford, and Humphrey, Duke of Gloster: the brothers of Henry V. Bedford was made protector of the realm, and did what he could to retrieve England's fortunes in France. During his absence Gloucester served as protector in England and chief counsellor to the little king.

198   Exeter, Winchester. Henry Beaufort, Bishop of Winchester, and Thomas Beaufort, Duke of Exeter, were sons of John of Gaunt and Katharine Swynford, and therefore great-uncles to Henry VI. They represented a rival branch of the House of Lancaster.

200   are all quite lost. The loss of the French provinces was not complete until 1453. Rheims and Orleans were lost in 1429; Paris in 1436.

200   several factions: the rivalries of Bedford, Gloucester, and the Beauforts rendered the little king's boyhood wretched, and greatly weakened the government both at home and in France.

200   flower-de-luces: fleur-de-lis, the flower upon the coat of arms of the kings of France, incorporated in the English arms after the Peace of Troyes.

201   the Dauphin: Charles VII., son of the mad king. He was later crowned king of France by Joan of Arc (1429).

201   York. Richard, Duke of York, was much loved by the people, who looked to him as the only man able to set the realm to rights. He laid claim first to the protectorate and then to the throne. He was killed at the battle of Wakefield (1460), but his son Edward won the crown.

201 **Salisbury**: Warwick's father-in-law.

201 **Warwick**: Richard Neville, Earl of Warwick, the most powerful nobleman in England, called for his part in the Wars of the Roses "the king-maker."

202 **his poor queen**: Isabella of France, daughter of Charles VI.

202 **Pomfret**: Pontefract.

203 **This Edmund, in the reign of Bolingbroke**: Edmund Mortimer, Earl of March, great-grandson of the Roger Mortimer who plotted against Edward II. Edmund was loyal to the Lancastrian line, but his name and claim were used by the Percys to justify their revolt against Henry IV. He was held a prisoner in Windsor Castle by Henry IV. Henry V. set him free, but he died without issue in 1424.

203 **Who kept him in captivity till he died.** Owen Glendower's prisoner was another Edmund, uncle of the foregoing.

204 **We thank you, lords!** York allows himself to use the plural pronoun as if he were already king.

204 **Blackheath.** Under the leadership of Jack Cade, a soldier returned from the French wars, the people of Kent, peasants and townsfolk, gathered at Blackheath, the moor where Wat Tyler had marshalled his troops seventy years before. The king fled to Kenilworth, the insurgents got possession of London and for several weeks held control of the government. They were finally induced to return to their homes by a royal proclamation, promising redress of grievances and pardon to all offenders: Deserted by his followers, Cade tried to escape, but he was captured and killed by a gentleman of Kent.

204 **fall.** Cade would derive his name from the Latin *cadere*, to fall. But how should a peasant know Latin? His English in this speech is absurdly confused.

204 **My father was a Mortimer.** Cade's assumption of the name Mortimer indicated his sympathy with the claims of York, but there is no evidence that he was in actual alliance with that powerful nobleman.

205 **three market-days.** The public whipping of rogues was often set for market-days, in order that as many people as possible might witness it.

205 **proof.** A coat of proof usually means mail, but here the Weaver,

naturally critical of garments, is punning on the well-tried or well-worn look of Cade's coat.

205 **burnt i' the hand.** Many criminal offences were punished with branding in old England.

206 **All the realm shall be in common.** An echo of the preaching of John Ball. The grievances of the people, as stated in the complaint of the commons of Kent, were political rather than social. They protested against the folly of the king's ministers and the waste of the royal revenue.

206 **let's kill all the lawyers.** The feeling against lawyers was due to the fact that deeds and charters were drawn up by them. They too often interpreted the law in the interest of the rich and powerful, and so wrought injustice to the poor.

206 **lamentable.** Note the pun.

207 **Emmanuel.** This name, meaning *God with us*, was often used to head both public documents and private letters.

207 **particular.** Punningly opposed to *general*.

208 **Sir Humphrey Stafford** and his brother William were in command of the troops sent to meet the rebels at Seven Oaks. Both were killed in that encounter.

208 **the filth and scum of Kent.** The "commons" were a large and well-organized army, so strong that they defeated the king's forces at Seven Oaks. The writer of this scene is entirely unsympathetic, and burlesques the insurgents.

209 **span-counter:** defined by Nares as a game "in which one player throws a counter, which the other wins if he can throw another to hit it, or lie within a span of it."

209 **the Lord Say.** One of the ministers responsible for the marriage treaty (1444) by which England's claim to Maine and Anjou was abandoned. He was beheaded by the rebels on their entry into London.

210 **out of order.** A calumny. Cade was a good disciplinarian and kept the people "wondrously well together."

210 **King Henry.** The battle of Towton Field was fought on Palm Sunday (1461). Henry passed the day in prayer at York. He was therefore not present at the battle, but his thoughts may well have been such as are described in the play.

213 **Edward and Richard.** The eldest and youngest sons of Richard

of York. Edward had already been declared king, but the battle of Towton Field secured his victory.

215 **the melancholy flood**: the Styx, over which Charon ferried the souls of the dead to Hades.

215 **my great father-in-law.** When Clarence turned traitor to Edward IV., he married the elder daughter of Warwick. Richard of Gloucester desired to marry the younger daughter, but Clarence protested because he did not wish to divide the inheritance. This was the occasion of the quarrel between the brothers.

216 **stabb'd me in the field by Tewkesbury.** According to tradition, Gloucester and Clarence slew Prince Edward of Lancaster, who was taken prisoner at Tewkesbury.

216 **my poor children.** The children of Clarence, Margaret and Edward, eventually paid with their lives the price of royal blood. Edward was executed for treason in 1499 and Margaret in 1541.

216 **good rest.** In Shakespeare's play, Clarence is murdered this night, drowned in a butt of wine, by the instigation of Gloucester. What is certain is his impeachment on the charge of high treason, his condemnation, and (1478) his secret death in the Tower.

217 **Buckingham.** Henry Stafford, Duke of Buckingham, was Richard's strongest and most helpful adherent. After the murder of the princes, Buckingham rebelled, was betrayed to Richard, and promptly executed.

217 **Cardinal Bouchier**: the archbishop of Canterbury, who had crowned Edward IV. and was yet to crown Richard III. and Henry VII.

217 **our crosses on the way.** The escort of Prince Edward had been met on his way to London by an armed force under Gloucester, and the little king's uncle, Lord Rivers, had been taken prisoner.

218 **my mother and my brother York.** Edward's queen had taken refuge in Westminster Abbey with her younger son. Richard joined his brother in the Tower soon after.

218 **Did Julius Cæsar build that place?** Cæsar built no stone fortresses in Britain.

219 **live long.** Apparently the prince catches only these last two words of his uncle's sinister mutter, but as the boy turns suspiciously toward him, Gloucester at once, like "the formal Vice" or regular jester of the old morality plays, gives a new twist to his sentence.

221 **shoulders.** The saucy-tongued little prince has at last stung his hated uncle by this reference to Gloucester's misshapen shoulders. York seems to hint at a likeness between the hunchback and a bear or other clumsy beast, such as was often ridden by a monkey at country shows.

221 My grandam: Duchess of York, the wife of the Richard who was killed at Towton Field and the mother of Edward IV., Clarence, and Gloucester.

225 Lord Stanley: the (third) husband of Margaret Beaufort, and friendly to Richmond. His desertion of Richard on Bosworth Field was the turning point of the battle. The execution of Stanley's son was immediately ordered by the king, but in the excitement of the hour the order was not carried out.

226 What heir of York is there alive but we? In point of fact, the children of Clarence were yet alive (but debarred from the throne because of their father's attainder), and there was still living a daughter of Edward IV., the Princess Elizabeth. Her marriage with Richmond combined the claims of York and Lancaster in the Tudor house.

227 Norfolk: Sir John Howard, who had received many favors from Edward IV., but who forsook young Edward V. for the usurper, by whose side he fell in the battle of Bosworth.

227 Surrey: son of the Duke of Norfolk. The Earl of Surrey led Richard's archers at Bosworth, but in time gained the confidence of Henry VII. and commanded the English army at Flodden (1513).

228 What said Northumberland. Richard, conscious that he deserves no loyalty, is always suspecting his followers and setting eavesdroppers upon them.

230 Catesby: an esquire much favored by Richard, even to the extent of the speaker's chair in his only Parliament. He was probably executed after the battle.

230 The king enacts more wonders than a man. Richard fought with the courage of desperation and performed prodigies of valor all in vain.

232 At Bewley, near Southampton. Warbeck, unable to make a stand against the king's forces under Lord Daubeney, fled with but three companions to Beaulieu in Hampshire, where he found refuge in a monastery. The place was surrounded by troops and the pretender, seeing defence was impossible, surrendered, casting himself on the king's mercy.

232 Not aiming at a crown. After the death of Henry VI. and his son, Henry Tudor was head of the House of Lancaster and nearest heir to the throne. His friends thought best to remove him from England, and sent him, a lad of fourteen years, to France, where he found refuge with the Duke of Brittany. There he remained till after the death of Edward IV.

233 He does but act. Warbeck was schooled for his part by Margaret of Burgundy, sister of Edward IV.

234 The hangman's physic. Henry treated the captured pretender with contemptuous toleration. Warbeck was made to confess his imposture and was then confined to the Tower. The discovery of a plot to get possession of the place brought him under condemnation. He was executed in 1499.

234 Innocent Warwick's head. Edward, Earl of Warwick, son of the Duke of Clarence, kept a prisoner in the Tower to prevent his claiming the throne, was involved in Warbeck's plot. He was beheaded in the same year.

237 our commission from Rome. The pope had authorized the cardinals, Wolsey and Campeggio (the Campeius of the play), to investigate the case, and to report the facts to him as a basis for his decision.

239 Upward of twenty years. Henry and Katharine were married on June 11, 1509. The divorce suit was begun on May 31, 1529.

240 these reverend fathers. The assembly at Blackfriars was an ecclesiastical court, held under the auspices of the papal legates. Katharine appealed from them to the pope himself.

240 You are mine enemy. Wolsey desired to secure an alliance with France by marrying Henry VIII. to a French princess. The first suggestion of a divorce probably came from him.

242 Griffith : Griffin Richardes, one of the queen's household officers.

244 Cromwell, Thomas : a clerk in Wolsey's employ and his devoted friend. Shortly after his master's disgrace, Cromwell won the favor of the king by suggesting that the divorce trial should be transferred from the papal to an English court, where the royal influence might secure a favorable decision. This act of defiance led to the complete separation of the English church from the jurisdiction of the Holy See. In the work of reformation that followed, Cromwell was the leading spirit. His authority was second to that of the king alone.

245   **Sir Thomas More :** one of the group of scholars who brought the New Learning to England. He was later beheaded because he refused to approve the act excluding Katharine's daughter, Mary, from succession to the throne.

245   **Cranmer is returned with welcome.** Cranmer had won the favor of King Henry by speaking and writing in favor of the divorce. He was recalled from a mission to the court of Charles V. and appointed archbishop of Canterbury in 1529. As primate of England, he presided over the court that finally granted the divorce, and a week later he crowned Anne Boleyn queen.

246   **the Lady Anne :** Anne Boleyn, a lady of Henry's court, whom the king had married even before securing the divorce from Katharine. She, too, thought Wolsey her enemy, and made the king promise not to see the disgraced minister.

248   **King James :** the great-grandson of James I., but a man of weak and pleasure-loving nature. The fatal defeat at Flodden was due to his foolish negligence.

259   **Sion House :** the family mansion of the Dudleys.

259   **Jane :** daughter of Mary Tudor (the sister of Henry VIII.) and the Duke of Suffolk. She was beautiful and learned beyond any woman of her time. The plot to place her on the throne was contrived by Northumberland, the head of the Protestant party, who arranged her marriage with his son, Guildford Dudley, and induced Edward VI. to declare her his heir.

259   **Our cousin king is dead.** Edward VI. died on July 6, 1553. His death left the Protestant party with no hope but Lady Jane, since the Princess Mary was a devoted Romanist.

259   **proclamation.** Edward's death was proclaimed, according to custom, by heralds, and the news was received, so Guildford seems to imply, with universal awe, since even great men, he says, fear death, and by such fears make it greater than it is.

259   **Our fathers grow ambitious.** Lady Jane herself had no ambition to be queen. When told that Edward VI. was dead and that she was to succeed him, she swooned away.

259   **not lords of what they do possess.** A change in the succession made all fortunes and estates uncertain, since the favorite of one king might suffer disgrace from the next.

259 **Castle of Framlingham** : in Norfolk. Here Princess Mary fled for refuge when informed that her brother had died and that the succession was claimed by Lady Jane. An armed force speedily gathered to her aid in sufficient strength to overcome all resistance Northumberland could bring against her.

260 **Sir Henry Bedingfield** : a nobleman who brought his retainers to Mary's support at Framlingham.

260 **Sir Thomas Wyatt** : son of the poet of the name, and a brave and chivalrous man. He was loyal to Mary until the Spanish marriage. This he regarded as a menace to the national independence, and he undertook to rouse the commons of Kent (January, 1554) by way of protest. The rising failed, and Wyatt was beheaded for the so-called rebellion.

261 **the council** : the Privy Council called to declare Lady Jane queen. Individual members of this body had already come over to Mary's side.

261 **the dukes at Cambridge.** Northumberland was arrested at Cambridge.

262 **O, who so forward, Wyatt, as thyself.** Wyatt's part, both in the proclamation of Mary and in the protest against the Spanish marriage, is exaggerated in the play.

264 **It was your father, great Northumberland.** Northumberland was executed in August, six months before the arrest of Suffolk.

264 **My father prisoner!** Suffolk had been pardoned for his share in his daughter's coronation, but, becoming implicated in Wyatt's Rebellion, was sentenced to death.

265 **'Tis the pleasure of the queen that you part lodgings.** Lady Jane herself refused to see her husband on the day of their execution, lest an interview should disturb the " holy tranquillity with which they had prepared themselves for death."

265 **Her beauty.** French ambassadors thought Mary " very handsome and admirable by reason of her great and uncommon mental endowments, but so thin and sparse and small as to render it impossible for her to be married for the next three years."

267 **Stafford,** Sir Thomas : a young nobleman who led a foolhardy attempt to proclaim Elizabeth queen and so rescue England from Spanish domination (April, 1557). He landed on the Yorkshire coast and seized Scarborough Castle, but the people would not come to his aid. He and thirty followers were arrested and shortly after executed.

267 Gardiner, Stephen: Bishop of Winchester. He had been in disgrace under Edward VI., but was recalled and made chancellor of the realm by Mary. He was bent upon the extermination of the reformers and even desired to establish the Inquisition in England.

268 our Parliament. Wolsey had ruled without a Parliament ; Cromwell had made the national assembly his tool. Gardiner, however, experienced great difficulty in securing legislation restoring the pope's authority over the English church. The statute against heretics cost him much pains, but was finally passed, December 15, 1554.

270 Woodstock. Elizabeth, the daughter of Anne Boleyn and heir presumptive to the throne, was the object of Mary's constant suspicions. The Protestant princess was brave and handsome and very popular, the rallying-point of the malcontents. After Wyatt's rebellion she was confined in the Tower, although Wyatt himself declared upon the scaffold that the princess had no part in the rising. She was declared innocent by the court of Star Chamber, removed to Woodstock (May 13, 1554), and held there, practically a prisoner, until July, 1555, when Mary was obliged to recognize her sister as successor to the throne. From that date Elizabeth was free.

273 Cole: Provost of Eton. He had preached a long sermon explaining the grounds for the execution of Cranmer.

273 Lord Williams : the vice-chancellor, who had presided over the execution of Latimer and Ridley in the same place a few months before.

273 Lord William Howard : admiral of the fleet and the most powerful of the queen's subjects. He had used his influence to protect Elizabeth from persecution and to secure her a fair trial.

273 Lord Paget : a gentleman of the moderate party. He had been favorable to the Spanish marriage as strengthening England in continental politics, but he would not go with the queen in her policy of restoring the pope's authority. He opposed the bill against heretics, arguing that men should not be punished for opinion merely.

273 Cranmer. He had been deposed from the archbishopric and tried for heresy in St. Mary's church at Oxford. He was sentenced to be burned alive, but the execution of the penalty was postponed from time to time in the hope that he might be induced to renounce his heresy.

Every influence was brought to bear to this end, his resolution was gradually undermined, and he finally declared his submission to the authority of the pope. He was too dangerous a man to be left alive, however, and recantation did not save him. When he came to the stake, Cranmer recalled his recantation in a dying address to the people, and thrust first into the fire the hand that had signed the act of submission.

276 **Sir Nicholas Heath:** chancellor after the death of Gardiner.

276 **Philip II.,** of Spain: the son of the emperor, Charles V., and heir to his dominions. The marriage with the queen of England had been a matter of policy on his part, and he quickly tired of his bride. He was only twice in England, the year immediately following the wedding, and for four months in 1557. The second departure is represented in the play.

276 **And you must look to Calais when I go.** When Mary was induced to join Philip in his war upon France, a French force was immediately sent against Calais. The town surrendered on January 6, 1558. The loss of Calais, the last of the English possessions in France, was bitterly mourned by Mary. "When I am dead," she said to one of her attendants in her last sickness, "you will find Calais written on my heart."

277 **your people will not crown me.** The marriage treaty, as framed by the Council, provided that if Mary should die childless, Philip's connection with the realm should cease. English statesmen did not intend that he should succeed to the throne, and Mary's effort to accomplish his coronation failed.

277 **Here swings a Spaniard — there an Englishman.** The Spaniards were so hated by the people that the men of Philip's retinue were frequently attacked. When the hot-blooded southerners retaliated by killing their assailants, they were brought before the courts and hung for murder.

278 **Burn more.** Mary had a woman's pity for the condemned heretics, but Philip, engaged in the suppression of the reformers in Spain and in Flanders, urged greater severity in England. During the three years of the persecution (1555–1558) three hundred persons were put to death for heretical opinions. Most of the martyrs were men of learning and station.

PAGE

278 Lady Clarence: the queen's favorite attendant.

278 papers. Papers with threats and taunts written on them were often found dropped in the palace.

279 my cousin Pole: Reginald Pole, cardinal, and legate from the pope. He was an ardent Romanist and believed that he had been born for the regeneration of England. Mary appointed him archbishop of Canterbury and followed his advice in all things. He, more than she, was responsible for the so-called Marian persecution. Pole was a far-away cousin of the Tudors, being the son of Margaret Plantagenet, the daughter of John of Gaunt.

280 We have made war upon the Holy Father. Philip had sent an army to Rome to force the pope to recognize him king of Naples. The pope avenged himself on England, Spain's ally, by recalling his legate, Cardinal Pole — a punishment keenly felt by Mary.

282 Sitting on the ground: an attitude characteristic of the queen in her last years of utter despondency.

282 Sir William Cecil: a loyal friend to Elizabeth, appointed chief secretary on her accession.

282 The Queen is dead. Mary died (November 16, 1558) a broken-hearted woman. Philip, who hoped to marry Elizabeth, sent a messenger, de Feria, to induce Mary to assent to her sister's succession. This was done, and the announcement that she was queen of England was made to Elizabeth not at Woodstock, but at Hatfield House.

284 Unto the presence of that gratious Queene. Elizabeth delighted in display, and was wont to dazzle men's eyes by the splendor of her dress and the magnificence of her retinue.

285 kings and kesars. Half the kings and princes of Europe sought her in marriage.

285 Maugre so many foes. Scotland, France, and finally Spain were open enemies.

285 She could it sternely draw. Elizabeth dreaded the costs and the hazards of war. By skilful diplomacy she secured for England thirty years of peace. When it became necessary to defend the land from invasion, the resources of the nation were fully adequate.

287 thou false woman. Elizabeth found her fair prisoner an embarrassing charge. The Romanists looked to her as the only means of securing the restoration of the old order in the church. Philip of

Spain was her powerful champion, and the pope was ready to use all the influence of the Holy See in her behalf. A series of conspiracies to assassinate Elizabeth, set Mary free, and place her on the throne convinced the Council that peace could only be secured by removing this dangerous captive. In 1584 Mary was tried, found guilty of treason, and condemned to execution. Elizabeth hesitated to sign the death-warrant, not so much for pity of her cousin's fate, as because she feared the consequences.

287 **My son! my son!** James Stuart, Mary's only child, was a baby when his mother fled from Scotland. He made merely a formal protest against her execution, being eager to keep on good terms with Elizabeth and so to win the succession.

289 **a warm summer day.** On July 29, 1588, the Armada was sighted off Plymouth.

289 **Plymouth bay.** Admiral Lord Howard and the valiant sea captains, Drake and Hawkins and Frobisher, lay here in hiding, with forty ships, waiting a favorable opportunity to attack the Armada.

289 **Edgecumbe.** The castle built on the promontory opposite Plymouth bay.

289 **the stout old sheriff.** The county sheriff was responsible for bringing the armed men of each county to the defence of the country.

290 **the Lion of the sea:** emblazoned on the royal banner.

290 **famed Picard field:** Cressy.

291 **Whitehall:** the royal palace in London.

291 **the royal city woke.** London, the prime object of the Spanish attack, was well-nigh defenceless. The best of her ships had been sent to join the queen's fleet.

294 **Capten, art tha sleepin'.** This poem is written in the broad and homely dialect of Devonshire.

294 **Plymouth Hoe:** the elevated promenade overlooking Plymouth Sound. Here, according to tradition, Drake was playing bowls with Lord Howard when the Armada came in sight.

294 **Yarnder lumes the island.** St. Nicholas, or Drake's Island, encloses the sound on the south, and renders the harbor a safe anchorage. Here lay the queen's ships awaiting the coming of the Armada.

297 **The little "Revenge":** the ship that had carried Drake's flag in the chase of the Armada.

302   the lands they had ruin'd.   The reference may be to the West Indies, where the natives were being exterminated by Spanish cruelty.

303   Essex: Robert Devereux, Earl of Essex, who succeeded to Elizabeth's favor after the death of Leicester.   Ambitious and self-confident, he grew restless under criticism and undertook to force the queen to remove the councillors hostile to his interests.   Defeated in this enterprise, he was condemned to die as a traitor.   Elizabeth was induced to sign his death-warrant.   (See Hon. Emily Lawless, " With Essex in Ireland.")

303   Dudley: Robert, Earl of Leicester, the favorite courtier of Queen Elizabeth from her accession to his death (1588).   (See Scott's " Kenilworth.")

304   kingly seed.   James I. had two sons, Henry, the much-lamented elder prince, who died in 1612, and Charles, who lived to succeed his father.

310   Vane: Sir Harry Vane, the younger, a man of noble birth, but a Puritan and an advocate of popular government.   He had gone to America with the thought of settling in Massachusetts Bay Colony, but returned to England in time to take an active part in the rebellion.

311   How he turns Ireland to a private stage.   As lord deputy to Ireland (1632–1641), Wentworth had worked for law and order according to English ideas, punishing disloyalty to the king, whether on the part of Romanists, Protestants, or corrupt English officials, with unsparing hand.   His unflinching administration of the law won for him many enemies and the nicknames, " Thorough " and " Black Tom Tyrant."

311   Power, power without law.   Vane exaggerates Wentworth's share in the arbitrary policy of the king.   The law that defined the rights of the subject was to Wentworth's mind not less sacred than the king's authority.   He had withdrawn from the reform party because he believed that their projects would work the ruin of the state.   His views of monarchy are thus stated in his own words: " Princes are to be the indulgent nursing fathers to their people. . . . (The people) repose safe and still under the protection of their sceptres. . . . The authority of a king is the keystone which closeth up the arch of order and government which contains each part in due relation to the whole, and which once shaken, infirm'd, all the frame falls together into a confused heap of foundation and battlement of strength and beauty."

NOTES 443

311 **Hampden**: John Hampden, a Parliamentarian, famous for his opposition to the illegal tax called ship-money.

311 **The Bill of Rights**. In the Parliament that met in 1628, Wentworth had stated the limits to royal authority which were embodied after his secession in the Petition of Right. The Bill of Rights was a document passed sixty years later.

312 **Hamilton**: the Marquis of Hamilton, a Scotch nobleman, intrusted by the king with the task of pacifying Scotland.

312 **The muckworm Cottington**: a member of the Privy Council and chancellor of the Exchequer. He was active in raising money for the Scotch war, and not over scrupulous as to the means used. Attacked by Parliament at the same time as Strafford and Laud, he resigned all his offices and so escaped impeachment.

312 **the maniac Laud**: William Laud, archbishop of Canterbury, was in full sympathy with the king. His zeal for restoring the old order in church and state rendered him hateful to the reform party.

312 **Rudyard**: Sir Benjamin, a scholar and man of letters. He was at this time in full sympathy with Pym and Hampden.

312 **Runnymead**. Vane refers to the conference at Runnymead, where the barons forced King John to grant the Great Charter in 1215. Charles had offered to ratify that same charter, but its provisions were deemed insufficient to the present needs of England.

313 **the League and Covenant**. The alliance between the Scotch Covenanters and the English Puritans, called the Solemn League and Covenant, was not concluded until 1643, two years after the death of Strafford. It should be distinguished from the National Covenant mentioned as "the League."

313 **Fiennes**: later Viscount Saye and Sele, an aristocrat but a Puritan. He was one of those who looked to America for the freedom that men despaired of finding in England. He had actually undertaken to plant a colony at Saybrook, Connecticut, but it had failed.

313 **Loudon**: John Campbell, Earl of Loudon, a Covenanter who had come to London as commissioner from the Scotch Parliament, to make terms with the king. He was in high favor with the Puritans.

313 **Pym**. John Pym was the leader of the reform party in the House of Commons, and possessed so much influence that he was nicknamed "King Pym" by Charles's friends.

PAGE

314 **Eliot.** Sir John Eliot was one of the most eloquent advocates of free speech and Parliamentary privilege. His brave championship of the Petition of Right drew on him the special anger of the king. He was thrown into the Tower, and there sickened and died (1632).

316 **the Queen:** Henrietta Maria of France. She was an ardent Roman Catholic and had much influence with the king. She encouraged Charles to persist in his arbitrary policy.

316 **not that awful head.** Strafford apparently anticipates that the struggle may end in the execution of the king. He entreats Pym's mercy, not for himself, but for the king. Pym is steadfast in refusing to regard anything save England's good.

317 **crop-headed.** The Puritans usually wore their hair short, and were called Roundheads. The king's troopers, on the other hand, were known as Cavaliers, or soldiers of fortune.

318 **Hazelrig:** a Puritan who was willing to carry the reform movement to its logical end. He fought through the civil war and voted for the death of the king.

318 **Rupert.** Prince Rupert of Bavaria, the son of Charles's sister Elizabeth. He was summoned to England on the outbreak of the war, joined the king at Nottingham Castle, and was immediately placed in command of the cavalry. His personal daring inspired his troops to brave deeds, but his heedless impetuosity lost as many battles as his courage won.

319 **Castle Brancepeth:** a picturesque castle in Durham, belonging to the Neville family.

322 **the wine-press.** The imagery is drawn from Isaiah liii.

322 **Man of Blood:** the term applied to King Charles by the Parliament.

322 **Astley:** Lord Astley, the royalist general, "an honest, brave, and plain man," and an able commander. He fought with the king in the battle of Stow (November, 1646), the last before Charles's surrender.

322 **Sir Marmaduke:** Langdale, in command of the king's horse.

322 **The General:** Fairfax, who was at this time in command of the Parliamentary forces.

323 **Stout Skippon:** major-general in the Parliamentary army and in command of the infantry. He was wounded at Naseby.

323 **brave Oliver.** The advent of Cromwell's forces turned the tide of battle against the king.

324   **Temple Bar**: the great gate at the entrance to the city of London where traitors' heads were exposed to the contempt of the people.

324   **those cruel eyes.** The reference is to the king, but Charles could not justly be accused of torture.

325   **Oxford halls.** This university town was the rallying ground of the king's party.

325   **Durham's Stalls.** The bishop of Durham was a stanch champion of the king.

326   **Tyranny.** The taxes levied by Parliament proved as burdensome as the "benevolences" extorted by the king. Men made "reformation" an excuse for private "revenge and robbery." The property of Cavaliers, sequestered by Cromwell's authority, meant more actual oppression than the king had ever dared to propose.

326   **Great Britain's heir.** Prince Charles found refuge in France (1646), where he tried in vain to procure help for his father. When Charles I. was condemned to death, the prince offered to sign a blank pledge that might be filled out as Parliament chose, if only the life of the king might be spared.

327   **bills of hate.** The House of Commons declared the king guilty of treason "against the Parliament and kingdom of England" before he was brought to trial.

327   **Felons attain more privilege than I.** The trial of Charles I. was held before a high court of justice appointed for this special purpose. The king refused to defend himself since he did not acknowledge the legality of the court.

327   **my mate.** Henrietta Maria had been the king's most trusted adviser during the twenty years of civil strife. After his surrender she fled to France and there gathered her children about her. She returned to England on the restoration of Charles II.

327   **his helpless right.** Charles stated in the words spoken from the scaffold his conception of good government. "For the people, and truly I desire their liberty and freedom as much as anybody whatsoever; but I must tell you that their liberty and freedom consists in having of government those laws by which their life and their goods may most be their own. It is not having share in government, sirs; that is nothing pertaining to them."

328   **the Highland host.** Montrose's followers were drawn from the

Highlands. They fought with hereditary hate against the Lowland clans.

329 Assynt. Montrose was delivered up to the Covenanters by Macleod of Assynt with whom he had taken refuge.

330 Whig west-country lords. Whig is a Scotch term used in driving horses. It was applied in contempt to the west-country gentlemen who marched on Edinburgh (1640) to protest against coming to terms with the king.

331 Of him who sold his king for gold,
The master-fiend Argyle.

The Lord of Argyle, leader of the Covenanters, was always consistent to his purpose of establishing the Presbyterian church in Scotland. By alternate craft and force he had induced Charles I. to concede the Scotch demands. When the civil war broke out, he approved the Solemn League and Covenant in accordance with which a Scotch army was sent to the aid of the Parliament. When Charles surrendered to the Scots (1646), Argyle undertook to induce him to accept the Covenant, but failing in this he saw no better way out of an embarrassing situation than to agree to the demand of Parliament that the king be given into their keeping. Four hundred thousand pounds was then paid to the Scotch commissioners, not as the price of the king's person, but for expenses of the Scotch army during the English campaign. No part of it came into Argyle's hands, and he was as much shocked as Montrose by the execution of the king. He had joined in the invitation to Prince Charles to return to Scotland, because he hoped to induce him to take oath to the Covenant. Failing in this, Argyle withdrew his support. The part he played was bitterly denounced by both Presbyterians and royalists, and his influence in Scotland was lost for all time. When Charles II. came to the throne, Argyle was charged with complicity in Cromwell's " usurpation," and condemned to death. He was executed on the spot where Montrose had died.

331 Saxon soldier. It was an Englishman who taunted Argyle with treachery.

332 the solemn hall: Parliament House.

332 Warristoun: Lord Warriston, lord advocate of the court, a Covenanter and a bitter foe to Montrose.

334 **Like a bridegroom.** " He was very richly clad in fine scarlet, laid over with rich silver lace, his hat in his hand, his bands and cuffs exceedingly rich, his delicate gloves in his hands, his stockings of immaculate silk, and his shoes, with their ribbons, on his feet ; and sark provided for him with pearling round about, above ten pounds the ell." — " Nicholl's Diary."

By this rich array his friends endeavored to atone for the shameful death to which Montrose had been condemned.

336 **Darwin stream.** The battle of Preston (1648) must here be referred to.

336 **Of hireling wolves.** Milton's sonnet was suggested by the attempt to induce Parliament to levy tithes for the support of the Presbyterian clergy. This proposition of a forced contribution for the maintenance of a state church was opposed by Cromwell, who held that neither king nor Parliament had power to bind a man's conscience.

338 **a week's garret in London.** Many royalists were in hiding even in London, the stronghold of the Roundheads.

341 **bigotry.** Charles II. had not sufficient interest in religion to be a bigot, but fear of the bishops induced him to give his assent to laws forbidding public worship differing from that of the established church and excluding Puritans and Romanists alike from political office. The policy of toleration maintained by Cromwell came to be deeply regretted.

341 **Marston Moor** (1644) was the first of Cromwell's victories, and Worcester (1651) his last.

345 **Cornish lads.** The southwestern counties were ripe for revolt because of the fierce cruelty with which the participants in Monmouth's rebellion had been treated only two years before.

345 **Trelawney** was a royalist, and his father had forfeited place and fortune because of his sympathy with the Cavaliers; but the king's Romanist tendencies had forced the bishop into opposition.

345 **Michael's hold :** Saint Michael's Mount, a fortified island off Land's End. It was held in awe by Cornishmen, because St. Michael, " the great vision of the guarded mount," had appeared here, and also because of its legendary giant, one of those whom " Jack the Giant-Killer " slew.

347 **our leader.** Graham of Claverhouse, Marquis of Dundee, gathered the Highlanders to the support of King James, as Montrose had rallied them about King Charles thirty years before. Now, as then, the Lowland clans favored the Protestant cause.

347 Magus Muir. The archbishop of St. Andrews had been barbarously murdered by an armed band of fanatic Covenanters at Magus Muir.

347 blighted hopes of Scotland. The Scots had hoped to establish the Presbyterian church in England, and to maintain a Stuart king upon the throne. Both hopes were frustrated. The events of the seventeenth century, moreover, had tended to subordinate the interests of Scotland to those of the southern kingdom.

348 their pale Convention: the assembly convened at Edinburgh to declare for William and Mary. The declaration was an act of rebellion in the eyes of James's allies.

348 the prince: William of Orange.

350 Jacobite. The adherents of the Stuarts were so called from the Latin form of the name James — *Jacobus*.

352 Hampton Court: a palace on the Thames a few miles above London. It was built by Cardinal Wolsey, but surrendered by him to Henry VIII., who greatly enlarged it. It was the favorite residence of the Tudor and Stuart kings and queens.

352 three realms obey. The union of Scotland and England (1707) converted the dynastic connection into permanent alliance between the two kingdoms. Ireland, too, was brought into closer relations with England. After the defeat of the Stuart rising (1691) the English supremacy was assured.

355 Prince Eugene, of Savoy, in command of the Austrian allies.

357 thy father. James III., as the Jacobites styled him, — "the Old Pretender," according to the Hanoverians, — was not a man to awaken enthusiasm. The meanness of his private life alienated all but the stanchest supporters. But Charles Edward, "the Young Pretender," was loved by all men who came in contact with him. With the courage of inexperience he undertook to recover his father's kingdom. "I go, Sire," said he, "in search of three crowns, which I doubt not but to have the honor and happiness of laying at your Majesty's feet. If I fail in the attempt, your next sight of me shall be in my coffin."

357 thy faith. Charles Edward might have won considerable support in England if he had been willing to renounce Roman Catholicism.

357 thy marble pile: the monument placed by George III. (1819) over the tomb of James III. and his sons in St. Peter's at Rome.

358 the latest Minstrel: Sir Walter Scott, who, toward the close of his life, when his mind was already clouded, visited Rome and at once insisted on going, feeble though he was, to the tomb of the Stuarts.

362 Chatham: William Pitt, "the Great Commoner," created Earl of Chatham for his distinguished statesmanship. He enabled England to play a part in the Seven Years' War (1756–1763) that secured to her conquests of the first importance. The French possessions in India and in America were ceded to England at the close of the war.

362 Wolfe: James, an English officer who had rendered notable service in Germany before being despatched to America to take command of the army sent against the French in Canada. He directed the attack on Quebec and lost his life in the moment of victory.

363 heart-sick of his country's shame. Chatham earnestly protested against the attempt to tax the American colonies without consent of their legislatures, and regarded the American resistance as justified. The disasters of the war that followed were keenly felt by the aged statesman. The immediate occasion of his death (1778) was the exhaustion consequent on a speech denouncing the American policy of the king's ministers.

364 The mighty chiefs sleep side by side. Pitt and Fox died in the same year (1806) and were buried in Westminster Abbey.

365 Tommy Townshend: an adherent of Pitt and for some time leader of the House of Commons. Members sent to the House from rotten boroughs had no sense of responsibility to the people and were ready to lend or even to sell their votes if sufficient inducement offered.

366 the Prince of all the land: the crown prince of Denmark.

368 our chief: Horatio Nelson, the most distinguished commander in the English navy. He had already won two victories over the French, the battle of St. Vincent (1797) and the battle of the Nile (1799).

368 Elsinore: a fortified town overlooking the harbor.

368 Riou: the captain of the *Amazon*, killed in the engagement. Nelson wrote of his death, "In poor, dear Riou, the country has sustained an irreparable loss."

369 our joy, and pride. Nelson's brilliant successes were due as much to the devotion of the sailors as to naval strategy. Many of his ships were unseaworthy and all were scantily provisioned, but the admiral managed to keep his vessels in fighting trim and his men in excellent health and spirits.

372 **a war embrace.** Nelson's ship, the *Victory*, while sailing past the French *Redoubtable*, got entangled in her rigging. So held together, the two vessels engaged in a terrible duel, the *Victory* firing broadsides into the *Redoubtable's* hull and receiving in return a rain of shot and shell upon her deck. Nelson, walking on the quarter-deck with Captain Hardy, was struck and mortally wounded. He lived to learn that the enemy's fleet was ruined.

373 **burial.** Nelson was buried with magnificent pomp in St. Paul's cathedral. Monuments commemorating his victory were built in London, Edinburgh, and Dublin.

374 **Blake** : the only English admiral to be compared with Nelson. He won famous victories over the Dutch navy in the days of the Commonwealth.

381 **the fell Invader.** The French army, with Napoleon himself in command, were marching up from the south to encounter the allied armies, Prussian, Dutch, and German, as well as English, assembled in the vicinity of Brussels.

382 **Each Hulan** : Uhlan, the name given to Napoleon's lancers.

382 **My Guard.** The Old Guard, Napoleon's picked troops, stood their ground till the French army was ruined past recall.

382 **their leader.** Napoleon was no coward, but as emperor of the French, he had no right to risk his life.

382 **the Chief.** Wellington was in command of the Dutch and German troops as well as the English.

383 **The cohorts' eagles** : the standard of Napoleon.

386 **Assaye.** Wellington had won fame in India before being sent to Spain. At Assaye (1803) he had defeated a force of thirty thousand natives with forty-five hundred English troops.

386 **Lisbon.** It was Wellington who planned the defence of Lisbon and drove the French troops from Portugal.

387 **Again their ravening eagle rose.** Napoleon was forced to resign his crown and retire to the island of Elba in 1814, but he escaped to France the following year and resumed his imperial state. The allies renewed the war. Napoleon was again deposed and exiled to the island of St. Helena, where he died in 1820.

387 **that loud sabbath**: the battle of Waterloo was fought on Sunday, June 18.

387 **the Prussian trumpet blew.** The Prussian troops under Blucher arrived in the moment of victory and completed the ruin of the French army.

389 **The minster.** The monarchs of England have been crowned in Westminster Abbey since the coronation of William the Norman.

389 **the Dead.** Many of the kings of England and the greatest English statesmen, generals, and men of letters are buried in Westminster Abbey.

390 **Dieu et mon droit**: God and my right — the motto on the royal arms.

393 **my own ideal knight**: King Arthur of the Round Table.

393 **the gloom of imminent war.** In November, 1861, England seemed likely to be involved in the American civil war by the seizure of the Confederate commissioners, Mason and Slidell, from the British mail steamer *Trent.* The Prince Consort died in December following.

393 **his sons.** Prince Albert and Victoria had four sons and five daughters.

395 **him that utter'd nothing base**: William Wordsworth, who had preceded Tennyson as poet laureate.

396 **rulers of your blood.** Queen Victoria's eldest son, Albert Edward, succeeded her as Edward VII. in 1901. The present Prince of Wales has two sons, so the permanence of the dynasty seems well assured.

397 **the lordly Few.** The House of Lords has not been abolished as the Radicals desired, but its influence in legislation has been less since the House of Commons began to really represent the people.

397 **the moiling men who delve in the mine.** The lot of the miner has been made easier by legislation requiring safety appliances. The Mines Act of 1843 forbade the employment of women and children underground.

397 **the weavers' band.** The wages of factory operatives have more than doubled in the past one hundred years. This has not been accomplished by act of Parliament, but by trade-union agitation.

397 **the factory-child.** By the factory act of 1833, children under thirteen years of age might work only eight hours a day, and no person under twenty-one years of age could be employed at night.

PAGE

397　the negro's stain. The slaves held in Jamaica and the Bahamas were emancipated in 1833, and Britain was cleared of further responsibility for this degradation of human beings.

398　kingly crown and mitre. Kings and bishops are no less revered at the beginning of the twentieth century than at the beginning of the nineteenth. Englishmen have learned how to combine popular government with monarchical institutions.

399　Reform. The Reform Act of 1832 was favored by the king, William IV., but was with great difficulty forced through the House of Lords.

410　Gordon, Charles George: accepted the difficult and dangerous post of governor of the Soudan, with the hope of suppressing the slave-trade. Thousands of captives were released by his orders and the wretched fellaheen welcomed him as a deliverer. The slave-dealers, however, revolted against foreign rule and the English government decided to abandon the attempt to govern the Soudan. Gordon was sent to bring out the garrisons of English soldiers and friendly natives. Surrounded by the Mahdi's troops at Khartoum, he sustained a siege of three hundred and seventeen days. The fortress was finally taken and Gordon put to death only two days before the relief expedition arrived at Khartoum.